Making Waves

Making Waves

HOW THE WEST INDIES
SHAPED THE UNITED STATES

Debbie Jacob

IAN RANDLE PUBLISHERS
Kingston • *Miami*

First published in Jamaica, 2017 by
Ian Randle Publishers
16 Herb McKenley Drive
Box 686
Kingston 6
www.ianrandlepublishers.com

© Debbie Jacob
ISBN: 978-976-637-954-4

National Library of Jamaica Cataloguing-In-Publication Data

Jacob, Debbie
   Making waves : how the West Indies shaped the United States /
Debbie Jacob.

   p. : ill., cm
Bibliography : p.
ISBN 978-976-637-954-4 (pbk)

1. West Indies – History   2. West Indians – United States
3. United States – Civilization – West Indian influences
4. West Indies – Civilization
5. Caribbean Area – Immigration and emigration
6. United States – Immigration and emigration
I. Title

972.9   dc 23

Cover and Book Design by Ian Randle Publishers
Illustrations by Jiore Z. Moore-Gayle
Printed and Bound in the United States of America

*For my daughter, Ijanaya,
whose support meant the world to me
on this journey and for my mother, Maria
Stefania Götz Bowman, who lived the life of
an immigrant twice.*

Contents

Foreword

I know the exact moment I thought of writing *Making Waves*. The idea hit me during a telephone conversation with New Orleans-born American soul singer Aaron Neville about his upcoming concert in San Fernando, Trinidad, in October 2007. While talking about his uncle, Chief Jolly, I told Neville that much of the music of Chief Jolly and the Wild Tchoupitoulas (a group of Mardi Gras Indians formed in the early 1970s) resembled Trinidad calypso and the Fancy Indian masquerade of Trinidad Carnival.

Neville agreed and said, "My brother Cyril used to say New Orleans was the northernmost Caribbean island. We all thought of New Orleans as an island that hooked on to the US. It's the melting pot of so many different cultures."

The idea began to take shape on a whole new level when Kendell and Richard, two of my students at the Youth Training Centre (YTC), decided to sit the Caribbean Examination Council (CXC) Caribbean History exam. When we opened our history books to check the chapters and the syllabus, we discovered – much to my horror – that one of the ten themes that divide the book into ten chapters was devoted to the US influence in the Caribbean. Our own history books seemed to suggest Caribbean islands had been nothing more than passive places waiting for the next colonial or neocolonial master to traipse through.

Neville's comment about the Caribbean colliding with New Orleans and those one-dimensional history books that flaunted US power haunted me, and this book, showing the reverse – the importance of the West Indies in shaping US history – began to take shape.

The full impact of these vignettes about the profound effect West Indians and the West Indies had on the US sunk in while listening to an audio version of David McCullough's biography *The Wright Brothers*, a very American story set in my home state of Ohio in the Midwestern US – a far cry from *Making Waves*. The story of Wilbur and Orville Wright, who are credited with inventing the aeroplane, is all the more vivid to me because I know the landscape of Ohio, but what really gripped me was the description of a journey to the Wright brothers' home in Dayton by beekeeper Amos Ives Root, who lived in Medina, just outside Cleveland. In the list of towns Root passed through, McCullough mentions Mansfield, the place where I was born. I couldn't stop listening to that line.

Finally, I realised what *Making Waves* really meant to me. Once upon a time these little islands, like the state of Ohio, had been an important place, bustling with activity, thriving with important events or inventions. It is hard for me to imagine prosperity and pride in Mansfield, a virtual ghost town now, littered with the skeletons of buildings that once symbolised affluence: Westinghouse, Mansfield Tire, the steel mill, Tappans and more.

The mere mention of Mansfield in *The Wright Brothers* reminded me of that lost sense of pride people once had in a thriving place. Although I and countless other Americans see ourselves in many books set in the US, there is something indescribably special about the place you call home being mentioned in a piece of literature. I hope that *Making Waves* proves that small places and small islands can have a grand history that should never be forgotten.

I sensed the power of the Caribbean from the time my Romanian-born mother, who grew up in Nazi Germany, had my father build a house next to the old farmhouse where we lived, in rural Ohio, so that we could have a proper bomb shelter. My dad, who was a farmer, a building contractor and a former Army Air Corps and Air Force radio operator in the Second World War, finally complied with my mom's wishes after the Cuban Missile Crisis in 1962.

At the age of ten, I stepped into that bomb shelter, which doubled as a very dark, windowless pantry illuminated by a single, naked, jaundiced light bulb. My grandmother, who had worked in an underground munitions factory in Germany during the Second World War, canned vegetables and fruit in glass jars. They were filled with peaches, peas, green beans, corn and homemade pickles made from the cucumbers and dill she grew in our backyard garden. She kept the shelves of our bomb shelter packed with this food just in case Fidel Castro ever acted up again.

My grandfather, who had worked on the Berlin–Baghdad Railroad during the war, listened to his shortwave radio even more after the Cuban Missile Crisis. My mother and my maternal grandparents developed a deep dread of Communism and Castro, and they reminded my brothers and me constantly that Castro was only 90 miles from our shore. I grew up knowing just how close the Caribbean was, and how it could collide with the US in the most unimaginable way.

NOTE

This list of famous West Indians who made an impact on US culture is not exhaustive. These are merely the people who have captured my imagination because of their extraordinary lives. Some of these West Indians are well known and impossible to leave out of this story; others have slipped through history's net, but their stories need to be recognised and remembered.

Introduction
EXPLORING THE MYTH

When he mounted a donkey and rode away from Granada, Christopher Columbus was sure his dream of exploring uncharted seas had finally come to an end. He had no idea that he would find support from an unexpected source in Queen Isabella's court, or that together he and the queen would be thrust into history for fashioning a myth that would wrongly define the Caribbean islands.

Columbus was "obsessed with his God-given task of finding Asia," said his biographer Laurence Bergreen; he wove "a tale that mixed astronomy and navigation with mythological history," said Isabella's biographer Kirstin Downey.

King João of Portugal could not take Columbus seriously and Henry VII of England "made fun of what Columbus had to say". Only Isabella, a devout Catholic obsessed with driving the Muslims out of Granada, considered Columbus's plan to reach the Orient by sailing west, and she had to be nudged to take the final plunge by an adviser in her court, Luis de Santángel.

Granada had just fallen to the Spanish Christians, in January 1492, and Isabella needed another adventure, another cause, another mission to keep her fractious country together. She finally gave Columbus her blessing. So it was that in August 1492, Columbus sailed west and landed on a "modest coral island in the Bahamas," claimed the emerald islands of the Caribbean one by one for the Spanish crown, and invented stories of reaching islands off Cipango (Japan).

It is unclear how long the obdurate Columbus believed his own stories about reaching Asia, but he had honed his skills as a storyteller on Europe's royalty, and he had promised Isabella gold and riches, which he scrambled to deliver in some shape or form. The islands were not exactly dripping with gold, but the myth of a God-given mission had been planted in the Caribbean, and it would loom large over the islands as the Spanish and the Portuguese sent missionaries to the New World. For them, these islands were merely uncivilised places waiting for European countries to "discover" and possess them.

The Spanish ruled supreme for about 125 years. They held on to Cuba, Puerto Rico, Trinidad, and Hispaniola until the French took the western half of the latter and named it Saint-Domingue. In 1623, the British established settlements in St Christopher (St Kitts), and they took possession of Barbados in 1625. In the 1630s, the Dutch arrived to take Bonaire, half of St Maarten, St Eustatius, Aruba and Curaçao, and the French occupied the rest of St Kitts, Guadeloupe and Martinique. The stage was set for innumerable battles, with Caribbean islands as pawns in a never-ending chess game of European wars.

Other countries claimed parts of the region as well. In 1651, the Knights of Malta bought St Croix, St Kitts, St Martin, St Bartholomew and Tortuga for 120,000 livres from the French West India Company. (The French bought back the islands in 1665 for 500,000 livres.)

Tobago changed hands about 30 times after the Courlanders, from modern-day Latvia, settled in Plymouth in 1654. Denmark had possession of St John,

St Thomas and St Croix from 1671 until it signed a treaty in 1916 to sell the islands to the US for US$25,000,000.

No matter who passed through the Caribbean, the myth remained the same: big countries had a right to possess tiny islands that passively waited for the next wave of colonialism to claim them.

But the islands were not blank slates. Many were home to the Taínos of the Greater Antilles and the Kalinagos of the Lesser Antilles, who had their own culture, rich with their own history and their own traditions and stories, many of which vanished with the vanquished tellers. Later, the myths and stories that came from Africa and Europe blended into a strong new creole voice that resonated throughout the region, but often went unnoticed in the history books, which focused on the colonising powers.

Even when West Indian islands were the possessions of European colonial countries, they wielded great power of their own. The islands produced masterful rebels who fought against slavery, prejudice and social injustice wherever they went. Thus, West Indians emerged as defining voices in US history from the 17th century to the Civil Rights Movement. The US proved a storyteller's paradise, not only in terms of the adventures of the first generation of Europeans who settled on the continent, but also for West Indian immigrants, particularly Afro-Caribbean immigrants fired up by the issues of slavery and prejudice.

This is the story of remarkable men and women from the West Indies who shattered the European myth about Caribbean islands and their people being helpless and insignificant. This is the story of how the West Indies shaped the US.

Chapter 1

PETER STUYVESANT:
The Dutch West India Company's Disappearing Act

On a crisp May morning in 1647, a one-legged man hobbled off a ship in the lower part of Manhattan, in the Dutch colony of New Amsterdam, which had been permanently settled about 21 years before. His arrival most likely seemed like a miracle – for him, though not necessarily for the people who greeted him.

Residents of the small Dutch settlement and some American Indians watched anxiously, shouted and clapped respectfully as the colony's guns saluted his arrival. Peter Stuyvesant limped towards the fort, mere steps from the riverbank where he landed. This was the place that the Dutch had purchased from Native American Indians for $24, and the crowd hoped Stuyvesant could make New Netherland thrive.

New Netherland had been founded in 1624, only four years after the Pilgrims and the *Mayflower* had landed on the east coast, and just six years before the Puritans arrived in Massachusetts Bay. The village hugged the wooden Fort Amsterdam, where the National Museum of the American Indian now stands, next to Battery Park and Bowling Green, and where the Dutch settlers once had their cattle market. By the time the British took over New Amsterdam, the city had reached as far as the modern Wall Street, named because that is where the Dutch had built a wall.

The population of New Amsterdam had dwindled from 3,000 in 1543 to about 1,000 just a year before

Stuyvesant's arrival. The settlement had its problems, so it was with great anticipation that the crowd waited for him to speak. They must have wondered about his wooden leg.

"I shall govern you as a father does his children," Stuyvesant said.

The crowd roared. With that, Peter Stuyvesant became the Dutch West India Company's new Governor of New Amsterdam.

In 1645, he had been appointed colonial governor and director general of all Dutch possessions in North America and the Caribbean, but that had turned out to be a nightmare that would forever loom large over his life. This was most definitely a new chapter.

When he looked around, Stuyvesant must have been shocked at the woeful state of New Amsterdam. A crumbling fort had deteriorated to mere ruins. The bare bones of a church blocked a clear view of his domain. Broken fences separated houses from narrow, crooked streets, and the place smelled like pigs, because the cramped quarters included pigpens. Windmills, gabled roofs and sprawling farms dotted the landscape. Stuyvesant clearly had his work cut out for him.

He ordered vacant lots around the fort cleared, and weeds replaced with colourful gardens; hog pens taken away; fences repaired. Governor Stuyvesant received help from Holland in the form of officers called *schouts*, much like modern-day mayors. He got two burgomasters and five *schepens* to preside over trials in the stone tavern that a previous governor had built. That became the *Stadt Huys*, or City Hall. With the appointment of these officers, New Amsterdam became a city. The main road, *Breede weg* (Broadway), passed through a gate in the wall and continued on past farms, fields and forests to the village of Haarlem. Ferrymen rowed goods and people across the East River to *Lange Eylandt* and *Breukelen* (Brooklyn), *Vlissingen* (Flushing), *Vlacke Bos* (Flatbush), and even *Staaten Eylandt* (Staten Island), a fur-trading post run by the Dutch West India Company.

Once Stuyvesant settled, he began to write letters to surrounding governors representing British power in the colonies, spelling out what he considered to be his, Dutch territory, and reminding them of their duty to give passage to Dutch ships.

British/Dutch relations seemed to be going reasonably well until January 1649, when Charles I was beheaded in front of crowds outside his own banqueting hall. The Prince of Wales and Duke of York escaped to Holland, where they were welcomed by their brother-in-law William, Prince of Orange. Tension mounted; war seemed inevitable. The British would undoubtedly try to take possession of Dutch colonies, including New Amsterdam.

On March 24, 1649, Governor Winthrop of Massachusetts died. Governor Eaton of New Haven suggested a governors' meeting to discuss political events and looming possibilities. There, Stuyvesant was informed that the British claimed all the territory between Cape Cod and New Haven. Lady Stirling, the widow of Lord William Alexander Stirling, insisted on maintaining her title and claim to his lands, including the whole of Long Island. When she sent an agent on her behalf, Stuyvesant arrested and threatened him, before sending him packing on a one-way trip to Holland.

No one could escape Stuyvesant's autocratic tendencies. He cracked down on dissenters who questioned his austerity. While the British and the Swedes quarrelled over rights to river passageways – including the Delaware and Hudson Rivers – a rumour surfaced among the British colonies that Stuyvesant supported American Indians in planned attacks against the British, though the American Indians he had supposedly enlisted objected vehemently to these accusations, saying they had never been approached.

By 1654 pirates – or British privateers, if you choose – and robbers preyed on Long Island. Restless British residents in the Dutch colonies itched for revolt, and Stuyvesant's Dutch subjects had grown tired of his heavy hand and stomping wooden leg, which he beat against the ground in his tirades. His decisions were final, and he did not take kindly to anyone questioning the law.

"If any one, during my administration, shall appeal [my decisions], I will make him a foot shorter and send the pieces to Holland and let him appeal in that way," Stuyvesant threatened.

He sent two men, known only as Melyn and Kuyter, to Holland as criminals. They appealed, won the right to be colonists of New Netherland, and had Stuyvesant summoned to The Hague to answer for his actions. When the two men returned to New Amsterdam, they decided on a public display of the innocent verdict awarded them in Holland, to match the public embarrassment they had suffered when they had been packed off to the motherland.

Stuyvesant certainly had his hands full. The American Indians in the area demanded the right to purchase guns, but Stuyvesant had laws passed preventing them from buying guns and alcohol. Everyone wanted more freedom, and now Oliver Cromwell, Lord Protector of England, decided to sail some soldiers into the picture.

New Amsterdam could not defend itself, and it would not take on any allies in the area. To do so, Governor Stuyvesant declared, would be like "inviting the Trojan Horse inside the walls". As tension mounted, unexpected news arrived: the British and Dutch had signed a peace treaty in Europe. New Amsterdam celebrated. Bells rang, residents cheered. But that was not the end of trouble. Stuyvesant had the Swedes to contend with. This he did with no emotion. The governor of the Swedes wrote to Stuyvesant after the fall of their Fort Christina:

> In Christina, the women were violently driven out of their houses. The oxen, cows and other animals were butchered. Even the horses were wantonly shot. The whole country was desolated. Your men carried off even my own property, and we were left without means of defence against the savages.

While Stuyvesant was off dealing with the Swedes, a former treasurer of New Amsterdam had shot and killed an American Indian woman he caught taking peaches from his orchard. Her people descended on New Amsterdam with a fury. They killed 100 Dutch settlers, took 150 prisoners, and destroyed over 300 houses and 600 cattle, as well as the grain New Amsterdam needed to live.

By this time the settlers of New Amsterdam had long realised that Stuyvesant was an impossibly intolerant leader, but a memorable one too. About a century and a half after his reign, the writer Washington Irving described Stuyvesant in his *Knickerbocker's History of New York* as "a tough, sturdy, valiant, weather-beaten, mettlesome, obstinate, leathern-sided, lion-hearted, generous-spirited old governor." Irving said Stuyvesant's voice sounded like it had come out of a barrel. Stuyvesant was also described as a "just leader and most satisfactory of all Dutch governors."

Just how much the citizens of New Amsterdam knew about their illustrious governor or the swashbuckling past that resulted in his austere, uncompromising behaviour is unclear.

He was born around 1612 in a small town in the flat farmland of Friesland in the northern Netherlands. His father was a serious Calvinist clergyman, but Stuyvesant proved rebellious. He had an affair with his landlord's daughter and had to abandon his degree in philosophy. (Some stories claim he was expelled from university for other, unknown reasons.)

Like many young men in trouble, Stuyvesant turned to the sea for a fresh start. Joining the Dutch West India Company would forever change his life. He signed up as a clerk and sailed away to the Caribbean. It didn't take him long to propel his way up the corporate ladder. He specialised in logistics, communication and transportation from Brazil and the Caribbean to New Amsterdam.

His leadership qualities brought him respect, but also enemies. A senior official, Jan Claeszoon van Campen, was not in Stuyvesant's corner. But van Campen's death in 1642 brought Stuyvesant good fortune, because with van Campen out of the picture, Stuyvesant climbed to his enemy's post as Governor of Aruba, Bonaire and Curaçao (the Dutch West India Company's American headquarters). He was only 30.

Ambitious as ever, Stuyvesant set out on a mission in April 1644 to reclaim St Maarten from the Spanish, leading a fleet of 12 battleships carrying more than 1,000 troops across the Caribbean. The Dutch had been busy conquering Portuguese territory in Brazil, and they were on the move.

"The stakes were high: control over the plantation economies of Brazil and the Caribbean, combined with control over the slave trade from West Africa, was a potent cocktail for profit—provided one could ignore or justify the resulting terrible cost in human misery," wrote Stephen R. Bown in his book *Merchant Kings: When Companies Ruled the World, 1600–1900.*

In that fateful month of April, when Stuyvesant sailed for St Maarten, his spies had insisted that the Spanish had neglected the island: there were not enough Spanish forces, and they could not be prepared in time for battle. Stuyvesant landed in St Maarten and demanded that the Spanish surrender. He found his spies were dead wrong. The Spanish had both troops and a plan. They would not surrender, and they answered his arrival with a flurry of cannon fire.

Stubborn to the bone, Stuyvesant ordered his men to attack and fought to rally his shocked soldiers. A cannonball from the fort burst through the fog of battle and shattered his leg, just below the knee. Still Stuyvesant wouldn't surrender, and ordered his troops to fight on. But the Dutch could not hold their ground. In the middle of the chaotic scene, Stuyvesant's soldiers carried him to the ship, where the surgeon told him his leg would have to go.

The raw stump festered, but miraculously, Stuyvesant survived, though he suffered from delirium, and the wound would not heal properly. In August, the struggling Stuyvesant, who feared for his future – not to mention his life – sailed for Amsterdam and arrived in December 1644, still suffering from fever and pain. He moved in with his sister and brother-in-law, and thrived in the cooler climate of Holland. There he met his future wife, Judith Bayard, the 37-year-old daughter of a Calvinist minister. By this time in his life, Stuyvesant felt more religiously inclined. He married within the year and worked hard to reclaim his position in the West Indische Compagnie –

the Dutch West India Company. Little did he know that he was soon to become the director-general of New Netherland.

Life in New Amsterdam meant living with the constant threat of the British on their borders. That is why Stuyvesant had transformed former Governor Kieft's fence, meant to keep in cows, into a wall that ran along the river. He also wanted to regulate the fur trade, but smuggling made that difficult.

"His despotic character and his blunt manners, coupled with his efforts at reform, won him many enemies," said Bown.

Still, for most, he was an improvement over the leader he replaced, Willem Kieft, who did not have Stuyvesant's leadership ability. Stuyvesant was a shaker and a mover. He cleared land and moved people who were in his way. He gave himself a deadline – three years – to straighten out Kieft's mess. He had planned to move on to another assignment, but became entrenched in New Amsterdam and ended up staying for 17 years.

Stuyvesant took the threats around him seriously. He had repaired the fort and posted guards in anticipation of the trouble he would have with the British or the Swedes. His strict demeanour meant he was dubbed 'The General', but it worked: New Amsterdam became an organised, thriving community. He made citizens clean their yards. He tackled the pigs, cattle, goats, and horses that wandered through the streets; forbade the sale of liquor on Sundays; introduced fines for knife-fighting; and threw violators in jail even for petty crimes. No more tossing rubbish, ashes, oyster shells, animal dung, or animal carcasses into the streets. He created garbage dumps, outlawed wooden chimneys and thatched roofs, established a police patrol, and developed a monetary system. He did not believe in handouts, and he would not support orphanages or hospitals. He taxed citizens. None of Stuyvesant's victories brought security, but his no-nonsense attitude went a long way in keeping the peace. He patched up many dicey situations with the American Indians.

The turning point for Stuyvesant came when Britain's King Charles II returned to power in 1660, after a decade in exile while England was under parliamentary rule. In 1664, the king decided to reassert Britain's claim in North America. He granted his brother James, Duke of York and Albany, a sizeable chunk of land, including Maine, Cape Cod, and the eastern shores of the Delaware and Hudson Rivers. He also gave his brother New Amsterdam: he knew well that it was the centre of Dutch commercial ventures in the western Atlantic.

Eager to claim his property in North America, James dispatched four ships, under the command of Colonel Richard Nicolls. This time, the Dutch didn't seem prepared for the attack, even though there were 20 cannon around the stone fort, 1,500 people living in New Amsterdam, and about 10,000 in the entire Dutch colony. They got wind that the British were coming. Time seemed to be on their side – and luck too, when the British ships got separated on the journey across the Atlantic. But they regrouped at Gravesend Bay on August 26. Stuyvesant sensed the urgency of the situation and sent for help, but the Dutch West India Company refused to send more soldiers or ammunition. The business-minded Dutch didn't want the extra expense. Instead, the company sent back a letter saying, "Don't worry." The Dutch also banked on the history of English settlers in North

America. They thought national loyalty would not match the value English settlers put on the religious freedom they had under the Dutch:

> We are in hopes that as the English at the north have removed mostly from old England for the causes aforesaid [religious freedom] they will not give us henceforth so much trouble, but prefer to live free under us at peace with their consciences than to risk getting rid of our authority and then falling again under a government from which they had formerly fled.

No one seemed to realise the Dutch settlers were tired of Stuyvesant's strict rule and thought they might fare better with the British; and so the four British ships, which had regrouped, cruised into the harbour of New Amsterdam. Appalled at the boldness he had witnessed, Stuyvesant wrote to Nicolls, reminding him that the two countries were not at war. The commander, he hazarded a guess, "was not apt to entertain any thing of prejudice intended against us."

Nicolls dashed off his own letter: "In his Majesties Name, I do demand the towne, Scituate upon the Island commonly knowne by the Name of Manhattoes with all the Forests there unto belonging, to be rendered unto his Majesties obedience, and Protection into my hands."

On the good side, Nicolls said he really did not want a skirmish.

Stuyvesant, a stickler for details, did not respond to the letter because it was unsigned. Nicolls re-sent his message, adding, "Your speedy answer is necessary to prevent future inconveniences...."

Stuyvesant knew he was outnumbered, and so did his subjects, who were not in the mood for a battle that would likely end in their deaths. Stuyvesant did not agree with them. He steadfastly clung to his position. "I would rather be carried out dead," he said, tearing up the terms of agreement in front of a horrified crowd. Noting their reaction, he slowly and methodically scoured the ground for the pieces of the letter he had ripped up. He gave the pieces to the mob, who glued them back together. Stuyvesant hobbled off on his wooden leg and headed for his fort.

Tension mounted. If Stuyvesant decided to fire one of those cannons, they would all be doomed.

On September 5, 1664, the citizens of New Amsterdam sent a petition with 93 important signatures asking for what they thought was the obvious: surrender, to avoid "...misery, sorrow, conflagration, the dishonour of women, murder of children in their cradles, and, in a word, the absolute ruin and destruction of about 1,500 innocent souls."

Stuyvesant knew all was lost. On September 8, 1664, he bowed his head to the beating drum and marched his soldiers out of Fort Amsterdam. A Dutch flag whipped in the breeze for the last time. A short distance away, the British soldiers waited. They entered the fort and raised their flag, and New Amsterdam became New York. Fort Amsterdam became Fort James.

Quietly, Stuyvesant boarded a ship and headed for Holland to explain why he had surrendered New Netherland. There, The Dutch West India Company blamed him for all its woes in the New World. The company "publicly accused him of cowardice and incompetence, and blamed him for the loss of the colony to the English." Stuyvesant denied the accusations.

Eventually, the Dutch allowed him to return to North America. He retired from public life and lived in New York for four more years after his imposed retirement, dying in 1672, at 60, on his farm in Bouwerie Village. Today, the street, on the lower east side of Manhattan, is called the Bowery. Stuyvesant was buried in St Mark's Church.

This was not the end of his story. Before Stuyvesant surrendered to the British, he insisted on a clause in the articles of transfer that said the citizens "shall keep and enjoy the liberty of the consciences in religion" – a statement that had a huge impact on New York. The English adhered to the clause, so that New York ended up resembling the Dutch settlement Stuyvesant had fashioned, unlike the other British colonies surrounding it. New Netherland was truly a special place, bold and radical in its religious freedoms, which would shape America for centuries.

Historian Colin Woodard wrote:

> Modelled on its Dutch namesake, New Amsterdam was from the start a global commercial trading society: multi-ethnic, multi-religious, speculative, materialistic, mercantile, and free trading, a raucous, not entirely democratic city-state where no one ethnic or religious group has ever truly been in charge.

> New Netherland also nurtured two Dutch innovations considered subversive by most other European states at the time: a profound tolerance of diversity and an unflinching commitment to the freedom of inquiry.

> It is no wonder, historians point out, that New York would be the place where so many immigrants would land and make this area the most densely populated place in the US.

New York became a melting pot, an example for the world. Woodard added:

> It was a cosmopolitan place with French-speaking settlers, Lutherans from Poland, Finland and

Sweden, Catholics from Ireland and Portugal, Anglicans, Puritans and Quakers from New England. There were Spanish – almost everyone imaginable. Other New England 'nations' banned Jews, but not New Amsterdam. American Indians roamed the streets and so did Africans, some slaves and some free. A Muslim from Morocco had been farming outside the walls for three decades.

Undoubtedly shaped by both his Dutch upbringing and his experiences in the West Indies, Stuyvesant had governed New Amsterdam to the end, and left a lasting legacy.

"Diversity, tolerance, upward mobility and an overwhelming emphasis on private enterprise—have come to be identified with the United States, but they were really the legacy of the United Provinces of the Netherlands," said Woodard. "Indeed many of the historic achievements of the American Revolution were accomplished by the Dutch nearly two centuries before the Battle of Lexington."

Hence, Woodard wrote that New York City would always follow its own path, much to the frustration of the other 12 colonies that joined with it to fight Britain for independence in 1776. New York would stubbornly and steadfastly forge its own identity.

"Later, the hamlet of Groenwijck would be absorbed into the expanding city and renamed Greenwich Village, which would be known as the federation's first and foremost bohemian district." From 1910 to 1960, Woodard tells us, "This enclave was a magnet for cultural revolutionaries of all sorts: anarchists, philosophers, free-verse poets, Cubist painters, feminists, gays, Freudian thinkers, hard-drinking writers, free-love playwrights and idiosyncratic musicians."

New Yorkers possessed an identity uniquely their own. As the small settlement of New Amsterdam burgeoned into the bustling city of New York, it became a reflection of the world – including a very visible West Indian population. Some of those West Indians – Alexander Hamilton, Marcus Garvey, Hazel Scott, Stokely Carmichael, Sidney Poitier, Shirley Chisholm, and even the first Puerto Rican to serve on the Supreme Court, Sonia Sotomayor, to name a few – would change the course of US history. And New York City would forever be a reminder of the connection between the Dutch West Indies and the US.

Chapter 2

TITUBA:
A West Indian Stirs the Cauldron in Salem

She admitted to flying on a stick with witches, and her confession sparked a witch hunt that still hangs like a spell over a New England town, in the northwestern commonwealth of Massachusetts. Tituba, a West Indian slave, along with the middle-aged Sarah Osborne and 38-year-old "semi-itinerant beggar" Sarah Good, were the first three people to be arrested for witchcraft in Salem. While a stubborn Osborne and a "caustic and insolent" Good insisted on their innocence, Tituba became the first Salem resident to confess to witchcraft, and she testified that all three women had travelled together to Boston.

In hindsight, Tituba's confession seemed as strange as the events that had erupted in Salem. Witches were not your common folk in Salem, or anywhere else, for that matter. They were generally social outcasts: strange, "deviant, cantankerous scolds and choleric foot-stampers...On all counts Tituba failed to fit the profile," wrote Stacy Schiff in *The Witches: Salem, 1692*. "She proved spellbinding, however," said Schiff.

Tituba's own testimony in a specially convened court suggested she had been a leader of witches: "I rid upon a stick or poale & Good & Osburne behind me we Ride taking hold of one another don't know how we goe for I Saw noe trees nor path, but was presently there," she told a spellbound court.

Tituba explained to a horrified courtroom how Sarah Good's spirit had transformed into a hog and a dog.

Her descriptions undermined the fabric of Salem life and eroded the self-confidence of those austere Puritans in charge. She saw animals – often dogs – turn into men, an obvious, metaphorical way to lower the status of those above her. When the questions transcended her own West Indian culture, Tituba often seemed to fumble for explanations. Asked to describe the devil, she said, "Like a man, I think." And of course, Tituba refused to serve that horrifying creature. She had heard talk of people serving the devil in Massachusetts and she would have heard descriptions of devilish deeds in religious circles, including the pious Christian home where she served, but the image of the devil did not quite fit into Tituba's own religious realm.

Tituba's testimony in 1692, at that specially convened court, set off the hysteria that sent 14 women and five men to the gallows. Nearly 150 women (and some men) were imprisoned for witchcraft. One person was pressed to death, and four others died in prison. Two dogs were killed for being witches.

No one would ever be able to explain exactly how a West Indian slave named Tituba set in motion those macabre events that culminated in the Salem witch trials. There had been such trials in New England before, but not on the scale of this one. Salem is the infamous one etched in our memories, even though few people realise the role of a West Indian slave in creating the chaos. Over 300 years after the witches' brouhaha, Tituba remains a controversial and elusive figure. Everything about her, including her race and birthplace, has been shrouded in mystery.

A popular historian of the 19th century, Charles Upham, wrote that Tituba had come from New Spain (Venezuela)

and was then sold in Barbados. But he was far from being a trustworthy historian (Upham lost a copyright case in 1839 for historical works he had pirated, squirrelled away for 11 years and then smuggled into England). His writings admit that the case for Tituba being from New Spain (Venezuela) had been based on local legend. So Upham may have been taking a stab in the dark, but he was close to figuring out Tituba's probable origins.

Most of what is known about Tituba can be found in testimony from the infamous trials, which were really a hastily put-together special court that listened to malicious gossip.

The trouble started on a late December day in 1691 when nine-year-old Elizabeth Parris and her 11-year-old cousin Abigail Williams engaged in a common adolescent game: telling fortunes by dropping an egg white into a glass. On a good day, this old English custom provided the girls with a taste of rebellion from their austere Puritan life dedicated to fighting the devil. On this day, much to the mischievous girls' horror, the egg white took the shape of a coffin. They panicked and took fright. By the time the New Year dawned, the girls had begun feeling horrific pains – a phantom illness no doctor could diagnose. Rumour had it the girls had been involved in blood rituals and had danced naked in the woods. After that, they became very sick for months.

Distraught over the girls' suffering, Tituba and a neighbour, Mary Sibley, concocted a witchcake, a mixture of rye meal and the girls' urine, which was baked in ashes and fed to a dog, which they thought was probably harbouring the witch.

But events spiralled out of control. Acting crazy and sometimes even possessed, the girls began to accuse Tituba of being a witch. She confessed when confronted and, pressured by Elizabeth's father, the Reverend Samuel Parris, "a tedious, mulish, sulky" man who was known in the area as a West India merchant before he preached his first sermon in November 1689. Tituba began to identify other witches, and implicated Good and Osborne. In Schiff's account, the embattled Amerindian slave claimed a tall, lean, white-haired man in a dark serge coat had threatened to decapitate her if she did not hurt the children. The grimacing, screeching girls in question – the supposed victims of the witchcraft – ceased their wailing and contortions during Tituba's testimony. The court took this as a sign of relief.

No one had ever previously bothered to pay much attention to Tituba. Even history slighted her by not garnering the facts concerning her life, but this everyone agrees: Tituba could put on a brilliant performance.

"She was a brilliant raconteur, the more compelling for her simple, declarative sentences. The accent may have helped," wrote Schiff.

On March 1, Tituba ended her testimony, with all the melodrama she could muster. The girls began to howl and convulse again.

If Tituba thought confessing to witchcraft was the end of her ordeal, she was dead wrong. It might have seemed like a good gamble, because witches were part of the local folklore, and no one could have predicted that Salem would take the stories to such an extreme. What is most strange is that Tituba would find herself at the centre of the conflict.

For Tituba's West Indian roots and cultural experiences did not include the European concept of witchcraft. She would have come into contact with obeah or voodoo practices among some of the African slaves she encountered along her journey. As an Arawak Amerindian, she would have encountered the spirits of the dead, *opias* or *hubias*, that wandered in the dark for the purpose of causing trouble. Worse than this were the *kenaimas* that struck lost people with sickness, misfortune or even death. Human in form, they appeared monstrous, with protruding eyebrows, and they sometimes sported two hideous heads. They could act alone or team up with a dead person's ghost; they were powerful spirits that lurked around every corner.

But although she was undoubtedly filled with stories of such colourful, maleficent characters, Tituba's knowledge of witchcraft did not harbour the sinister vision of broom-riding witches wreaking havoc on innocent Christian girls. For Tituba, witchcraft became a vehicle for her fantastic stories, which often featured animistic tales recalled from her own Amerindian religion. In many ways, Tituba was simply a West Indian who loved telling a good tale. Caught up in the drama spinning out of control around her, and quite possibly relishing her unforeseen power to send members of upper-class society into a tizzy, Tituba began to conjure up stories of midnight trips with witches flying on sticks to Boston, where they plotted the demise of Salem's young souls.

"Tituba the storyteller prolonged her life in 1692 through an imaginative ability to weave and embellish plausible tales," wrote her biographer Elaine Breslaw.

Her stories of shapeshifters and witches captured the imagination of the court, no one ever realising the double entendre that in hindsight seems to represent her own capture and demise under the evil force of slavery. Tituba also called upon her own cultural experiences to dramatise her testimony.

"Tituba had lived in a Barbados society among Africans and Amerindians who incorporated the trance, image-magic, divination and similar techniques into their religious ceremonies," wrote Breslaw.

By the time the judges – and everyone else who seemed to be under Tituba's spell – got a grip on reason, it was too late. The damage had been done. Innocent people had been executed. In the end, the Salem witch trials became a lasting symbol of mass hysteria and unmitigated ignorance, showing exactly where that deadly combination could lead. The well-documented trials became public record; but whatever information there was on Salem's star witness vanished or became distorted over time.

Then, strangely enough, Tituba re-emerged in 20th-century literature as a Barbadian slave with African roots. She appeared in *The Crucible* by playwright Arthur Miller. When American novelist Anne Petry wrote *Tituba of*

Salem Village in 1964, Tituba appeared on the cover as a slave of African descent. Guadeloupean writer Maryse Condé conjured up images of her as a black woman in her award-winning novel *I, Tituba, Black Witch of Salem*.

Then historians began to set the record straight about Tituba's identity. She was neither a witch nor an African slave. There had been no complaints about her engaging in witchcraft before the Parris girl and her cousin dabbled in predicting the future. As for her race, trial transcripts refered to Tituba as "Tituba Indian" and "that Indian woman", and to her husband as "John Indian".

Tituba was certainly a slave, and the stereotypical image of slaves being solely of African descent comes from the 18th and 19th centuries, when African slaves populated North America and the West Indies. But not all West Indian slaves had been black or African. In Barbados, Tituba's probable residence before the Parris family took her to Massachusetts, there had once been a small population of European indentured white servants and Amerindian slaves. Amerindians had been brought to Barbados by the English shortly after they colonised the deserted island in 1627.

"Within a few years, a small group of Arawaks had been persuaded to move to Barbados from the Guiana coast of South America to teach the islanders how to grow appropriate crops," wrote Breslaw. Once they reached Barbados, Breslaw says, the Amerindians were enslaved. They were not suited to hard labour, and most died quickly, but some settlers preferred Amerindian women to work with their children and in their houses.

Records suggest that Tituba was an Arawak slave kidnapped from Guyana (then British Guiana) and brought to the island. Her name seems to be from a language associated with the Arawaks. History has recorded stories about these slave trips from South America. In one such story, Captain Peter Wroth of Kent in England set sail from Barbados in July 1674 for the northeast coast of South America. He captured some children in that voyage, and while it is far-fetched – but not impossible – to pinpoint this as Tituba's journey, Wroth's trip certainly shows how she could have been an Amerindian from South America.

It is reasonably certain that Tituba lived in Barbados, because there is a handwritten document dated 1676 about a slave girl named "Tattuba", listed as a child in a 1676 inventory. Tattuba changed owners a few times before showing up as a possession of the Reverend Parris, and was between 13 and 18 when Parris left Barbados in 1680. At the time of the Salem trials, 12 years later, Tituba was said to be between 25 and 30 – an age that corresponds with the Barbados records.

Dreams had a purpose in Tituba's Amerindian culture, and she used her dreams – or stories about dreams – during the witch trials. In Barbados, she would have been in close contact with African slaves, who had their own rituals and own stories. Tituba had come from a culture in Guiana and met up with a culture in Barbados that possessed a rich history of storytelling, and she recognised the role of stories in anchoring people to their culture and their homes even after they had been enslaved. A storyteller had a special position in Amerindian and African cultures, and Tituba's stories, packed with symbolism, gave her the opportunity to elevate her own status. She told a better story than the other women defendants, and that made the difference between life and death. She relied on her own cultural experiences to save herself, even though she was the first to "confess" to engaging in witchcraft.

Her life was not easy after that. Unwilling to see his daughter as mischievous, let alone conniving or deceitful, Parris attempted to save face and protect his daughter by placing full blame for the girls' strange behaviour on Tituba and other "witches". A defiant Tituba admitted to being a witch, but insisted she had confessed because her master required her to do so. Throughout the trial, there was a sense that she had some control over a situation that had reached the point of hysteria. She knew how to deal with the tales of evil spirits, and the other women did not. For 13 months, she languished in a crowded, dirty, lice-infested cell because of her stories. But the two women Tituba accused of being witches made out far worse: Sarah Osborne died in prison on May 10, 1692, and Sarah Good was executed on July 16, 1692.

As for Tituba, "To dispose of his reluctant witch, Parris simply refused to pay [Tituba's] jail fees," said Breslaw.

Miraculously, she survived the trials; although, having been the first to confess to witchcraft, she was the last to be released from prison.

Schiff wrote:

> Having lent the previous year its shape, having introduced flights and familiars into the proceedings, having illuminated New England with her pyrotechnic confession but neither questioned nor so much as named since, she appeared before the grand jury for having covenanted with the devil on May 9, 1693. It declined to indict her.

Breslaw's account varies from Schiff's – at least, the dates do not match. Breslaw said, "An unidentified person paid [Tituba's] jail fees of about £7 and took her away in April 1693." This would have been a fairly cheap way of obtaining a slave.

Tituba's fate after her release is unknown. "Tituba vanishes from the public record after that point," says

Breslaw. Tituba's husband, John Indian, also disappeared. Puritans rarely split up married slaves, so he might have been sold along with her. Their four-year-old daughter, Violet, remained with Parris and was left as a legacy in Parris's will.

But although after the trials, Tituba seemed to disappear from the face of the earth, her name is forever etched in history as the slave responsible for creating the mass hysteria that led to the infamous Salem witch trials. Over 300 years later, it is still a story that only a West Indian could have concocted.

Chapter 3

JEAN BAPTISTE POINT DU SABLE:
The Haitian in the Onion Field

He paddled his canoe north from the steaming swamps of New Orleans and up the murky Mississippi River. No one knows exactly where Jean Baptiste Point du Sable came from or how he reached that place far to the north that the Potawatomie Indians called Checagou. Some reports say a Choctaw Indian accompanied him on his fateful trip.

Du Sable's story became legendary, particularly the part about where exactly he came from. Nehemiah Matson, an early historian specialising in the history of Illinois, claimed du Sable came from French Canada; but du Sable had said he was from Saint-Domingue (modern-day Haiti). He might still have known about the Mississippi before he began his journey: Haitians were not strangers to the area, and Haitian slaves worked along the river.

Navigating a place in history for a free Negro from Saint-Domingue would have been difficult had du Sable not left a trail of evidence that proved he had been living in the far northern corner of the Midwest in a strategic spot near the Mississippi. He first settled in Peoria, Illinois, 165 miles southwest of modern-day Chicago, but by 1779 he had settled in Checagou, named, by the American Indians, for the surrounding wild-onion fields. There, in the mucky, smelly, sludgy land off the Mississippi River, which no one else seemed to be able to tolerate for its smell and foul conditions, du Sable envisioned the rich, fertile future a full eight years before John Kinzie would be given the credit for "discovering" the place that would be called Chicago. Du Sable came to the area with little or nothing more than the canoe that he most likely travelled in, and he noticed something that no one else saw: a place of promise.

Du Sable must also have had the uncanny ability to charm his way out of danger and into a bundle of business deals with traders passing through from Canada, and trading posts in Detroit (Michigan) and even as far as Green Bay (Wisconsin). Only a strong and confident man with a mesmerising personality could have transcended the cultural barriers that existed in the area. Du Sable met all the challenges and did business with all those who came his way: French trappers, American Indians, British soldiers and American rebels.

Trappers, traders, and soldiers described du Sable as a "large, handsome man". There are no contemporary pictures of him, except a sketch that surfaced centuries later. Later images of du Sable show strong features: a very exaggerated, alpine nose, a ruddy complexion suggesting a white man weathered by the elements, and a rugged face framed with unruly hair that fell in wild waves. But such a picture does not suggest his biracial parentage, which is not in dispute.

Out of an undefined piece of territory, du Sable built a home. He constructed buildings and became a wholesaler. The area he settled was not a promising place.

"And the weather was impossible. Great blasts of heat from the open prairie were succeeded, in turn, by icy blasts of air from the lake. Rainy seasons alternated with dry spells. The Indian trails were either muddy holes or powdery rows of dust, which rose up and smote the eyes and seeped into the membranes of the nose. A great stench covered all," wrote Lerone Bennett Jr, scholar and social historian.

The Mississippi and other rivers in the area were slow and clogged with vegetation. It would be more than a century before American writer Samuel Clemens would invent the pseudonym of Mark Twain, along with the whole romantic notion of the vast and mighty Mississippi and the large, bellowing steam engines dotting its course. For du Sable, the area was merely mud. Before him, the French had passed through long enough to make a map, but they saw no reason to settle in this forlorn place.

Jean Baptiste Point du Sable claimed to have been born in St Marc, Saint-Domingue, around 1745, to a French father and African slave mother. Given Saint-Domingue's complicated social strata, he could have been a free coloured man or a former slave who made his way to New Orleans, as did many of his compatriots.

Once du Sable had made the epic journey up the Mississippi, he maintained excellent relations with Native Americans and lived among indigenous tribes, where, in 1778, he married Catherine, the daughter of Potawatomie Chief Pokagon, in a tribal ceremony as well as in a Catholic church in Cahokia, Illinois. Jean-Baptiste and Catherine had two children, Jean-Baptiste Jr and Suzanne.

Set on the north bank of the Chicago River at its junction with Lake Michigan, du Sable's estate consisted of a modest-sized home with a fenced-in yard bordering a waterway. He had a dock for his canoe, a horse mill, a bakehouse, a dairy, a smokehouse, a poultry house, a workshop, a stable and a barn. His house had a large fireplace, a stove, a large French walnut cabinet with four glass doors, a couch, four tables, a bureau, seven chairs, candlesticks, two mirrors, and two paintings (he once owned 23 European paintings). He also had a churn, a coffee mill, scales, weights and a large featherbed – even though he lived 100 miles from the nearest settlement, and over 900 miles from the bustling New Orleans. He had two mules, cattle, hogs and hens. He shot duck, deer, pigs, wild turkey, rabbits, raccoons and opossum.

And he possessed an extraordinary vision of the future in this land. He set up a trading post and sold flour, pork and bread in exchange for cash. But with success came trouble. Charles de Langlade, a pioneer in Wisconsin, organised Indians to try to capture du Sable. He fled the area and settled in River du Chemin, in Michigan City, Indiana.

This episode in his life could have been a matter of greed or of political differences. The British had pegged du Sable as a danger because he had sided with the Americans during their Revolutionary War. Historical evidence suggests that du Sable had ties to Colonel George Rogers Clark of Virginia, who was sent to Illinois and Indiana to win the territories for the Americans. The British felt he was a spy for Mayor Godfrey de Linctot, Clark's assistant.

In 1779, the British lieutenant Thomas Bennett arrested du Sable on suspicion of treason and sent him to Mackinac. "I had the negro Baptiste Point au Sable brought prisoner from the River du Chemin," he wrote.

But du Sable had friends and customers who spoke for him. He remained in detention for the remainder of the American Revolution; however, because of his good character, he was sent to the Pinery, a trading outpost on the St Clair River, south of modern-day Port Huron, that had been established by British Lieutenant Governor Patrick Sinclair. When the British received news that the manager of the Pinery had been mistreating the indigenous people of the area, Sinclair appointed du Sable manager, and he worked there for three years.

Eventually having quite possibly charmed his way back to freedom, in 1784, he returned to Checagou to reclaim his abandoned property and to re-establish his trading post. His business thrived, and he lived in peace among Native Americans and white traders travelling through the area. Historical accounts by white traders, British governors and military officers described him as a wealthy man of good character, sound business acumen, and many friends.

But in May 1800, du Sable sold all his property to Jean La Lime, a French-Canadian fur trapper from St Joseph, for £6,000. The sale was recorded in Detroit and witnessed by John Kinzie (four years later, Kinzie would purchase the estate from La Lime). No one knows why du Sable decided to pack up and leave the area he had made his home. He returned to his land in Peoria for over a decade, and then retired to St Charles, Missouri, where he died on August 28, 1819.

His place in history was largely ignored or forgotten until the Du Sable Heritage Association (DHA), which is affiliated with the Association of Haitian Physicians Abroad, decided to keep Du Sable's historical legacy alive. The DHA organises cultural and educational activities, and is even constructing a Du Sable Park in Chicago. Du Sable's original land, carved out of a wilderness, is prime property in Chicago today. It makes up the foundation for the Tribute Towers, the Wrigley Building, the Palmolive Building and the Magnificent Mile. As long ago as 1963, the real estate he once owned was estimated to be worth at least US$1 billion.

Du Sable kept impeccable records, which appear in everything ever written about him. His deeds are recorded in the Wayne County Courthouse in Illinois. The reports of British officers and the journals of travellers and traders also recorded their transactions and notes about du Sable (sometimes called Au Sable, De Sable or Du Saible). Milo M. Quaife, an author who writes about Great Lakes history, and Fr Thomas A. Meehan, another scholar, documented du Sable's religious records. All of these formed the foundation of the writings about him.

So there is no doubt of du Sable's place in history. The great mystery is exactly how he ended up in Chicago. This we know: what would later become the midwestern state of Illinois was originally controlled by the French, who imported a large number of slaves from Saint-Domingue to mine lead along the Mississippi River. Baptismal records prove the presence of these slaves; but by all accounts du Sable was born a free man and was never one of them. Many settlers trekked across the wilderness, including French trappers from Canada who traded with the American Indians, but the stories that surrounded Du Sable all point to his being a free negro from Haiti, born around 1750.

Little, if anything, is known of du Sable's life in Haiti, unless you want to believe the dramatic tale that author Lawrence Cortesi relates. With a cryptic reference to an interview with du Sable's grandson by Nathan Matson and a footnote crediting the Wisconsin Historical Collection, Cortesi spins a yarn that goes like this:

> Jean du Sable and his friend Jacques Clemorgan sailed on the *Suzanne* with no clear-cut dreams except to make their fortune off the cargo they carried across the Gulf of Mexico.

Neither of them foresaw disaster. But when the
Suzanne was within a day's reach of New Orleans,
grey, low-hanging clouds raced across the sky,
darkening the horizon, and brisk winds suddenly
whipped up the ocean....

Beaten by waves, the Suzanne capsized, and both
men found themselves tossed into the sea.

"Save yourself, Jean," Clemorgan ordered, but du Sable
would not abandon his childhood friend, who came from
a neighbouring plantation in Haiti. After collapsing into
a 12-hour sleep, du Sable searched the desolate beach
on which they had landed for a piece of driftwood to fix
Clemorgan's broken leg. He found no wood, but looking
off into the horizon, he saw a ship sailing towards them.
So he vowed to swim to it and bring back help.

"In a letter many years later, Clemorgan recounted this
incident, saying he owed every year of life beyond age 21
to his negro companion," wrote Cortesi.

There's more to Cortesi's story. He says the ship,
which was Dutch, took them to New Orleans, where
Clemorgan got a job in a merchandising house and du
Sable met a sympathetic priest, Fr Pierre Gibault, who
offered him room and board in exchange for working as
a groundskeeper. There du Sable remained for a year.

Then came a meeting that changed du Sable's life. In
February 1765, a Potawatomi American Indian named
Choctaw came to the mission. He had travelled from
the Great Lakes region to New Orleans to sell furs, but
found himself cheated out of his money. From Choctaw,
du Sable learned of the French influence on the Indians
in the north.

"Besides the explanation of his Christian background,
Choctaw...spoke of freedom in the northern wilderness
– no slaves and no masters – and of the beautiful rivers

and lakes, the sea of plains, the endless forests. Finally, Choctaw spoke of the riches in furs awaiting those strong enough to hunt for them," says Cortesi.

Choctaw sold du Sable on the idea, but neither man had any money. Du Sable turned to Clemorgan, who loaned him money for a dugout canoe, traps, and guns. The motley trio set off on their 600-mile trip up the Mississippi to the French settlement of St Louis. There, Cortesi claims, du Sable and Clemorgan built a cabin and began learning the trapping trade. They thrived in St Louis because they built a reputation for being honest traders even with the American Indians. It was a bustling town with an inn, two saloons, livery stables, two general stores, and surrounding cabins. Choctaw suggested they take the pelts to New Orleans, where they could make more money, and du Sable made two trips to New Orleans a year.

When he returned in May 1769, he got the surprise of his life: The French had secretly signed away Louisiana in a treaty, and it now belonged to Spain. Du Sable hated the Spanish because they had killed his mother. (His father had served on a French privateer that took great pleasure in attacking Spanish ships.)

While an angry du Sable weighed his options, a runner from Cahokia burst into the room to tell him that Chief Pontiac had summoned him. An Indian brave sent by the British had stabbed Pontiac in his sleep, and he was on his deathbed, but wanted to see Choctaw and du Sable before he died. The two men followed Pontiac's messenger.

According to the legend, this is when du Sable headed towards his adventures in the north. The rest is Chicago's history of its West Indian connection.

Chapter 4

JOHN PAUL JONES:
The Secret in Tobago

He was a Casanova with sea legs, and he charmed politicians and ladies from Europe to the Caribbean. In the Age of Sail, when one man's pirate was another man's hero, John Paul Jones, an ambitious, hot-tempered Scot, became a contemptuous pirate to the British and a decorated hero to the Americans during the Revolutionary War (1775–83).

You could say Jones had the best of luck and the worst of luck. His good luck gave him opportunities that seem to fall into his lap. Bad luck – including a dark secret hidden in Tobago – set the course of Jones's swashbuckling life, which eventually led to his being given the title of "Father of the US Navy" – nearly 125 years after his death.

John Paul Jones was born on July 6, 1747. At 13, when he apprenticed himself for seven years to the captain of the brig *Friendship*, he signed on with his birth name: John Paul. The sea offered the best opportunities for non-aristocratic boys like Paul, whose father worked as a gardener on the 1,400-acre estate of Arbigland at Kirkbean, Kirkcudbright, Scotland. John Paul had no dancing or fencing lessons while growing up – two useful skills for the time – but he had the good sense to educate himself, and he was bossy.

Paul had his first stroke of luck when Robert Benson, captain of the *Friendship*, trained him to use the octant, a navigational tool that charts a ship's course on the trackless sea. In the wrong hands, an octant could lead to a mutiny, but the captain felt safe training a boy. Paul crossed the Atlantic eight times in three years on the *Friendship* before it was sold for debts. No longer obligated to fulfil his apprenticeship, he took a job as third mate on a slaver, the *King George*, and sailed the Middle Passage to deliver slaves to the Caribbean.

Paul hated the work. He asked to be paid off in Jamaica after three years and was lucky enough to get a free passage home on the *John*. During that voyage, both the captain and the first mate died of fever contracted in the West Indies. So, at 21, Paul became the unpopular captain of the *John* (he would never get along with any of his crews). On his second voyage as captain, Paul's infamous temper surfaced. He ordered the ship's carpenter, Mungo Maxwell, flogged with a cat-o'-nine tails. As the crew and Paul watched, Maxwell received 12 strokes.

When the *John* anchored in Tobago in mid-1770, Maxwell filed charges of assault and unjust abuse in the Admiralty Court. After the court found Paul not guilty, Maxwell quit the *John.* But in early November, Paul sailed to Kirkcudbright and was arrested as soon as he went ashore. In jail, he learned Maxwell had died on his return voyage to Scotland. So Maxwell's father, a prominent figure in Kirkcudbright, had had Paul arrested, claiming his son had died from the beating he had received under Paul's command.

After posting bail in the spring of 1771, Paul set off for the Caribbean to clear his name. He got a letter from the judge at the Admiralty Court in Tobago saying Maxwell's wounds had not been life-threatening, and a letter from the captain of the ship on which Maxwell had sailed home stated Maxwell had died of a fever.

Paul quickly regrouped. He loaded his new ship, the *Betsy*, with butter and wine to take to the West Indies; then he noticed the *Betsy* needed repairs. While waiting for them to be completed, he contracted a fever, and by the time he recovered, the butter had turned rancid. Short of cash, Paul proceeded as planned and arrived in Tobago around Christmas 1773. There, his cantankerous crew demanded their pay. Paul said they would get paid when they returned to England. The ringleader, never identified by name, confronted him.

The only record of what happened on that fateful day comes from a letter Paul wrote years later, on March 6, 1779, to American patriot Benjamin Franklin. Paul had misunderstood a cryptic letter Franklin had written to him about a prank on Paul that Franklin had been privy to in France. Thinking Franklin had found out his secret in Tobago, Paul wrote, "It has been my intention for more than Twelve Months past to communicate to you; which however I have put off from time to time on reflecting that the account must give you more pain than pleasure..."

Paul began to spill the story about his last trip to Tobago. "The brute, a principal in embezzling the Master's liquors, confronted me with the grossest abuse that vulgarism could dictate."

Always tactless and impatient with his crews, Paul offered the ringleader some "frocks and trousers" from the ship's supply. Enraged, the ringleader threatened to seize the ship. Paul ran into his cabin "intending" to take a board to ward off the attack, but grabbed his sword instead, which just "happened to be on the table. The ringleader having thrice my strength grabbed a cudgel. I was thunder struck with surprise."

An angry crew gathered to watch the fight. The *Betsy* rocked and creaked. Paul backed away until his heel hit the edge of the hatchway.

"The assailant raised his arm high, and threw his body forward to reach the Master's head with the descending blow, the fatal and unavoidable consequence of which was his rushing upon the sword," wrote Paul.

The ringleader was dead. Paul claimed he fled the scene to find a justice of the peace and turn himself in, but was told he could not because no charges had been laid. He could not go before the Admiralty Court, because the judge was not on the island. Paul hopped on a horse and galloped from Scarborough to Courland Bay, where he caught a ship. From there, he disappeared, travelling incognito, as friends advised, for fear of being extradited back to Tobago to stand trial.

In the winter of 1774, Paul surfaced in Virginia, where he had once visited his brother. He was now John Paul Jones, and his brother was dead. Alone, Jones hooked up with two radicals, Thomas Jefferson and Patrick Henry, who talked of freedom for the American colonies.

Jones courted southern belles. He joined the Masons and then the American Revolution. On December 7, 1775, he was commissioned First Lieutenant in the Continental Navy, serving aboard Esek Hopkins's flagship, the *Alfred*. He got command of the *Ranger* on November 1, 1777.

The fledgling US navy was no match for the mighty British, and Jones was never able to get a decent ship. When the Continental Congress of the newly formed US sent Jones and other representatives to France to woo French support, he hoped to procure a sleek ship, but waited in vain, busying himself with trysts that he had to be rescued from by American diplomats. Early in 1779, the French gave Jones a battered old East Indiaman, *Duc de Duras*. Jones spruced up the ship and dubbed it *Bonhomme Richard*, the French translation of *Little*

Richard, a publication by his mentor, Benjamin Franklin. Commanding four other ships and two French privateers, he sailed on August 14, 1779. His plan: to raid the English coast. This proved difficult because his crew, privateers by nature, were more interested in loot than any mission to burn English ships. But Jones craved fame.

On September 23, 1779, in the dark of night off Flamborough Head in the cold and treacherous North Sea, Jones engaged the British HMS *Serapis*. With jagged cliffs 450 feet high as a backdrop, the *Bonhomme Richard* cornered the *Serapis*, a far superior ship. The *Serapis* fought relentlessly. The *Bonhomme Richard* survived three hits from Captain Landais of the *Alliance*, a ship in Jones's own squadron. Jones appeared to be doomed, but when asked to surrender he supposedly shouted, "I have not yet begun to fight!" For this, he was later immortalised in American history books.

With the aid of superb French marksmen, Jones captured the *Serapis*, and Captain Pearson surrendered. The battered *Bonhomme Richard* sank the next day, after its one and only encounter.

This was the legendary battle that defined Jones's career. By now the British had deemed Jones a pirate, but in France, where he travelled after a stop in Holland, he became a hero. The French warmly welcomed him.

Historian and socialite Mrs Reginald de Koven, who collected and compiled John Paul Jones's letters, wrote:

> All Paris whose pleasure it was to celebrate the new ideas of liberty...now rose to greet and to honour the victor of the Serapis. Eulogistic reports of his conduct in Holland had been sent to the King from his ambassador at The Hague, the Duc de la Vauguyon, insuring a most favourable reception at court; the report of his astonishing exploits was

on every tongue, and the curiosity to see the hero
of the hour waxed so keen that it penetrated even
into the petits appartements of Versailles.

It was said that Marie Antoinette, and a "bevy of her
ladies...hastened to place herself at one of the glass
partitions of the palace to catch a glimpse of him as he
passed by." Marie Antoinette invited him to her box at
the opera. He spoke little French, but that proved no
hindrance. John Paul Jones had become a star.

"The public received me," he wrote in his journal for
Louis XVI, "at the opera, the theatres, and wherever I
passed, with enthusiasm and the warmest applause."

His popularity did nothing for his cause to procure
proper ships to fight the British in the American revolt.
Jones spent most of the war hoping the US colonies would
realise the need to boost their naval power. After the war,
Jones returned to the US. There was no prize money for
him, and the American navy no longer officially existed.
He had no funds to purchase the estate he wanted, so
he returned to Philadelphia to serve Congress in any
capacity it chose. He offered plans to build the American
navy, but was ignored.

With Congress's blessings, Jones fed his insatiable
ego by serving as a rear admiral in the service of
Russia's Empress Catherine, but her cronies constantly
undermined his efforts and took credit for his victories,
so Jones retired to Paris in 1790. He died alone on July
18, 1792, at 45, and was buried in Paris without fanfare.

Shortly after his death, a message arrived from the US
government for Jones to deal with the Barbary pirates
who had seized some American ships. The call to service
came too late.

John Paul Jones was forgotten until US President Theodore Roosevelt decided to build the greatest navy in the world. He needed a symbol for that navy, and Jones fitted the bill. In April 1905, anthropologists found Jones's grave in the abandoned St Louis Cemetery in Paris, which had been turned into a foundation for lower-class housing. Jones was given a coffin similar to Napoleon's and a huge parade through Paris. Four American cruisers brought his remains back to the US and seven battleships escorted the coffin up Chesapeake Bay. On January 26, 1913, Jones was laid to rest in the crypt of the US Naval Academy Chapel in Annapolis, Maryland.

All this for a man the US Continental Congress had ranked 18th in a list of sea captains. He had really only accomplished two, single-ship battles. He died with unpaid accounts, and all he took away from the Revolutionary War was "empty praises of Congress". His sketchy list of achievements makes his popularity baffling.

There is no doubt that the events of Tobago determined Jones's destiny. Had it not been for that "unfortunate incident", as Jones always referred to the murder he committed, he might have settled in Tobago, where he had investments. Instead, his misfortune turned to good luck; and, through legend more than accomplishment, he secured a place in history as the father of the US navy.

Chapter 5

JOHN HANCOCK:
Fame, Fortune and the West Indies Connection

On May 9, 1768, John Hancock's ship the *Liberty* slipped into the Boston port at sunset. No one walking down the bustling streets or along the busy wharf could have possibly pinpointed the significance of that event. No one – not even Hancock – could have guessed how the *Liberty* would set in motion a chain of events which would spark a momentous protest that would lead the American colonists one step closer to revolution.

Sure that they would find the *Liberty* stuffed with cases of Madeira wine, but tired after a long day's work and unwilling to work in the dark, British customs agents made the mistake of waiting until morning to inspect the ship. The next day they were shocked to find it almost empty. Someone wanted them to believe that the ship had come into Boston only a quarter filled. Baffled by the eerily empty ship, the customs agents who had been present on the dock during the night insisted they had not seen any wine being unloaded.

Irate and outsmarted, the customs agents knew their hands were tied. John Hancock, a lucky man his entire life, had seemingly bypassed the customs. He ordered the *Liberty* reloaded with cargo bound for England. But as it was about to sail, the *Romney*, a British man-of-war, sailed into Boston harbour. The captain was looking for trouble.

"The town is a blackguard town and ruled by mobs...I will make their hearts ache before I leave," said the captain.

Inspired by the captain's swagger, no doubt, a customs agent who had searched the *Liberty* a month before changed his original story, and now claimed he had been held aboard it against his will on the night of May 9, when, he said, he "heard the squeal of tackles hoisting goods." Fearing for his life, he claimed, he had remained silent.

That was the excuse the British needed to seize the *Liberty*. The word spread fast, and Boston bubbled over with rage. Down at the port, a mob of about 500 "sturdy boys and negroes" rushed to the wharf, where marines from the *Romney* had stormed the *Liberty*. The enraged colonists ripped paving stones from the streets and heaved them at the marines. A man who worked for Hancock ran up Beacon Hill to deliver the startling news to him: the *Liberty* was slowly being dragged away from the shouting mob.

The hot-tempered Samuel Adams – always ready to whip a mob into a frenzy – saw the *Liberty* as the excuse he needed to stir up trouble, but Hancock could not muster the spirit yet to become a revolutionary. He still held out hope for a reconciliation with the British, who were desperate for ways to make money out of the colonists to pay England's debts from the war with France, which had spiralled out of control. The British had felt they were entitled to money from the Stamp Act, which proved impossible to enforce. So, not willing to give up the revenue they expected from the colonists (who were smuggling goods from the West Indies and Europe and keeping false records of their imports), the British made another futile attempt to collect money on imports through the Townshend Act. Now, Boston and the British were sizing each other up, and the tension could be cut with a knife.

Throughout the summer of 1768, Hancock, known as "the patriot in purple", could only stand on shore and watch his well-guarded *Liberty* rocking on the waves. He must have been thinking about how he had got to this point in his life.

John Hancock had once been a devout British subject who dreamed of being the first Lord Hancock, with a sprawling estate housing a castle. Instead, as one of Boston's most famous citizens, living in the Commonwealth of Massachusetts, he became the first American rebel to sign the Declaration of Independence. The moment he signed his name big and bold, Hancock assured his place in history. Who would have guessed that he would be given the privilege of being the first to sign such an important document?

He did not have the most engaging personality among those who framed the famous document nor the fame of the politicians who became heroes of the American Revolution. Hancock did not have the daring reputation of the fledgling country's chief military officer, General George Washington, or the flamboyant style of one of America's founding fathers, the plantation owner Thomas Jefferson. Hancock could be considered cunning and smart, but he did not possess the intelligence of Washington's right-hand man, Alexander Hamilton (who happened to have been born on the West Indian island of Nevis); nor did Hancock have the political savvy of another founding father, John Adams, cousin of Samuel Adams.

As a matter of fact, Hancock has been described as "vain, arrogant, egotistic, hypersensitive, petulant, exhibitionistic, capricious, vacillating, intemperate, susceptible to flattery, improvident, and somewhat of a demagogue and faker," by his biographer, Herbert Allan. When this first major biography of Hancock, *John Hancock: Patriot in Purple*, was published in 1948, Karl Lehman, of New York University, wrote a scathing review in the *William and Mary Quarterly* claiming, "One of the most notable lacunae of American history has been a good biography of John Hancock. Many people have begun the task but have abandoned it when they came to the conviction that, as John Adams [the second US President] phrased it, Hancock was 'a man without head and without heart' or as James Truslow Adams put it, was 'an empty barrel.'"

But the man who would become most famous for his signature had something more important than the other revolutionaries, a trump card that forced even those who despised him to turn to him. The rebels needed John Hancock like no other patriot in the struggle for freedom because he was rich; and while everyone at the time knew that, it seems to be a secret that was buried in history. Hancock possessed enormous wealth – much of which came to him under the table, so to speak – and he revelled in it.

> John Hancock did not set out to be a rebel, let alone found a new nation. He was quite happy with the old one, which had made him rich and powerful—the head of one of North America's largest mercantile empires...Hancock loved wealth. He adored all the foppish trappings it could buy: the fashionable wigs, frilled shirts, silk and velvet jackets and breeches—and the shoes with silver or gold buckles that sparkled as he strode along Boston's Hancock Wharf.

He was a wholesaler, warehouser, importer, exporter, shipbuilder, shipowner and operator, investment banker, realty developer and manager, and merchant.

"The Hancocks were no different from other merchants; they were just better at the game – more daring, more willing to take risks, and sometimes more clever at analysing market conditions and minimising those risks."

Britain, virtually bankrupt from a century of war with France and Spain, wanted to squeeze Hancock and the colonies, so it came up with an ingenious or ingenuous plan: a tax on tea. The colonies, fed up with England, revolted – and John Hancock was right there.

While the new Americans fought for their survival, Hancock "...lived as an aristocrat – even in the face of enemy cannon fire – and he continued to ride through Boston in his splendid gilded coach," writes Hancock biographer Harlow Giles Unger. It was a far cry from the life he had once seemed destined for.

Born on January 12, 1737, Hancock, who would become second president of the Continental Congress and the first elected governor of Massachusetts, showed early signs of wanting to become a preacher like his father and grandfather, after being educated at Harvard. But when his father died unexpectedly at 41, in 1844, Hancock's life took an entirely different turn. His uncle, Thomas Hancock, had built a thriving business in Boston, but he had no heirs, and did not want his life's fortune to fall into strangers' hands, so he and his wife Lydia decided to adopt John.

Overnight, John Hancock became a wealthy teenager. His uncle enrolled him in the Boston Public Latin School, which prepared boys for Harvard University. There, students learned to be proper British citizens, respect the king, and speak fluent Latin and Greek, as well as read and recite the Bible in those languages. Boys mended quills instead of playing. They learned about the businesses of Boston.

"Boston's merchant plutocracy turned their city into a mercantile utopia. It was by far the busiest, most important, and best-developed port in the colonies... More than 500 ships sailed out of the harbour each year," wrote journalist and historical writer Unger in *American Tempest*.

By 1736, Uncle Hancock's business, which had started with bookbinding, had grown into a lucrative general store, with everything from cloth – calico, chintz, muslin, cotton, taffeta, and silks – to staples like sugar, tea, corn, and rum. The retail store grew into wholesaling and spread throughout the 13 colonies. Thomas Hancock also turned to investment banking, selling whale oil. He sent his whaling ships to the most remote areas of New England and Newfoundland, and traded rum for oil. His first ship sailed from Boston in 1729, only five years after he had started his little stationery store. The ship carried rum, beer, cotton, hemp, and other commodities to whaling towns in New England and Newfoundland.

"Thomas Hancock's oil ventures made him rich beyond his wildest dreams. Within five years he had commissioned five ships to handle his trade, ordering 5,000 or more gallons of rum from New England distillers," said Unger in *The Merchant Kings*.

But in 1737, the whale-oil business crashed. Quickly, Thomas Hancock sold his ships and invested in real estate, buying up Beacon Hill and much of Boston.

"Two years later they began a life of splendour never before seen in New England," wrote John Hancock's biographer Allan.

And of course, there was molasses. Thomas Hancock owed much of his success to the growing popularity of rum in colonial America, and John Hancock's fortune reached back to the Molasses Act of 1733. "Rum, by then, had become New England's most popular drink, and New England distillers imported the vast majority of molasses to make their rum from the French and Spanish sugar islands of the Caribbean," said Unger.

This was because sugar production in the British West Indies cost from 25 to 40 per cent more than in the other islands.

According to Unger:

> Rhode Island's 30 distilleries imported nearly 900,000 gallons of molasses a year; 60 distilleries in Massachusetts produced 2.7 million gallons of rum a year and imported about one million gallons of molasses annually...But only 30,000 gallons came from the British West Indies. Noting this, the British decided to impose a sixpence-a-gallon duty on foreign molasses. Preachers and doctors were happy, but not colonial American businessmen.

The molasses-smuggling business was lucrative enough for merchants to persevere. They bribed underpaid customs officials and waterfront workers to undervalue ships' cargoes. The frustrated English knew what was going on, but were hard pressed to stop it as ships slipped in and out of Boston Harbour. During Governor Jonathan Belcher's term, 1.5 million gallons of molasses were smuggled into New England, and the colonists boldly refused to pay a three per cent tax.

In addition, "Hancock sent New England's salted fish to the French West Indies, where his agent traded it for low-cost molasses to send to Holland for distillation into cheap rum that he bought and shipped back to New England," said Unger.

The colonists had been sabotaging the British with their molasses trade as far back as the French and Indian War, which had begun in 1754. Massachusetts merchants had prolonged the war by smuggling essential goods to the French forces, not only undermining the British military effort but also depriving the British treasury of revenues to help pay for the war. They purchased molasses and smuggled it to New England distillers, who had paid for it with contraband war matériel for French forces.

Thomas Hancock's merchant bank had become New England's largest enterprise. By 1758 he was the primary financier and procurement officer in America for the British military, and the defence ministry at London appointed him His Majesty's Agent for Transports. The House of Hancock handled the payroll for generals and civilian governors, and, "always quick to sense which way the trade winds were blowing...gradually broadened the scope of his merchandising to include Nova Scotia, the West Indies, Holland and Spain."

The secret of Thomas Hancock's mushrooming success lay in imports from St Eustatius, a Dutch West Indies isle near Nevis and St Kitts. Records show that he smuggled goods through St Eustatius as early as 1749, even with Britain trying to bear down on this practice.

Sir Francis Bernard promised that he would end illegal molasses-smuggling when he became governor of Massachusetts in 1760. He seemed to be successful: within months of his appointment, merchants were importing duty-free British molasses. But then John Temple, a customs officer, realised that "Salem merchants were importing more cane from the English island of Anguilla in just a few weeks than the island's entire annual crop," says Unger. The merchants had been bribing customs officials with their boatloads of molasses from the French West Indies.

In 1764, the British, in dire straits over the war, decided to raise taxes and crack down on the colonists. As John Hancock's money spread through the colonies supporting revolutionary ventures, his popularity grew and he began winning elections. At a town meeting on October 28, 1767, everyone decided to support Hancock's call to boycott British luxury goods: gloves, shoes, gold, silver thread, and silks.

On April 8, 1768 three weeks after he was re-elected as selectman, Hancock's ship the *Lydia,* carrying tea, paper and other dutiable goods, came into Boston harbour. Hancock told his men to remove the customs agent, who would certainly cause trouble.

The British realised how important Hancock's money was to bankrolling the rebels in Boston, and charged him with not paying tariffs. Early in August 1768, Hancock went to trial, represented by his boyhood friend John Adams. The court dismissed the smuggling charges and Hancock won his case, but the British had seized the *Liberty*. No one wanted to cross Hancock, who by that time symbolised freedom to Bostonians, so no one would buy the ship.

But, always adept at enraging the colonists, the British armed the ship, and sent her on runs up the New England coast to snatch smugglers. Restless and growing increasingly intolerant of British decisions, the merchants and ship owners of Newport dispatched a mob to burn the *Liberty*. By then, the British had forced Hancock's hand and he was financing the patriots in their struggle against them. The events involving the *Liberty* propelled him to the forefront of the American revolution, though he would elude his enemies – the British – throughout the war.

On January 22, 1774, residents of Boston thinly disguised themselves as American Indians, stormed the port and tossed crates of tea into the harbour. Two weeks after the *London Chronicle* reported on the uprising, England's attorney general formally charged John Hancock and others with high treason.

On March 5, Hancock addressed a crowd. "Looking every inch an aristocrat from his dress and powdered wig to his smart pumps of grained leather, his dark eyes were penetrating, his mouth was firm, his chin determined," said Unger.

It was the most important speech of his life. He demanded that everyone give up tea, and said about the British: "Prepare to fight for your houses, lands, wives, children, liberty and God so that those noxious vermin will be swept forever from the streets of Boston."

He quoted a passage from the Bible, stepped down from the pulpit, shook Sam Adams' hand and stepped into the American Revolution with all his heart and soul. He packed up his ships with enough goods to clear his debts in England. Hancock wanted to keep his good name.

"Hancock and other men of great wealth in Congress made huge loans from their own personal sterling reserves to purchase essential supplies during the American Revolutionary War," said Unger.

Adams knew how to raise money, and "Hancock's desk was the central command post for the entire Continental Army with Hancock...serving as liaison between the various commanders, General George Washington and Congress." In 1774, Hancock was elected to the Provincial Congress of Massachusetts and simultaneously to the Continental Congress. When Peyton Randolph resigned in 1776, Hancock assumed the position of its president.

On July 4, 1776, the members of the Continental Congress left for the day. Hancock was to sign the Declaration of Independence. He received a corrected copy, sat at his desk in an empty chamber and signed his name with a quill pen. The Secretary of Congress, Charles Thomson, a Pennsylvania delegate, was by his side. When the copies came out the next day, they bore only Hancock's large signature, smack in the middle of the bottom of the document. It was a signature that could have cost him his life. If the colonies had lost their struggle, he would have been nothing more than a treasonous merchant who instigated people to rebel while he sneaked everything from tea to molasses into New England.

By 1778, poor health and repeated bouts of gout had taken a toll on Hancock, and he asked General Washington for permission to return to Boston. He was taken back by the rebels as a hero. Bells rang, and 13 cannon sounded for the 13 colonies from the fortress on the hill and ships in the harbour. Soldiers saluted as he was escorted into Boston.

Hancock presided over town meetings and resumed his opulent lifestyle, riding in an "ornate yellow chariot that sparkled like gold in the sunlight...with all the state and pageantry of an Oriental prince," said Unger. He continued:

> The chariot had been taken as a prize from the Civil Usage, a pirate vessel. He was attended by four servants dressed in superb livery, mounted on fine horses richly caparisoned and escorted by 50 Horsemen of the Corps of Cadets with drawn sabres, one following his carriage.

Hancock retired from business in 1777 owing to his gout, but continued public service in his native state by participating in the formation of its constitution. He was elected to the governorship of the state, where he served for five years, and then declined re-election, but rallied and returned to public office. On October 25, 1780, John Hancock donned his crimson velvet jacket with gold trim and gold buttons and embroidered white vest and rode his gilded chariot past cheering crowds to his inauguration as the first Governor of the Commonwealth of Massachusetts.

He died on October 8, 1793, at 55, and was buried in an unmarked grave until Massachusetts erected a memorial for him, which was dedicated on September 19, 1896.

When he died, the once-wealthy Hancock left a small estate. He had spent most of his fortune on the revolution, rebuilding Boston and forming state institutions and charities. But it had been a sweet life, thanks partly to molasses from the West Indies.

Chapter 6

ST EUSTATIUS:
A Thorn in the Side of a Colonial Giant

As the 16-gun converted brig-of-war the *Andrew Doria* appeared on the blue carpet of sea unfurling towards the tiny West Indian island of St Eustatius, Johannes de Graaff knew that one signal from him would send a bold and defiant message to Europe. That decision, a mere gesture, would put him in hot water. It would also ensure his place in history.

It was strictly business. Politics would have to take a side. Other European nations – the Spanish, French and British – stirred up political trouble in the Caribbean with their endless cycle of wars, but the Dutch usually created their own brand of trouble through trade. They undermined European governments by paying little attention to other countries' trade laws.

Take, for instance, this ship sailing towards St Eustatius. Its mere presence was enough to risk the wrath of the good governor's sworn enemy, the British, because the Dutch had proclaimed themselves neutral in Britain's latest war on North American soil. But this was business. Anyway, what was a little political turbulence in the Caribbean, which was defined by political turmoil?

So it was settled. Governor de Graaff would defy the Dutch stand of neutrality, decided way over in Europe, and would propel St Eustatius, only seven square miles, into the maelstrom of the American Revolution, where 13 colonies along the Atlantic seaboard up north had decided to fight for their independence from Britain. De Graaff stood poised and ready.

Suddenly the sound of squawking birds gave way to growling cannons belching clouds of smoke. St Eustatius had recognised and answered the call of the *Andrew Doria*, and with that it became the first country in the world to recognise the United States of America.

Soon, St Eustatius had Europe buzzing. The Dutch revelled in their newfound riches from the thriving trade with the rebelling American colonies. They had to dodge the British, who forbade trade with the colonial upstarts who dared to fight for their freedom. British spies stationed in the Caribbean relayed tall tales and sketchy information about the trouble-making St Eustatius back to England.

A merchant in the seaside town of Campveere wrote about a favourite way to take ammunition to the Americans, by loading it on the coast of Africa, then proceeding to St Eustatius, where it was instantly snatched up by American agents.

"Seldom has an island port had a more meteoric career, or shown a more striking contrast between insignificance in time of peace and resounding prosperity in war-time than that presented by the little volcanic island of St Eustatius," said J. Franklin Jameson, an early American naval historian. "Its tale is worth telling...partly on account of the close association of its fortunes with those of the American Revolutionary War, and the important part which it played in enabling our forefathers to sustain that difficult and unequal struggle."

In a lecture at Newport Naval Academy in the mid-1800s, Jameson said the island had a reputation for being "a bold, little, rocky and rather infertile place." It did not produce more than 600 barrels of sugar a year. There was only one landing point, but the Dutch realised its strategic importance and turned the island into a centre of commerce.

Many Europeans did not even know St Eustatius existed, but English politicians and businessmen certainly knew of it. Edmund Burke described it in the House of Commons in a long-winded speech of 1781, when Britain contemplated how to deal with this thorn in its side:

> The island is different from all others. It seemed to have been shot up from the ocean by some convulsion, the chimney of a volcano, rocky and barren...Its proprietors had, in the spirit of commerce, made it an emporium for all the world, a mart, a magazine for all the nations of the earth. It had no fortifications for its defence: no garrison, martial spirit or military regulations. Its inhabitants were a mix of all nations and climates; its utility was its defence. The universality of its use, the constant neutrality of its nature, which made it advantageous to all nations of the world, was its security and its safeguard.

Before the American Revolution, St Eustatius, as Burke had pointed out, had little need for defence, because its neutrality protected it. Of course, those in the know would have realised that St Eustatius had a habit of cutting political corners for its own business purposes. Now, however, the island had become a source of political gossip.

Sir Joseph Yorke, the British ambassador at The Hague since 1751, possessed some secret information about the Dutch traders, which he shared in letters, and those letters show that St Eustatius played a far bigger role in America's independence than most people had imagined. A Dutch rear-admiral, who spent 13 months in

Statia (another name for St Eustatius) between 1778 and 1779, reported 3,182 vessels sailed from the island. An English observer claimed that in 1779, 12,000 hogsheads of tobacco and 1,500,000 ounces of indigo came from North America to be exchanged for naval supplies and other goods.

Jameson said:

> Many passages in the diplomatic history of the American Revolution show that St Eustatius was one of the chief, and at times the quickest and safest, means of communication between our [the US'] representatives abroad and the Continental Congress and its officials at home.

John Adams, the rebel who would become the second president of the US, often mentioned St Eustatius, and it is clear other merchants in the rebelling states did as well. According to Jameson:

> An informant of Lord Suffolk at Rotterdam tells [Adams] in March, 1777, that Messrs Willing and Morris of Philadelphia have written to a Rotterdam merchant, their correspondent, and that he can write by way of St Eustatius, as they will henceforth have regular means of intercourse with that island.

"As early as March 1776, Abraham van Bibber, agent of the state of Maryland at St Eustatius, [was] taking care of cargoes sent or underwritten by the state,'" Adams wrote to the President of Congress in 1779 about two Boston agents in Amsterdam [who spent)] all winter buying gunpowder and military supplies.

By March 20, 1775, the States General of the United Netherlands had, at Yorke's insistence, issued a proclamation. But even when the Dutch officially bowed to pressure and prohibited sales of military supplies to the colonies, the trade continued. A letter from Yorke to

Lord Suffolk of December 30, 1774, reads, "By the end of the year 1774, it was noted that there had lately been a prodigious increase in the trade from St Eustatius.

"Skyrocketing prices for gunpowder proved to be a great temptation for Dutch merchants."

Desperate and exasperated, Yorke wrote to Suffolk that a Dutch merchant had been warned by British authorities in a letter dated October 22, 1776, that: "[If] you continue [to trade], we will cut off your supply of saltpetre from Bengal."

When Johannes de Graaff became the new governor of St Eustatius, there was apprehension in the American colonies. After all, he had been given his post in order to run a tighter ship, as the last governor had been far too slack in allowing illegal trade with the rebels. But soon, merchants posted letters of assurance: the new governor had no intention of shutting down trade with the American colonies. A Captain Colpys wrote to Mr Young on November 27, 1777, that since the arrival of the new governor, the ports had been opened without reserve to American ships.

> As the Dutch have discover'd that their laws when put in force must ruin their Merchants. I am on the best terms with His Excellency the Governour and have his word and Promise relative to some particulars that gives me great Satisfaction and puts much in our powers. I was not so happy some times agoe, and every bad consequence to apprehend on our new Governour's taking command, but we are as well fixed with him now as we were with the former...The Governour is daily expressing the greatest desire and Intention to protect a trade with us here.

There is no doubt that American colonies depended on St Eustatius for vital supplies necessary to wage their

war, but the end of the American Revolution contributed to the island's decline. An independent US had less need for tiny St Eustatius because it could buy whatever it needed from whatever country it chose. St Eustatius also depended heavily on the slave trade, until it was abolished by the Dutch in 1821. St Eustatius's important role in importing crude sugar also decreased, and the island began to slide into oblivion.

Today, St Eustatius is a tourist island that markets its rich history, including its role in the independence of the US.

Chapter 7
GEORGE WASHINGTON:
How Barbados Saved the General

George Washington carefully guarded a secret that could be more important than the clandestine attack he was planning. Bracing himself against the wind that whipped the Delaware River, the stately Washington, who towered over his men at six foot two, surveyed the motley group of 2,400 farmers and fishermen shuffling across the icy ground towards McConkey and Johnson's ferries, in the American colony of Pennsylvania.

It was 3:00 p.m. and a desperate, sombre Washington commanded his battered, hungry, and shivering troops quietly to load sturdy boats and rafts with cannon, guns, ammunition, and horses on that brutally cold Christmas Day of 1776. On that dreary, overcast day, Washington had decided to attack the Hessians – German mercenaries hired by the British – stationed across the flooding Delaware River, which was littered with chunks of floating ice. He knew it was a daring act that could change the course of the American Revolution. For the last five months the struggling colonies had lost every battle. They could not lose this one.

Once they landed on the other side, his loyal troops penetrated needle-sharp sleet in the dark night. Looking regal as usual and, as always, immaculately dressed, Washington ordered a march to Trenton, New Jersey, where he shocked the holiday spirit out of a garrison of 1,500 Hessians, who never suspected anyone would attack in the middle of a bitter storm. Attack they did, with Alexander Hamilton, a West Indian, playing a major role in the battle. When the skirmish ended, the Americans emerged victorious, and the course of American history changed dramatically. Washington's leadership was never in doubt after that surprise attack. He had taken Trenton in less than an hour.

But historians now recognise that Washington, who would become the only commanding American general of the Revolutionary War and the first President of the US, owed much of his success and his unique place in history, including the day he crossed the Delaware River, to a much earlier crossing: a trip to Barbados, in the eastern Caribbean, that Washington had made with his half-brother, Lawrence. It was the only trip he ever took outside the continental US, and it undoubtedly had a profound effect on him and consequently the American Revolution.

Washington's voyage to the Caribbean came about because of his special relationship with Lawrence, a father figure to him from the age of 11, when Washington's father died. While growing up, young George had learned a lot about war from Lawrence, who was 14 years older than him. They were, at that time, loyal British subjects.

In 1739, Spain had goaded Great Britain into war when the Spanish coastguard went overboard by storming a British merchant ship and mutilating British captain Robert Jenkins. The British retaliated with the War of Jenkins' Ear. Lawrence, a loyal British subject in the American colonies, had become the captain of a Virginia company under Admiral Edward Vernon, whose 9,000 men challenged the Spanish at Cartagena, Colombia. After the war ended in 1748, George learned the details of the battles through the stories Lawrence told when he returned to Virginia. He could not have guessed how important the Caribbean would become in his own life.

The horrific conditions at sea had contributed to Lawrence's lung ailments, which developed into tuberculosis. Desperate for a cure, Lawrence decided to sail for Barbados, because he had heard that doctors there had had success in treating lung diseases. With its flourishing sugar plantations and commerce, Barbados was Britain's prize colony in the Caribbean. On November 2, 1751, the Washingtons sailed into Carlisle Bay on a merchant ship, the *Success*. There they found the bustling Bridgetown, well known in Virginia because of its commercial ties with the US.

George and Lawrence expected to be the guests of the Gedney Clarke family. But they had to abandon that plan because the Clarke family was in quarantine for smallpox, so they rented a two-storey Georgian-style house on the Garrison Ridge at the top of Bush Hill. Via wills, deeds and old maps, the Barbados National Trust (BNT) has combed through the work of historians Eustace Shilstone and Warren Alleyne and government archivist Michael Chandler to decide conclusively that a building known as Bush Hill House was where the Washingtons stayed.

George, an impeccable record-keeper and dedicated diarist, wrote of his journey to Barbados, as well as his stay there. He did not miss writing about a single day, no matter how commonplace the events. The first part of his journal charts the weather and events like catching supper from the ship. In his diary, he kept track of the volatile weather on the voyage, which ranged from clear and calm to great winds and even a suspected hurricane. It appears that Washington did not have the best spelling and grammar, though.

He wrote:

> 19th. October: Hard Squals of Wind and Rain with a fermented Sea jostling in heaps occasion(ed) by Wavering wind which in 24 hours Veer'd the Compass not remaining 2 hours in any point...It was universally surmised their had been a violent hurricane not far distant....

On November 1, Washington wrote, they were greeted with the cry of "Land...at 4 am: we quitted our beds with surprise and found...land plainly appearing."

Good news followed on November 4.

> Early this morning came Dr Hilary, an eminent physician recommended by Major Clarke, to pass his opinion on my brother's disorder, which he did

> in a favourable light...In the cool of the evening
> we rode out accompanied by Mr Carter to seek
> lodgings in the country, as the Doctor advised...
> beautiful prospects which on every side presented
> to our view The fields of Cain, Corn, Fruit Trees & in
> a delightful green.

The Washingtons received many invitations and appeared to enjoy socialising. Washington made further observations on the island:

> The Governor of Barbados seem[s] to keep a proper
> State: Lives very retired and at Little expence is
> said he is a Gentleman of good Sence As he avoids
> the Errors of his predecessor he gives no handle
> for complaint but at the same time by declining
> much familiarity is not over zealously loved...There
> is seve[ral] regular Risings in this Island one above
> another so that scarcely any part is deprived of a
> beautiful Prospect: both of sea and Land which is
> contrary to the observation on other Countrys is
> that each Rising is better than the other below....

Initially, Lawrence's health seemed to improve, but two weeks after they arrived in Barbados, George came down with smallpox and was confined to his bed for three weeks. Washington must have cursed his luck. He had been enjoying Barbados, and he undoubtedly appreciated the freedom from the constraints of a widowed mother. Washington's life depended on Dr John Lanahan, who declared him completely recovered on December 12, 1751.

There was also an unexpected, positive side to Washington's illness.

"In retrospect, his brush with a mild case of smallpox was a fantastic stroke of luck, furnishing him with immunity to the most virulent scourge of eighteenth-century armies," wrote historian Ron Chernow in *Washington: A Life*.

Ten days later, Washington decided to return to the US. He had been saddled with the responsibility of taking care of his mother since his father had died, and his work in Virginia undoubtedly weighed heavy on his mind. When the new year rolled around, Lawrence moved to Bermuda, a cooler climate, but realising he was going to die, he went home to Mount Vernon, the family home on the banks of the Potomac River, where he died in June 1752. George was undoubtedly wracked with grief at the loss of his protector.

Ironically, Lawrence's decision to go to Barbados probably saved George's own life and career. It also saved the American Revolution. Smallpox left Washington's face scarred for life (his portraits kindly leave out this fact), but experiencing the disease in Barbados gave him information he probably would not have garnered in the American colonies: he had learned about immunisation and quarantining smallpox patients while in Barbados, and used that knowledge to help inoculate and protect his soldiers when an outbreak threatened the fledgling US army. He swiftly quarantined sick soldiers and prevented a total catastrophe. "Because he had contracted smallpox in Barbados, Washington was spared the fate of at least a quarter of his army, who still succumbed to the disease. If he had got smallpox during the Revolutionary War, he would have been removed as the commanding general or, worse yet, might have died, leaving the American rebels to find a new leader."

Writing in *His Excellency George Washington*, in 2004, historian Joseph J. Ellis says:

> Historians have long known that more than two-thirds of the American casualties in the war were the result of disease. But only recently – and this is rather remarkable – have they recognised that

the American Revolution occurred with a virulent smallpox epidemic of continental scope that claimed about 100,000 lives...When historians debate Washington's most consequential decisions as commander in chief, they are almost always arguing about specific battles. A compelling case can be made that his swift response to the smallpox epidemic and to a policy of inoculation was the most important strategic decision of his military career.

This was the secret that George Washington guarded on that fateful crossing of the Delaware.

There is no doubt that the events of American history would have changed drastically without Washington in charge. Historians agree there was no one else with his leadership skills and astute military mind. There was no one else who possessed Washington's symbolic stature as father of the country. No one had his selflessness or rare wisdom in understanding the importance of relinquishing power when necessary. Another man as the first president could have steered the colonies towards a monarchy or allowed them to disintegrate into chaos. When he took office, the US was a weak and fragile confederation of fiercely independent states, held together mostly through his and Alexander Hamilton's views on a strong federal government.

Standing outside Washington's home – not the one in Mount Vernon, Virginia, that he became known for, but the 18th-century plantation house near Carlisle Bay that he and his half-brother Lawrence rented in Barbados – it is not difficult to realise how important that trip to the Caribbean was to Washington's life and the American Revolution. You could say Barbados played a vital role in America's independence.

Today, the house is preserved as a museum that captures elements of colonial life with furnishings that would have been common for the era. Mahogany, oak and cherrywood antiques, plain pine floors covered with Turkish carpets, royal creamware china, and canopied mosquito-netted beds capture the colonial period. Upstairs, a museum recreates life in Barbados in the 18th century. Visitors can view a 15-minute film that re-enacts the Washingtons' trip from Virginia, and can stroll through the spacious grounds.

The important events of George Washington's life all flow together. From his plantation home on the banks of the Potomac River, where he heard stories of battles in the Caribbean from his brother Lawrence who took him to Barbados – in the only real respite he ever had in his life; to the Delaware River, which became a solidifying point in his military career when he captured Trenton, the astute and observant George Washington certainly realised how water had shaped his life.

It is not difficult to imagine that fateful trip to Barbados crossing his mind on more than one occasion during the American Revolutionary War. Surely on that icy, cold Christmas Day, far away from his wife Martha and the home he cherished, Washington was visited by memories of Lawrence and those warm nights in Barbados.

Chapter 8

ALEXANDER HAMILTON:
The West Indian Who Defined the US

Early on the morning of July 11, 1804, Alexander Hamilton, one of the most famous men in the relatively new country of the United States of America, sneaked out of his house with a pistol, rowed a boat across the Hudson River with his friend Nathaniel Pendleton and his doctor, David Hosack, to the village of Weehawken, New Jersey, climbed a narrow path up a granite cliff – and came face to face with his long-time arch-enemy, Aaron Burr.

This would not be a secret government meeting about America's political misfortunes. Burr and Hamilton had not planned to discuss their political differences or Burr's smouldering resentment of Hamilton's backing his opponents, or his penchant for ignoring Burr's opinions.

For Burr, Republican Vice President of the US under the Democratic-Republican President Thomas Jefferson, the last straw came near the end of his vice-presidency, when Hamilton opposed Burr's run for Governor of New York. Burr challenged Hamilton, and the two met on that fateful morning for a duel to the death, although Hamilton insisted in the letters he left behind that he never intended to kill Burr.

Known as one of the most brilliant men of his time, Hamilton, by all accounts, was striking, both physically and intellectually. He was described as not very tall – about five foot seven – muscular, and having the golden looks of an Adonis. He had red hair and eyes so blue they appeared violet (like the famous eyes of the late movie actress Elizabeth Taylor). George Shea, in *The Life and Epoch of Alexander Hamilton*, described him as having "...a mouth infinite in expression, its sweet smile being most observable and most spoken of; eyes lustrous with deep meaning and reflection, or glancing with quick, canny pleasantry, and the whole countenance decidedly Scottish in form and expression...His political enemies frankly spoke of his manner and conversation, and regretted its irresistible charm."

Hamilton had studied at King's College, had fought in the Revolutionary War, and had become General George Washington's right-hand man – both during the war and Washington's two terms of office. He was fluent in French, and one can only imagine how this helped Washington with the Americans' French allies, especially General Lafayette. Hamilton had turned Wall Street into the stock exchange it is known as today, served as the Inspector General of the US army, and launched the US Navy into existence. He played a big part in saving the floundering US when he and future President James Madison championed what appeared an impossible feat: getting the 13 original colonies, now states, to scrap the Articles of Confederation and support the writing of a new Constitution that would give the federal government more power. It would be 32-year-old Hamilton and 36-year-old Madison who would mainly shape that Constitution.

But the man who had accomplished so much threw away what most likely would have been an even brighter future when he accepted Burr's challenge to a duel. Hamilton's brilliant mind told him that Burr had nothing to gain from killing him.

Hamilton fired the first shot. Burr "heard the ball whistle among the branches and saw the severed twig above his head," wrote historian Ron Chernow. Hamilton had thrown away his shot. He had carried out his plan of the previous night, to give Burr a chance "to pause and to reflect".

Burr aimed his pistol and shot to kill.

Hamilton crumpled to the ground.

"This is a mortal wound, doctor," Hamilton, now paralysed, said to Dr Hosack, struggling to examine the injury. The doctor propped Hamilton up on a reddish-brown rock: the bullet had fractured Hamilton's ribs, damaged his liver and lodged in his heart. Hamilton drifted into unconsciousness and the doctor could find no pulse. Hosack and Pendleton carried Hamilton out of the woods.

Hamilton rallied. "My vision is indistinct," he said.

In the boat, rowing back to New York, Hamilton spotted the pistol he had carried to the duel – his son's, the same pistol used in the duel that had killed his son three years earlier.

"Take care of that pistol. It is undischarged and still cocked. It may go off and do harm," he warned.

"Pendleton knows I did not intend to fire at [Burr]," said Hamilton.

As the boat reached the dock, Hamilton rallied yet again. "Let Mrs Hamilton be immediately sent for. Let the event be gradually broken to her, but give her hopes," he said.

William Bayard stood at the dock waiting for his friend. His servants had told him that Hamilton had rowed away at dawn. When he saw Hamilton in the bottom of the boat, he burst into tears.

His friends rushed to bring Hamilton's wife, Elizabeth, and their seven children to Hamilton's bedside. They carried him to the second floor of the Bayard house. While he lay there, gravely wounded, Hamilton thought about his childhood in the West Indies: he now made last-minute provisions on his deathbed for his cousin Ann Mitchell, who had helped him get his education.

"Mrs Mitchell is the person in the world to whom as a friend I am under the greatest obligation. I have [not] hitherto done my [duty] to her," he said.

On July 12, 1804, shortly after noon, 31 hours after he had been shot, Hamilton died. He was 49 years old.

Hamilton's shocking death had been preceded by a remarkable life, a truly unbelievable one for a boy who had been born on the small British West Indian island of Nevis on January 11, 1755.

His mother, Rachel Faucett Lavien, had left her unhappy marriage to Johann Michael Lavien to live with Hamilton's father, James Hamilton, by 1752. When he was ten, Alexander's father took the family to the Danish island of St Croix, where he had got a job as head clerk in Christiansted, the capital. But shortly after the move, James Hamilton disappeared, wandering from island to island. Alexander knew nothing more about his father until 1771, when he discovered a story in the Christiansted newspaper that his father had been shot in the thigh in a slave rebellion in Tobago, when 30 Koromantyn slaves tried to annihilate the island's white population.

By the time he was 13, Hamilton's mother had died of yellow fever. Some sources say Hamilton's older brother, James Jr, inherited the mother's meagre estate; others say she died intestate. She had run a little store, selling goods to those living on sugar plantations, but had struggled to make ends meet. She left no cash, and a few bills. Alexander received a slave named Ajax from his mother's estate, and the boys' uncle reportedly bought Rachel's books and gave them to her sons.

It was all like a bad dream for Alexander, who had suffered from yellow fever alongside his mother. A cousin, Peter Lytton, was appointed guardian, but he committed suicide less than a year after Alexander and his brother went to live with him. Left at the mercy of other relatives, Hamilton received little schooling. But he loved reading and became fluent in French – his mother was of French descent and probably spoke French at home.

Looking back on his tumultuous life, Hamilton was undoubtedly aware of Nevis's rich history, and while there was little left to idealise in the once affluent, sugar-producing colony, Nevis still possessed the idyllic surroundings of an island that smelled of cinnamon and burning sugar cane. Living there, Hamilton was aware of the delicate balance of nature and the vulnerability of small islands used as colonial pawns in Europe's wars. French Huguenots settled there to escape from Catholic persecution under Louis XIV. Nevis had once been fought over by European nations. Hundreds of thousands of barrels of sugar had been exported from there. Earlier, Nevis had been important for its timber, and before it became a sugar island, there had also been tobacco, indigo, ginger, and cotton.

Hamilton would have known how colonialism created the volatile history of the tiny island, and before he came to the American colonies, he would have known about the revolt in Basseterre, St Kitts, over the British Stamp Act in 1765. He knew how Britain depended on its colonies for revenue. He knew about colonialism. Hamilton grew up with slavery around him, and also the stories of his father's native Scotland, which had filled him with "yearning for an aristocratic heritage he would never be allowed to share," said his biographer William Sterne Randall.

Two merchants, David Beckman and Nicholas Cruger, took note of Hamilton's intelligence and gave him a job as a clerk in their business in Christiansted, St Croix. Soon, he was moving up in the firm. By the time he was 16, he was running the operations when his bosses travelled. His dreams of becoming a physician vanished by the time he was 17, as he became fully entrenched in the firm. He was an astute businessman, who kept impeccable records, and he even learned the ways of the sea – the tides and weather – so that he could export sugar and molasses to the American colonies.

Bored with his low-level clerk position, which he felt did not make enough use of his intelligence, Hamilton began writing pieces for the newspaper. He would discover on St Croix just how powerful his pen could be, and had already captured the attention of many people. Hugh Knox, a Scotch-Irish Presbyterian minister, noted his intelligence and decided that Hamilton must be educated. After Hamilton had submitted a piece to the newspaper on a hurricane that devastated the island, the Reverend Knox arranged for Hamilton to study in the American colonies. Other people rallied to support Hamilton. His boss, Cruger, and his associate Cornelius Kortright and others on the island pitched in to assign the revenue of four annual cargoes to Hamilton's upkeep in the American colonies.

That Hamilton would come to North America to study was a stroke of unbelievable good fortune for the American colonies.

"Few West Indians were educated in North America. The Nevis-born Alexander Hamilton was untypical... One study identifies only 18 West Indian graduates of mainland colleges between 1650 and 1790," wrote Andrew Jackson O'Shaughnessy in *An Empire Divided: The American Revolution and the British Caribbean.*

Hamilton arrived in Boston and proceeded to Elizabeth-town Academy in New Jersey – Princeton University today. There, he mastered Latin and Greek. When Princeton refused to allow him to accelerate his programme, he switched universities, opting for King's College, now Columbia University. He enrolled in 1774 and turned his attention to political writing.

The American Revolution was just around the corner. Hamilton joined the New York provincial militia, and then New York's Provincial Congress ordered an artillery company in 1776 and appointed 21-year-old Hamilton commander. He was now Captain Hamilton.

"Hamilton's tendency to be noticed came to the fore. Looking even younger than his years, and very often giving the impression that he was lost in thought, the new captain somehow made his men look like models of discipline," said author Charles Cerami.

George Washington quickly noticed Hamilton, and on March 1, 1777, promoted him to be his aide-de-camp. Hamilton never really left Washington's side after that. From 1777 to 1781, he served as Washington's main secretary, drafting letters and reports. He followed Washington into battle, but dared to rebel, insisting on going back into the battlefield as a commander, and even resigning his post with Washington to get his way when need be.

For Hamilton, Washington was a father figure – even more so than for most of Washington's admirers and supporters – because Washington provided the admiration, support, and stability that Hamilton had never experienced as an illegitimate child with a wayward father who had deserted the family. But Hamilton did not cling to Washington's coat-tails. He contributed immensely to Washington's callings, in and out of war – and not just the official Revolutionary War – and he followed his own mind.

In 1782, Hamilton defended the former loyalists who had sided with the British in the American war of independence. This was not a popular decision among American colonists, and it did not endear Hamilton to Aaron Burr, but it did show Hamilton's fierce individuality and sense of fairness, as well as his understanding of the complicated dynamics of a newly formed independent country that had once been divided into loyalists and rebels. He helped save the new country from a bitter split.

In 1788, he convinced New Yorkers to ratify the US Constitution. He then served as the nation's first Secretary of the Treasury, from 1789 to 1795. From 1798 to 1800, France and the US fought an undeclared war, in which the US lost over $12 million in ships and cargo to French privateers and frigates. When Washington came out of retirement to head a US army of 10,000 men, he appointed General Hamilton field commander. Hamilton was always there to save the young nation.

"Hamilton was...the proponent of banks, factories and stock exchanges. [He was the cornerstone] of American nationalism and believed states should be controlled by a strong central government, and a professional military..." said Chernow. He added:

> He had a pragmatic mind and he was a prolific writer, taking lofty principles and making them understandable. He came up with a budget system to fund debt, a tax system, the central bank, customs service and the coast guard. He argued for a dynamic executive branch and an independent judiciary. Nearly everyone described him as a genius. He was a pivotal force in four consecutive presidential elections and defined much of America's political agenda... He produced 22,000 pages of legal and business papers...

> Today we are indisputably the heirs to Hamilton's America, and to repudiate his legacy is in many ways to repudiate the modern world.

Hamilton's contribution to the development of the US is astounding and immeasurable. His personal life seems contradictory to his stellar professional life, however. He had been embroiled in needless scandals, one of the biggest a romantic tryst that his wife must have heard about. He had his enemies and his detractors.

"Even some Hamilton admirers have been unsettled by a faint tincture of something foreign in this West Indian transplant; [US President] Woodrow Wilson grudgingly praised Hamilton as 'a very great man, but not a great American.'"

Nevertheless, British statesman Lord Bryce called Hamilton "the most interesting in the early history of the Republic". President Theodore Roosevelt called Hamilton "the most brilliant American statesman who ever lived, possessing the loftiest and keenest intellect of his time." President William Howard Taft praised Hamilton as "our greatest constructive statesman".

As Chernow reminds us, "Hamilton is the foremost political figure in American history who never attained the presidency, yet he probably had a much deeper and more lasting impact than many who did."

For all of his personal shortcomings, including the bad judgment and haughty pride of becoming involved in a duel with Burr, Hamilton possessed a softer side he hid from the brutal world of politics. He never gave up on his father, and never wrote bitterly about the man who abandoned him. In letters to his brother, he wondered what had happened to his father; later in life, when he was famous and settled, he found his father and pleaded with him to come to New York to live with him.

Because of Hamilton, the developing country of the US got a good, strong start. It had the highest credit rating in the world and a net worth estimated at $1.8 billion because of the financial system that Hamilton set up as Washington's Secretary of the Treasury.

Washington and other statesmen get the credit for winning the war of independence, but you could say

Alexander Hamilton, a brilliant young man from a tiny West Indian island, put the US firmly on its feet. He knew there was much work to do, and he worried about the country even on his deathbed: "If they break this union, they will break my heart," he said.

His life – and for that matter his death – had been defined by his West Indian roots. "He was incapable of turning the other cheek," wrote Chernow. "With his chequered West Indian background, he had predicated his career on fiercely defending his honour."

His enemies saw Hamilton as a West Indian upstart and not an American, but his legacy lives on both in Washington, DC, and in New York City. In 2015, Secretary of the Treasury, Jack Lew, announced that the Bureau of Engraving and Printing would feature changes to the $10 bill, which currently carried a picture of Hamilton. (That picture was taken from John Trumbull's 1805 portrait in the collection of the New York City Hall. Hamilton, the first Treasury Secretary, has been on the $10 bill since 1928. When the changes are made, his portrait will either appear on the flip side of the bill, which will feature the picture of a famous woman from American history; or Hamilton will appear by himself on a separate series of notes.)

At the same time, over in New York City, Hamilton was making waves in the Broadway hip-hop musical entitled *Hamilton*, based on Chernow's 800-page biography. Throughout 2015, the musical was described as "the hottest ticket in town". Latino performer and composer Lin-Manuel Miranda was "making headlines and winning awards with a show that is hailed as transforming both theatre and the way Americans think about 18th-century history," Reuters journalist Jill Serjeant wrote.

By November 2015, the CBS news magazine *60 Minutes* reported that ticket pre-sales had hit $56 million. Recognising the immense popularity of Hamilton and yielding to verbal protests about having Hamilton share the spotlight on the $10 bill with Harriet Tubman (the woman chosen to be represented on US currencies), the US Treasury Department announced there would be no changes to the $10 bill. Instead, Tubman's picture would replace former President Andrew Jackson's picture on the $20 bill.

Centuries after his death, Alexander Hamilton continues to make history, and now he is even a pop-culture star.

Chapter 9
SOUTH CAROLINA:
Nothing Sweet from Barbados Comes

When the news travelled to Barbados in 1660 that Charles II had been restored to the English throne, Sir John Colleton sailed for London, along with other hopeful subjects, to carry a request he felt reasonably assured the king would not turn down. After all, Colleton had remained steadfastly loyal during Charles II's exile. During the civil war, he had raised money and commanded a regiment to support the king. He lost a fortune, many of his men, and his own personal security; then retired to Barbados, where he hoped to recover his losses by applying for a royal charter for some land directly south of the state of Virginia, on the Atlantic sea coast of North America.

That charter, dated March 24, 1663, changed the course of US history. News spread quickly upon Colleton's voyage to England and his subsequent return to the West Indies, where about 200 men formed the first group of Barbadian Adventurers. They saw this quest to settle the South Carolina coast as a necessity, not just an adventure. Land was becoming scarce and quite expensive in Barbados, thanks to the growing need of sugar plantations to expand their boundaries.

Barbadians were not the first to attempt settling in the inhospitable area that would become South Carolina. The Spanish tried from 1521 until 1562. In 1564, a group of Huguenots – French Protestants – abandoned the settlement they had founded two years before. The

Spanish tried again in 1566, but American Indians resisted them and by 1587, the Spanish had given up.

The Barbadians persevered. On November 1, 1670, a letter written by Lord Ashley referred to a new settlement, Charles Towne, at Albemarle Point, which feared attacks by the Spanish. That aside, the colonists were said to be happy and settling in "a very rich and fertile soyle".

By 1671, immigrants from Barbados made up at least half the new arrivals in South Carolina. It took time for their settlements to become lasting landmarks, but by 1678 Barbados was shipping about 10,000 pounds of sugar to South Carolina in exchange for beef, pork, and lumber. Their economic links continued to grow.

Warren Alleyne and Henry Fraser wrote in *The Barbados-Carolina Connection:*

> Apart from politics, the Barbadians exercised other influences that were to have a more far-reaching effect on the social development of the area that would become the state of South Carolina. In Barbados, the social order was based on slavery, and the planters who migrated to South Carolina took their slaves with them.

"During the early decades of its establishment, the South Carolina settlement had been little more than the dependent servant of an island master - in short, the colony of a colony," says historian James Wood.

Colleton's third son, James, was most involved in the Barbadian venture in North America. The South Carolina Historical Society records that:

> James Colleton appears to have frequently come to South Carolina, and taken a great interest in its settlement; and in 1686 was commissioned Governor, but after a stormy administration, was in 1691 by the parliament called at Charles Town

by the acting Governor Seth Sothell, banished, and
thereupon returned to Barbados.

South Carolina's history changed dramatically when
rice came into the picture during the 1690s. With it came
slaves who knew how to grow it. Introducing slaves
into the South Carolina landscape had always seemed
natural to West Indians, who had a history of using them
on their sugar plantations. Importing slaves was a cruel
and heartless business, but slavery became entrenched
in South Carolina culture. It would become a distinctive
feature that would lead the state to be the centre of the
Deep South, with undeniable Caribbean roots.

One proof of this was the Gullah language, which could
be traced to Africa and possibly the West Indies. Gullah
had uncanny similarities in accent and content to the
Bajan (Barbadian) dialect. With an influx of slaves from
Africa, often arriving via the Caribbean, South Carolina's
black culture had a language to develop its own unique
way of expression and some form of unity in a plantation
culture that worked hard to prevent communication
among the enslaved. Gullah could not be suppressed.
In the 19th century, Edgar Allan Poe tried to capture it
through a character named Jupiter in a short story called
"The Gold Bug", published in 1843.

With the development of Gullah, coastal South Carolina
arguably became the birthplace of "black English" as a
distinct American dialect. Along with the Geechee dialect
of the Georgia Sea Islands, it offered a distinctive voice
for the growing slave population, and it would become
important as a means of communication in the largest
slave rebellion in the US, which came close to succeeding.

Nowhere else in the US became frozen in time and
frozen in infamy like the area known as the Deep South.

This was the cradle of slavery; this was the heart of the Confederacy. When Abraham Lincoln won the election of 1861 and became the 16th President of the US, South Carolina became the first state to secede from the nation. The beating heart of the Deep South, it led the way for 11 other states to follow it down that divisive road. The way of life that these states fought to preserve, on opulent plantations that counted on the labour of brutalised slaves, was the worst the West Indies had to offer the US.

"The Deep South was founded by Barbados slave lords as a West Indies-style slave society, a system so cruel and despotic that it shocked even its 17th-century English contemporaries," wrote historian and journalist Colin Woodard in *American Nations: A History of the Eleven Rival Regional Cultures of North America.*

Of the other regions in the US sometimes referred to as nations by Woodard, South Carolina and the Deep South that formed around it stood apart from the rest of the country in an appalling way. He argued that the Deep South was one of those 11 "nations" that made up the US. South Carolina's brutal political system spread "apartheid and authoritarianism," wrote Woodard, across the Southern lowlands: Georgia, Alabama, Mississippi, Florida, Louisiana, western Tennessee, the southeastern part of North Carolina, Arkansas, and Texas. He continued:

> For most of American history, the region has been the bastion of white supremacy, aristocratic privilege, and a version of classical Republicanism modelled on the slave states of the ancient world, where democracy was a privilege of the few and enslavement the natural lot of the many.

Its wealth came from land, trade, and slaves – and its roots could be traced to Barbados, the easternmost island of the Caribbean. For some time, that island had been inhabited only by wild pigs. On a whim, John Powell decided to explore the island when he sailed the *Olive* from Brazil back home to England in 1625. When he landed with ten African slaves, he found little besides wild hogs. As Barbados was settled and began to grow crops like tobacco and cotton, no one paid much attention to this small island in the middle of nowhere.

But when sugar entered the picture, everything changed. As sugar plantations grew, they squeezed small farmers out of their land, and by the 1660s, these farmers, who had arrived in the 1630s, were migrating. A report on Barbados published in 1667 claimed 12,000 "good men, formerly proprietors, had gone off the island together with tradesmen..." They scattered through the Caribbean and North America, especially South Carolina, write Alleyne and Fraser.

> ...along the coastal plain of the North American continent (where) there is a broad wedge of land which stretches from the hazy base of the Appalachian Mountains to the uneven rim of the Atlantic Ocean...[A] low triangle of green and brown, spread out like a fan between the Savannah River and the sea.

Along the way on this tumultuous journey, the Deep South grew both politically and culturally, giving the world blues, jazz, gospel, rock and roll, and Caribbean food, including barbecue. Although most Americans no longer remember South Carolina's Barbadian connection, it is there, deeply rooted in the state's culture. There are scholars who make persuasive arguments that as a result, African American culture constitutes the periphery of a larger Creole Caribbean basin that extends down to Brazil.

Up until the Civil War, the South seemed to be winning the race to be the wealthiest area of the US. It had cotton, sugar, and an ability to push westward. But by the middle of the 19th century, what Woodard calls "Yankeedom"– an area in the north commonly referred to as New England – began receiving a flux of immigrants, who pushed westward as far as Ohio. Yankeedom and the Deep South had emerged as superpowers within the US. They were the wealthiest "nations" and "neither could abide living in an empire run on the other's terms," said Woodard.

But the balance between slave states and free states was beginning to tip. When South Carolina seceded from the Union, it was joined by Mississippi, Alabama, Georgia, Florida, Louisiana, and Texas in the Civil War mayhem of 1861. Other states would follow. South Carolina sealed its fate and any dreams of leading a new country separate from the US when it fired on Fort Sumter and started the war. Different factions in other areas of the US – the different "nations" Woodard identifies – joined together against the Deep South.

The southern Confederacy would surrender in 1865, but its political and social demise did not obliterate its cultural roots. As time passed, South Carolina became more set in its ways, a reactionary enclave rooted in its Barbadian past, which strongly believed in a strict hierarchy and a society defined by racism: white over black. The Deep South, steeped in the brutal conservatism of the West Indian plantation system, grew into the antithesis of New Amsterdam, now known as New York City.

Woodard argued:

> From that single square mile tucked inside the tolerant cocoon of New Netherland would spring much of what the religious conservatives of South

Carolina and the Dixie bloc would later mobilise against: the gay rights movement, modern art, the beatniks and their hippie successors, left-wing intellectualism and the antiwar movement. Like 17th-century Amsterdam, New Netherland provided a sanctuary for heretics and freethinkers.

Thus, in many ways, the political and social divide in the US today can be traced back to the difference in histories of New Amsterdam, with its Dutch-Caribbean roots, and the Deep South, with its Barbadian beginnings. The cultural clash had been there from the start. The two areas shared West Indian origins, but had nothing else in common. They had only come together in the American Revolution to fight a mutual enemy, the British. Once independence was achieved, they clashed throughout history, their positions virtually etched in stone.

Chapter 10

TOUSSAINT L'OUVERTURE:
From Slave to Iconoclast

The slaves who had congregated inside a wooded area at Bois Caïman – the Crocodile Forest – slit the black pig's throat, solemnised the secret they had kept for months in a vodun ceremony led by the Jamaican-born Boukman Dutty, picked up their guns and sabres, torched their masters' plantations, and killed anyone in their path. But the man who would become the most famous revolutionary of them all could not be found.

Toussaint Bréda surely knew about the plan for revolution in Saint-Domingue, because his job as a coachman meant frequent trips away from the Bréda plantation, where he certainly heard both gossip and news. As a devout Catholic, he might have quietly and uneasily looked on at the vodun ceremony that took place that fateful night of August 16, 1791, but Toussaint was eerily silent and absent from the action.

Two days later, as the revolt began, with more slaves joining Boukman's bloody cause, the Bréda plantation somehow remained miraculously untouched by the violence. The trusted coachman Toussaint kept the slaves from revolting. Only 22 of the 318 of them fled to join the revolution, and Bréda kept the plantation's white French mistress alive. He rallied the slaves to salvage some sugar cane that seemed to have caught fire from a neighbouring plantation, so that when the French manager, Bayon de Libertad, returned to Bréda, he found the slaves boiling vats of sugar under

Toussaint's supervision. It was an extraordinary sight: there in the midst of the chaos, even anarchy, which gripped the French colony, Toussaint Bréda behaved as though nothing had happened.

As black clouds of smoke from sizzling canefields burned, the rebellion spread. The embittered slaves slaughtered anyone who got in their way, including fellow slaves who hesitated to join their cause. In eight days, the slaves destroyed 184 plantations. By late September, over 200 plantations had been attacked. Fifty miles on either side of Le Cap there was nothing but ashes and smoke, and 1,200 coffee plantations in the mountains had been sacked.

This had become an "exterminating war". Both sides seemed bent on wiping out each other in the most unimaginably brutal manner. On the slaves' side, the man known as Jeannot whipped a white prisoner with over 400 strokes, rubbed gunpowder in the bleeding wounds, and gave his prisoner only one glass of water and three bananas a day as food. He roasted other prisoners alive. When his superior, Jean-François, rode into camp, he gave Jeannot a quick military trial, tied him to a tree and shot him.

Plantation owners clamoured to board ships to flee the looting, burning, and torture that engulfed Saint-Domingue. They headed for Philadelphia, Pennsylvania; Charleston, South Carolina; and New Orleans, Louisiana, and they carried first-hand stories of the destruction that fed fears in the US.

The refugees probably did not tell the story of how greedy, heartless managers of Saint-Domingue's plantations grew rich by squeezing the life out of slaves, or that just below the overseers at the top of the slave hierarchy were drivers, themselves enslaved, who were willing to engage in their own brutality to protect their coveted positions of power. They most likely left out the fact that about half the slaves who arrived in Saint-Domingue died within a few years, while half the children born there died, or that the birth rate among slaves hovered at three per cent.

At the time of the revolution, two thirds of the slaves had been born in Africa and most of the others who lived in Saint-Domingue were no more than a generation away from Africa. When the revolution began, 90 per cent of the population was slaves. Salaried administrators and overseers managed many of the plantations – not plantation owners, who lived a high life in France. The hired staff was notoriously thoughtless and cruel. Brutality led to more brutality and proved impossible to curtail once it ran out of control.

Into this picture came Toussaint Bréda. Within a month, this beloved former slave – born on May 20, 1743, the eldest son of Gaou Guinon, an African prince captured by slavers – took the journey that would lead to his metamorphosis into Toussaint L'Ouverture. He disappeared into the mountains, and with him vanished the life he had once known.

Somehow, Toussaint Bréda had managed to escape the worst horrors of slavery. His godfather, the priest Simon Baptiste, had taught him to read and write. Bréda knew French and some Latin as well as Kreyòl. He had caught the attention of de Libertad, who gave him a fair amount of freedom to travel about and access to his library. Bréda became known as a skilled horseman, earned his freedom, kept his job as a coachman, and bought a small coffee plantation. He legally married Suzanne Simon, a

Catholic, and had two sons, Isaac and Saint-Jean. When chaos engulfed Saint-Domingue, Toussaint L'Ouverture moved his family to Santo Domingo, the Spanish side of the island.

It took little time for L'Ouverture to be noticed among the revolutionaries. His skill at taking care of horses was recognised, and he served Georges Biassou, initially as médecin general. Soon, L'Ouverture climbed the ranks to become a legendary leader known for his keen sense of timing and astute sense of alignment. His success could be considered nothing less than an impossible feat, even considering that by 1789, there were an estimated 500,000 slaves in Saint-Domingue, and they outnumbered the white masters by at least 12 to one.

The complicated, colour-based, stratified society of the plantation owners (*grands blancs*) and the artisans, sailors, and merchants (*petits blancs*) along with mulattoes, and a mixture of blacks and whites, labelled according to their varying percentages of black blood, assured constant undermining and posturing for power in Saint-Domingue. This would be a battle of religion, too, pitting Catholicism against vodun.

"The insurrection of 1791 required community and leaders, and there is little doubt that religious practices facilitated the process of organisation. Once the insurrection began, religion helped inspire insurgents and solidified the power of certain leaders," wrote historian Laurent Dubois in *Avengers of the New World: The Story of the Haitian Revolution*.

The slaves beat their drums, shook calabashes, clapped their hands, played the four-stringed instrument called the banza and danced the calenda for their religious-induced sense of power. Before the revolution, this had been the pressure valve that allowed them to defuse the tension and escape from the memories and threats of being branded, whipped, mutilated, and tortured. Slave owners cut off hands and other body parts and rubbed hot pepper, salt, lemon, or ash into open wounds or burnt flesh. For control, plantations cultivated a culture of torture, and no one could forget the stories of the past, especially the story of the man who turned into a legend.

In January 1758, a slave named Makandal had to kneel in the plaza of Le Cap wearing a sign that read: "Seducer, profaner, poisoner." He was tied to a post and set on fire, but he broke free. The crowd cried, "Makandal saved!" and when panic broke out, soldiers cleared the plaza so they could tie him to a board and burn him. But Makandal had said he could change form, and so the slaves believed he had flown away as a fly.

Toussaint L'Ouverture would become a legend in his own right: a colourful combination of man and myth, brave enough and educated enough to know the horror stories of others who had made their bid for freedom, like Vincent Ogé, who had appeared in the French National Assembly in October 1789, arguing for free men of colour to vote in local assemblies in Saint-Domingue.

When Ogé returned home, he organised supporters in Dondon and stormed a couple of towns, but his rebellion was put down by the soldiers. He was broken on the wheel and his head displayed on a pike. These were the images indelibly stamped in L'Ouverture's mind, but still he wanted the French to recognise him as a fellow citizen, even to the extent of aligning himself and his troops with France during his own revolution.

Following France's decision to emancipate the slaves, L'Ouverture fought with France against Spain, and from

1794 to 1802 he was the dominant political and military leader in the French colony. Operating under the self-assumed title of General-in-Chief of the army, he led the French in ousting the British. He was ruling Saint-Domingue as an independent state. L'Ouverture drafted a constitution in which he referred to the 1794 abolition of slavery, and appointed himself governor for "the rest of his glorious life". But he faced problems from all sides. According to Trinidadian writer C.L.R. James:

> A growing army and the confidence of free black labourers meant power. But L'Ouverture saw early that political power is only a means to an end. The salvation of San Domingo [Saint-Domingue] lay in the restoration of agriculture. This was an almost insuperable task in a disorganised society depending on the labour of men just out of slavery

and surrounded on every side by the rabid greed
and violence of French, Spaniards and British.

L'Ouverture's actions eventually aroused the ire of
Napoleon Bonaparte. It is tempting to blame some of
Napoleon's decisions about regaining control of Haiti
on his wife, Josephine, who was from Martinique, but
no historian has ever found evidence of this. In 1802,
Napoleon dispatched his brother-in-law Charles Leclerc
to capture L'Ouverture and return the island to slavery
under French control. This Leclerc could only accomplish
by trickery.

A letter for Toussaint dated June 7, 1802 arrived from
General Brunt.

> You must assist me in securing free communication
> to the Cape, which has been interrupted since
> yesterday. We have arrangements to make
> together, my dear General, which it is impossible
> to do by letter, but which an hour's conference
> would complete. If I were not worn out by labour
> and petty cares, I should have been the bearer of
> my own letter.

It was a trap. When L'Ouverture arrived, he was taken
into custody, sent to France and imprisoned at Fort de
Joux.

L'Ouverture never tired of appealing to France's honour
with letters reminding the French of his loyal service.
But he lived the rest of his life in that cold, remote,
impenetrable fort perched precariously on the rocks,
and died on April 7, 1803. The day after his death, two
physicians of Pontarlier performed a post mortem and
certified that he died of apoplexy and pleuropneumonia.
He was buried in a grave under the chapel of the fort.

Independence for Saint-Domingue would follow
L'Ouverture's imprisonment, under the leadership of

Jean-Jacques Dessalines, one of L'Ouverture's generals. So Dessalines, who stepped into L'Ouverture's place after he was tricked, gets the credit as the liberator of Saint-Domingue, but Toussaint L'Ouverture laid the important groundwork, and without him, it is safe to say, there would not have been a successful revolt.

"As the leader of the only successful slave revolution in recorded history, and as the founder of the only independent black state in the western hemisphere ever to be created by former slaves...Toussaint L'Ouverture can fairly be called the highest-achieving African-American hero of all time," writes American novelist and L'Ouverture biographer Madison Smartt Bell.

When the revolution began in 1791, no one could have foreseen the death and destruction, or even the outcome of independence. L'Ouverture had been captured because the French played on the one quality that most defined his life: fairness. L'Ouverture went to his death remembering his revolution as a noble struggle and fighting for an audience with Napoleon.

From his cold, dank, lonely prison cell in a French dungeon at Fort de Joux he had written:

> The colony of Saint Domingo, of which I was commander, enjoyed the greatest tranquility; agriculture and commerce flourished there. The island had attained a degree of splendour which it had never seen. And all this—I dare say was my work.

> At the time of the evacuation of the English, there was not a penny in the public treasury; money had to be borrowed to pay the troops and the officers of the Republic. When Gen Leclerc arrived, he found 3,500,000 francs in the public funds. When I returned to Cayes, after the departure of Gen Rigaud, the treasury was empty...

I have neglected nothing at Saint Domingo for the welfare of the island; I have robbed myself of rest to contribute to it; I have sacrificed everything for it. I have made it my duty and pleasure to develop the resources of this beautiful colony. Zeal, activity, courage—I have employed them all.

The island was invaded by the enemies of the Republic; I had then but a thousand men, armed with pikes. I sent them to labour in the field, and organised several regiments by the author of Gen Laveaux...

I was once rich. At the time of the revolution, I was worth $648,000 francs. I spent it in the service of my country...I purchased my one small estate....

In the dungeon of Fort Joux 17th September 1802

Toussaint L'Ouverture became a beacon of hope for slaves everywhere. On March 18, 1862, a New England abolitionist, Wendell Phillips, gave a lecture in the Smithsonian Institution which painted a picture of L'Ouverture as a freedom fighter. He received a standing ovation.

L'Ouverture had been a key leader in Haiti's quest for independence, making it the only successful slave rebellion in history. His presence looms large; yet no one knows exactly what he looked like. Paintings often portray him as a caricature of a black man dressed in an overly ornate French general's uniform, or as a squat, balding, brown-skinned man with a receding hairline, no neck to speak of, and eyes too wide and empty to see the world for what it was. Even in one of the best portraits of him, an English portrait from 1802 that appears in Carrie Gibbons' *Empire's Crossroads: A History of the Caribbean from Columbus to the Present Day*, a lugubrious L'Ouverture with a pot belly looks like a defeated man, with his dark, drooping eyes and sad mouth. There is no hint of the pride or accomplishment that he would have felt in the earth-shattering accomplishments that would assure his place in history.

His boldness was legendary. When he was whisked away to France, he said, "You think you have rooted up the tree of liberty, but I am only a branch; I have planted the tree of liberty so deep that all France can never root it up."

Matthew Clavin wrote in his history of L'Ouverture's impact on the American Civil War:

> The significance of L'Ouverture iconicism in transatlantic abolitionist print culture cannot be overstated. The Haitian Revolution had a profound effect on the United States throughout the first half of the 19th century. In an era that saw both the expansion of slavery and the growth of a movement to destroy the institution, it was both a resonant and polarising symbol.

L'Ouverture inspired slave uprisings throughout the western hemisphere. Slave owners could never live in any semblance of peace after he came on the scene. His presence instilled fear far and wide. And because of Toussaint L'Ouverture, American President Thomas Jefferson would engage in clandestine negotiations that would forever change the landscape of the US.

Chapter 11

SAINT-DOMINGUE CHANGES AMERICA'S LANDSCAPE

Thomas Jefferson had been shocked when he received a French visitor at the unfinished White House (then called the Presidential Palace) in July 1801. Louis André Pichon, a charming young diplomat – but with a rank lower than ambassador – had unexpectedly called on the red-haired, freckle-faced third President. But Jefferson, who had lived for a while in France, loved all things French, so he felt inclined to entertain the chargé d'affaires.

After all, Jefferson had defended the French Revolution in spite of its violence, which led to the beheading of Louis XVI. Surely Pichon knew that Jefferson had stood virtually alone against General Alexander Hamilton's Federalist Party and its stern, anti-French-Revolution position. The Federalists felt the Republicans – led by Jefferson – had sold out the US by writing off millions of dollars in claims by US merchants who had lost goods to French privateers when the French turned on the Americans after the Revolutionary War. It was not a fair trade, the Federalists thought, simply to exchange this multi-million-dollar loss for the French accepting the US bowing out of the Treaty of 1778. That treaty had basically guaranteed American support for the French if they should decide to fight the British.

Pichon revealed his surprising reason for the French visit to Jefferson: he wanted to know exactly what was the US policy towards the volatile island of Saint-Domingue. By that time, Toussaint L'Ouverture had emerged as the undisputed leader in the slave rebellion and France was seriously thinking about reclaiming its most prized possession, with its lucrative sugar, coffee, and indigo plantations (of course, those plantations had been destroyed for the most part by now). "If we decide to take back Saint-Domingue," Pichon wanted to know, "how would the US feel?"

Jefferson reportedly smiled and assured him that France could surely starve out L'Ouverture.

The other founding fathers of the US would have been shocked at Jefferson's flippant dismissal of L'Ouverture, particularly the second president, John Adams, who believed that L'Ouverture was a buffer against British and French colonialism in the Caribbean. The US could not truly be free, Adams's supporters felt, unless it could halt the endless cycle of islands changing hands among the European powers like pieces on a chessboard. Adams had even supported L'Ouverture's army with food and ammunition to help them defeat the British when the latter tried to seize Saint-Domingue. Alexander Hamilton's friend Edward Stevens had gone to Cap-François, Saint-Domingue's main port, to advise L'Ouverture.

Knowing this, Pichon might have been sceptical about Jefferson's casual approach, but Jefferson claimed that most Americans were entrenched in their own problems, with struggling politics and a struggling economy, and they could not be bothered to think seriously about Saint-Domingue. He conveniently left out the fear in the back of everyone's head of what a successful slave revolt could mean to slaves in the US.

But Jefferson warned that the British would try to crack down on Saint-Domingue if France settled its differences with Britain, because the British could not afford to let other slave economies in the Caribbean rebel as Saint-Domingue had done. Britain would want to make an example of the island. A cornered L'Ouverture, Jefferson predicted, could resort to piracy.

Pichon rushed home to France to relay this conversation to Napoleon. What he possibly did not know was that Jefferson was more convinced than ever that the US needed to get possession of the Louisiana Territory, because he did not want that land, bordering on the western side of the US, to be part of the colonial game. And he would really have liked all the European countries – including France – out of Saint-Domingue. The trouble there was too close for comfort.

The chess game on American soil had begun, and the French were determined that the Americans would be the losers. They plotted a deal with their Spanish enemies at San Ildefonso, the Spanish king's country palace. Napoleon would make the king's son-in-law the king of Etruria, a new kingdom created just for him, with one condition: the Spanish would never give the Louisiana Territory to another country. (France had ceded it to Spain in 1762.)

Although he was busy conquering Europe, Napoleon still thought of Saint-Domingue as France's crown jewel. Megalomaniac that he was, he sometimes had visions of a French empire beyond the Caribbean that included land along the Mississippi, throughout the blue Caribbean waters, and down to South America. The American states hugging the Atlantic coast would merely become France's weak border in North America, if Napoleon had his way. The ambitious Napoleon already dreamed of possessing the Spanish-owned Florida and all the territory along the Gulf of Mexico westward to Louisiana. From there,

Napoleon reasoned, he could launch his Caribbean navy. Only Toussaint L'Ouverture stood in the way of his plan: Napoleon needed to regain Saint-Domingue because he needed the revenue from that once booming economy. So the French leader sent his brother-in-law, General Charles Leclerc, and 20,000 troops to occupy Saint-Domingue – with permission, of course, from the British. Once the French army arrived, Jefferson promised, the US would support a blockade against L'Ouverture.

Jefferson had no clue that some of those French troops were destined for Louisiana. Meanwhile, the gossip about the secret treaty with the Spanish was beginning to drift westward to the US. Word was that the deal had already been made, and Louisiana and the Floridas were out of the Spaniards' hands and in the possession of France. The US had no problems with the Spanish in Florida. Busy with their own problems in Europe, the Spanish allowed the Americans to use the Mississippi River. It was the French whom the Americans did not trust.

Secretary of State James Madison decided to approach Pichon, who claimed he was unaware of any deal between the French and the Spanish. But the cool Madison, who was always able to get his point across, left Pichon in a mad scramble to get a message off to France that war could break out, with the British siding with the Americans. Jefferson and Madison nervously decided to dispatch Robert Livingston to France to meet with Napoleon.

Leclerc moved towards Saint-Domingue in late January 1802, much to Madison's horror. The US was playing its own games, sending diplomats to Saint-Domingue to congratulate L'Ouverture and denying that it supported any opposition to L'Ouverture's government.

L'Ouverture sensed something was up because of the size of Leclerc's fleet, and Leclerc threatened Henri Christophe, one of L'Ouverture's generals, who was in charge of Cap-François. Christophe refused to surrender the city. Instead, he burned it, killed the white inhabitants and then abandoned the port. Leclerc got the shock of his life when he discovered that most of the food for the island was on American ships or in American warehouses, and the Americans unexpectedly turned the screws by demanding outrageous prices for it. Desperate for supplies, Leclerc dispatched an agent to New York and Philadelphia to borrow a million francs to purchase the food, but American banks refused to give him a loan. Angry and fed up, Leclerc seized the food and threatened to seize American ships. Pichon ran back to Jefferson to beg for a loan. Leclerc was not faring well. He took the Spanish section of the island easily, but L'Ouverture remained elusive and his lieutenant Jean-Jacques Dessalines terrorised the countryside, murdering white people and anyone who tried to help them.

On February 1, 1802, Leclerc decided to tackle L'Ouverture at Gonaïves. Chaos ensued, with some of L'Ouverture's generals defecting to Leclerc. Christophe changed sides on May 1. The French forces were now free to concentrate totally on the rebels, since they had signed a treaty with England, and L'Ouverture called for peace.

Then came L'Ouverture's downfall. It stunned the US. The French had to trick L'Ouverture to catch him, but they finally had him out of the picture.

Meanwhile, France continued to deny it had obtained Florida and the Gulf Coast lands, including Louisiana, from the Spanish. The US tried to get the French to sell it the northern part of the Louisiana Territory, claiming the US could be a buffer between the French and the British in Canada. The French would not fall for it. Then the US tried to play off the British against the French, and the British would not fall for that. Jefferson's dream of the Louisiana Purchase seemed to be fading.

Meanwhile, yellow fever was wiping out Leclerc's army. He depended on Napoleon to send more troops. Thinking Saint-Domingue was safe now that L'Ouverture was out of the way, merchants and former plantation owners returned to the island, only to find an uneasy situation, especially since Napoleon had announced his intention to reinstate slavery there and in Guadeloupe. Leclerc lacked men and money, and his health deteriorated.

Now that Jefferson was no longer enamoured by all things French, the government stood by while American merchants capitalised on the situation, trading guns, ammunition, and food to the rebels in Saint-Domingue. With lies and secrets came rumours, the most vicious being that the French were dumping slaves from Saint-Domingue in the US so that they could incite rebellions among slaves in the south. Talk of the French presence in Louisiana stoked the fire. The US was adamant: it did not want a French occupation of Louisiana.

Edward Livingston, the US representative to France, was chipping away at France's confidence by pointing out that its money woes had been made worse by a decade of war in the West Indies. Guadeloupe, Martinique, and French Guiana all needed huge investments to build back devastated economies. So what use was the vast Louisiana wilderness to France? It would cost too much to develop. Napoleon was beginning to grasp this point of view, and he was desperate for money.

This was when Jefferson sent James Monroe to France to help Livingston complete the negotiations for the acquisition of New Orleans and West Florida. Monroe and Livingston were authorised to pay US$10 million for New Orleans and the ports of Florida.

Napoleon offered the entire Louisiana Territory – larger than the area of Great Britain, France, Germany, Italy, Spain, and Portugal combined – for US$15 million. Although Monroe and Livingston were not authorised to make such a large purchase, they knew a good deal when they saw it, so they began negotiations. Monroe was successful, and the Louisiana Purchase became one of the greatest real-estate deals in history.

On April 30, 1803 the US contracted to pay France $11.25 million, plus a cancellation of debts of $3.75 million – that is, a total of $15 million – for 828,000 square miles of land west of the Mississippi River known as the Louisiana Territory. The lands stretched as far west as the Rocky Mountains (including Denver), and from the Gulf of Mexico to the Canadian border. Many states were carved from this territory, including Arkansas, Iowa, Missouri, Kansas, Oklahoma, Nebraska, parts of Minnesota, and Louisiana west of the Mississippi River, including New Orleans, as well as large parts of New Mexico, South Dakota, northern Texas, and some parts of Wyoming, Montana, and Colorado. The Louisiana Purchase nearly doubled the size of the US. In January 1803, Jefferson secretly called on his cabinet to help develop a plan for exploring these lands beyond the muddy waters of the Mississippi. It was an unbelievable acquisition that had depended on much secret manoeuvring.

Historian Thomas Fleming wrote:

> Without Secretary of State James Madison's hard-headed realism about Santo Domingo [Saint-Domingue], the French might have pressured Jefferson into keeping his promise to starve the black rebels into submission – and General Leclerc's army would have arrived in Louisiana more or less on schedule in 1803. Without Ambassador Robert R Livingston's...diplomacy...the French might have thought that they could manipulate the United States' attitude toward Spain's cession of Louisiana. Without Special Envoy James Monroe's willingness to risk bankruptcy and the wintry North Atlantic bearing Jefferson's ultimatum, Napoleon might have decided to take [the French bishop and diplomat] Talleyrand's advice and ignore the countless letters...of the US minister.

At least as important in the genesis of the great event were the black men and women of Santo Domingo [Saint-Domingue]. Their refusal to resubmit to the humiliations of slavery was a crucial factor in upending Napoleon Bonaparte's grand design.

Toussaint L'Ouverture and the slave revolt in Saint-Domingue had been the catalyst for this remarkable real-estate deal, which forever changed the landscape of the US.

Chapter 12

DENMARK VESEY:
The Man Who Bet on Freedom

When Denmark Vesey and his supporters met secretly in Charleston, South Carolina, on a hot, sultry Saturday in May 1822, they felt confident about their plans. The oppressive heat had been driving some of the rich plantation women and their children northwards out of the city. This could be helpful, the conspirators thought as they finalised their plans to meet in Charleston on Sunday, July 14.

Rural slaves who supported the mesmerising African priest known as Gullah Jack would steer their canoes, filled with provisions from their gardens, toward Charleston. Underneath their produce they would hide their hoes, hatchets, axes, and spades. They would congregate three miles north of the city, at an ideal location, Bulkley's Farm – the centre of the plot because the slaves could reach there by river and avoid the city watch and rural patrols. It would not look suspicious, because slaves often congregated there to roast a fowl, sing psalms, and pray.

On Bull Street in Charleston, artisans mingled with pedestrians, but they did not take any jobs. Vesey had quit taking carpentry work. Everything was looking up. The dream just might come true. Vesey's luck just might hold out. It all seemed possible – especially to those conspirators just ten blocks away at the Market Wharf who dared to stand in front of the *Sally,* in port from Cap-Haïtien.

And then it happened: William Paul, a minor recruit, a foot soldier, so to speak, could not contain his excitement. There, in the fish market, he pointed out the *Sally* to someone he barely knew, Peter, a 55-year-old mulatto cook. Peter was just the type of person Vesey had warned everyone to avoid: a loyal slave who would want no part of a slave rebellion.

"I don't understand such talk," said Peter. He wanted to hear nothing about a planned uprising and escape to Haiti. He stopped William from saying more, but before William could warn Peter to forget what he had said, Peter disappeared.

With him went Vesey's rebellion.

Peter's master was not in Charleston, but he confided in a friend, a free man, William Penceel, who dealt in the slave trade, and a few days later, Peter's master returned and Peter divulged the plot. The governor, shaken when he was notified, was sufficiently terrified to request federal troops, who made their presence in Charleston known. The conspirators fell like dominoes – especially after officials tortured them. Vesey hid, but he was caught on June 22 and put on trial with the other conspirators.

Tortured slaves turned against Vesey, but the real turning point came when a witness fingered Vesey in court. Vesey denied knowing the French wigmaker who testified against him, but when shown the wigs that had supposedly been made for him, a visibly shaken Vesey murmured, "Good God". Silence engulfed the courtroom and then Vesey admitted he knew the wigmaker.

Denmark Vesey's luck had finally run out. Once, when he was known as Télémaque Vesey, he had been lucky enough to talk his way out of being a slave in Haiti.

History has recorded the story of Denmark Vesey's good fortune and the bad luck that led to his ultimate demise, but the details of his life in between remain sketchy.

No one even knows what Denmark Vesey looked like. No one ever described him, even in the 164 pages of court testimony presented at his trial in Charleston, South Carolina, in June 1822.

What we do know is this: "Denmark Vesey in 1821 organised the most elaborate and well-planned slave insurrection in the history of the United States. Had the rebellion succeeded, it would have been the most violent," says his biographer David Robertson. Vesey had reportedly recruited 9,000 slaves to his cause, and he had written to Jean-Pierre Boyer, the president of the black republic of Haiti. Robertson continued:

> He planned to seize the US arsenal and ships in Charleston, then the fifth largest city in the nation, and sail for [Haiti]. Relying on faith – not luck – [Vesey] preached a black liberation theology: violence justified the means to an end. He preached a common black brotherhood that connected Africa, the US and the West Indies, the place where he was born.

Vesey had joined the newly formed African Methodist Episcopal Church in 1817 and quickly became a speaker there. He preached straight from the Bible, especially the book of Exodus. At almost every meeting, he read a certain Bible story: the one about how the children of Israel were delivered out of Egypt. He believed that slaves had the God-given right to revolt and in a new beginning for African slaves.

It was a confidence born from the luck that had afforded him a few new beginnings in his own life. His good fortune rescued him from being a slave in Haiti when it was still Saint-Domingue. In 1771, Captain Joseph

Vesey, a slave trader, took the 14-year-old boy, then called Télémaque, from the Danish island of St Thomas in the Virgin Islands, where he was born, to Cap-Français in Saint-Domingue, where his new owner rejected him because he suffered from epilepsy. Miraculously, cleverly, or through luck, Vesey seemed never to have another seizure after leaving Cap-Français. History does not record any medical problems like seizures once Captain Vesey took back his slave. Denmark sailed with Vesey until the captain eventually retired to Charleston; most accounts say they sailed the Caribbean for 20 years.

In 1799, Vesey won a lottery and bought his freedom for $600. He would have been a happy man if he could have bought the freedom of his wife and children too, but he was not allowed to. Slave owners did everything they could to keep free slaves from manumitting their families. In 1815, the citizens of Charleston moved to block black Methodists who had been secretly pooling money to buy freedom for enslaved congregants.

To add insult to injury, the white population decided to build a hearse house on top of a black burial ground.

> Over 4,000 black members left white churches in protest, and formed an African Methodist Episcopal Church in Charleston. Denmark Vesey followed them, leaving the segregated Second Presbyterian Church, where slaves were taught the words of St Paul: 'Servants, obey your masters.' In the AME Church, Vesey found the freedom to preach his beliefs.

By 1821, Vesey was plotting the rebellion with the popular slave Gullah Jack. Then everything came crashing down around them. The trial at the Court of Magistrates and Freeholders horrified the people of Charleston. Witness after witness swore Vesey's plot had been fuelled by the Haitian Revolution. One claimed Vesey had been "in the habit of reading to me all the passages in the newspapers that related to [Saint-Domingue] and apparently every pamphlet he could lay his hands on, that had any connection with slavery." Another witness claimed Vesey had said, "We can conquer the whites, if we were only unanimous and courageous, as the [Saint-Domingue] people were."

Vesey's company of black supporters, the court heard, included 300 "French negroes" from Haiti who were refugees from the revolution. French-speaking conspirators said they were willing and able to provide spears, swords, bayonets, and firearms for Vesey's uprising, and the terrified courtroom observers heard how he had modelled his revolution after the one in Haiti by declaring that no white person – including women and children – should be spared. Newspapers rushed to print the news that came out of the court.

By August 9, 35 men had been hanged. A total of 77 were executed or imprisoned, and Judge Lionel Kennedy had sentenced Vesey, telling him,

> The court were (sic) not only satisfied with your guilt, but that you were the author, and original instigator of this diabolical plot. Your professed design was to trample on all laws, human and divine, to riot in blood, outrage, rapine and conflagration, and to introduce anarchy and confusion in their most horrid forms. Your life has become, therefore, a just and necessary sacrifice, at the shrine of indulgent Justice. It is difficult to imagine what infatuation could have prompted you to attempt an enterprize so wild and visionary. You were a free man....

A tear streamed down Denmark Vesey's face. He was led to a dank cell that he shared with two co-conspirators,

Peter Poyas and Jesse Blackwood. Like the other citizens of Charleston, Judge Kennedy hoped that Vesey would repent before he died, but, surrounded by the singing of psalms coming from other cells, he waved off the preacher, saying, "It was a Glorious cause to die in...It is no use to say nothing more."

When the violent thunderstorms of July came, militia companies still patrolled the streets. On July 2, warden John Gordon marched Vesey, Poyas, Blackwood, and others out of their cells. They shuffled slowly forward in their heavy leg irons and climbed onto a cart for a two-mile ride to Blake's Lands, a piece of marshy ground in the north. Vesey stared straight ahead.

News of the plot had reached far and garnered the wrath of many people. President James Monroe refused to recognise the Republic of Haiti after he heard of it. Shock waves travelled fast and furious across the US, still settling into its independence. Vesey became the faceless threat to white people far across the country. He represented the face of the revolution in Saint-Domingue and its original charismatic leader, Toussaint L'Ouverture. According to one account of the official investigation into the Vesey plot, published in 1822, the revolution there had been mentioned nearly 20 times in witnesses' statements.

Those curious onlookers who had packed the court learned that Vesey had lived as a free man in Charleston for 22 years before the revolt; he was close to 60 at the time of the plot, and was a relatively well-to-do carpenter, respected for his work. He had no formal education, but spoke and wrote English and French, as well as Creole, Spanish and other European languages.

The white inhabitants of Charleston tried to obliterate the memory of Denmark Vesey and bury their terror at the thought of what he could have accomplished. The African church was burned down, and the city passed laws with harsher conditions for the slaves. This, Charleston hoped, was the end of Denmark Vesey's story. But it would not go away. In June 1861, there appeared a detailed account of Vesey's planned revolt and its suppression, titled *Denmark Vesey*. Its author, a frequent *Atlantic* contributor named Thomas Wentworth Higginson, was a minister in Cambridge, Massachusetts, and a committed abolitionist.

Gradually, Denmark Vesey's legacy turned from insurgent to freedom fighter. In 1976, the city of Charleston commissioned a portrait of him, but artist Dorothy B. Wright did not know how to paint him because she could find no description of him anywhere. She solved the problem by painting Vesey standing at a church pulpit, his right index finger raised above the lace cuff of his shirt as he addressed the congregation of the church – with his back to the viewer. In 1996, there was a movement to put up a monument to Vesey, and in February 2015 the committee overseeing the project unveiled it in Charleston's Hampton Park. Vesey stands tall and proud, with a strong, determined face. In his hand, he carries a bag of carpenter's tools.

Four months later on June 17, 2015, a gunman walked into Charleston's Emanuel AME Church and shot worshippers gathered for a mid-week prayer meeting. Nine black church members, including the Reverend Clementa Pinckney, were fatally shot.

This was the church associated with Vesey; the same church burnt to the ground when Vesey's plot had been exposed. When it was rebuilt, it became a monument to freedom, a place where many civil-rights leaders spoke from the pulpit.

"For nearly 200 years [this church] had been the site of struggle, resistance and change," wrote the *Washington Post* after the attack. When traditional newspapers and the electronic media carried stories of that hate crime against innocent members of a black church, they resurrected the story of Denmark Vesey, the former slave from St Thomas who had been accused of the heinous plot to murder citizens of Charleston. This time, the reports firmly established him as a freedom fighter who died as a martyr for the abolition of slavery. Clearly, the attempt to rob Vesey of his place in history had failed.

Chapter 13

JEAN LAFFITE:
The Legend of a Pirate

He was the ultimate nuisance and an unlikely hero, a loose cannon. Mannerly and highly noticeable – with gleaming, white teeth, extraordinarily pale skin for a seaman, dark hazel eyes, dark hair, and a face framed by side whiskers down to his chin – the well-proportioned, six-foot-two Gulf Coast corsair Jean Laffite flaunted his pirate power by brazenly breaking New Orleans' laws. Sporting clever disguises, he sneaked in by night – for both business and pleasure – and snaked his way into the moral and economic fabric of the city – before he became the legendary saviour of war-torn New Orleans.

Jean Laffite and his brother Pierre have gone down in history as smugglers, merchants of contraband, revolutionaries, spies, privateers, or pirates, and even heroes. Along the way to both infamy and glory, Laffite impressed people with his undeniable charm and ran his crew with a strict but fair rule. Stealthy, like a cat, elusive and even difficult to really know, Jean Laffite nevertheless left an indelible impression on those who had the pleasure of meeting him. Described by his biographer William C. Davis as an "easy and genial conversationalist [who] liked to tell stories of his experiences, no doubt with embellishments," Laffite kept order among his pirates – not an easy feat in an ever-changing community of miscreants both on and off the sea. He stood for hours telling stories with one eye shut, a quirky, puzzling and undoubtedly intimidating habit. One look into his "liquid brown eyes made quadroon women swoon," says Davis in *The Pirates Laffite: The Treacherous World of the Corsairs of the Gulf.*

But who was Jean Laffite? And where did he come from? Davis says his surname can be traced back to the "fertile reaches between the river Garonne and the Pyrenees Mountains that separated France from Spain."

His brother Pierre seems to have fallen into line as a merchant and tradesman, as most of the Laffites were in that area. But, straddling two countries, the Laffites were well positioned to be smugglers, and an acquaintance of the brothers claimed that is exactly what they did.

There was little to keep them in France after their father, also named Pierre, died in 1796. The Laffite brothers disappeared. By then many residents of this turbulent region were making their way to the New World to seek their fortune.

Pierre seems to have surfaced as a merchant in Le Cap, a sea port in the French West Indian colony of Saint-Domingue. When fighting broke out on June 20, 1793, Pierre could have been in Le Cap to see 2,000 mariners and political prisoners rebel from their ships and spill over onto Saint-Domingue's soil to attack government buildings.

Pierre left for Savannah, Georgia, returned to Port-au-Prince in 1794 when the British threat had passed, and seems to have traversed the area, making yet another stop in Saint-Domingue in 1802 on his way to Louisiana. It is a safe bet Pierre was on one of those French privateers' ships busy whisking away white refugees and depositing them in Cuba and New Orleans; they certainly had a thriving business in Saint-Domingue's chaos. At some point, Pierre scoped out New Orleans to carry out the family tradition of working as merchants. But New Orleans was about to be cut off from the West Indies, and American politics would close the door to Pierre's dreams.

Still, there is no sign of brother Jean, who would be remembered as a legendary figure who played a huge role in US history.

"From the moment of his birth in Pauillac to more than 20 years thereafter, Jean Laffite's life is a complete mystery," says Davis.

While Pierre was well-grounded, so to speak, as a merchant, Jean took to the sea.

"He felt at home on the small sailing feluccas with their mainmast and triangular sails, the single-masted schooners, and even the larger merchant brigantines that carried most of the oceanic and Gulf trade. Where and how he acquired his seamanship is part of his mystery, though likely he started on the Gironde estuary on vessels owned by or trading with his father," says Davis.

By 1802, Jean could have been in Saint-Domingue at the same time as Pierre. Records show more than one Captain Laffite by 1806. One of those privateering captains was most likely Jean under a thinly disguised name. Could he have been the captain of the French privateer *La Soeur Chérie* when it sailed to Louisiana in 1804, along with its two prized vessels? *La Soeur Chérie* and its "Captain La fette" were allowed to enter the Mississippi River because the captain told a convincing sob story about a damaged ship and deserting crew, when his real intention was to unload slaves and smuggled goods. The ship, sold to the authorities as a Spanish prize, was actually an American one seized by the good Captain Laffite while it had been trading with British Jamaica. By the time Governor William Claiborne got wise to that fact, "Captain La fette" and *La Soeur Chérie* had sailed. Pierre, who was being hunted by his creditors, mysteriously disappeared about the same time as Captain La fette sailed away.

It would be the first of endless missions in which the brothers Laffite would outsmart the authorities. Always up to some trickery, Jean was on an island 50 miles south of the city, a "wild and scarcely inhabited place", called Barataria Bay. Thanks to the pirates who congregated there, the place lived up to its Spanish name, meaning "cheap goods", while its picaresque reputation found its roots in Sancho Panza's fictitious island in Miguel de Cervantes' novel *Don Quixote*. Barataria offered some much-needed peace of mind for pirates on the run, and the sand dunes and other inhospitable conditions made it difficult for their enemies to navigate.

Meanwhile, New Orleans was a goldmine for pirates. The city needed illegal slaves. The women, who fancied themselves fine Frenchwomen, needed fancy clothes. Everyone needed cheaper goods, which pirates could furnish.

"All that was needed was daring men to grasp the opportunity. By 1809, (Pierre) Laffite decided he would be one of them," said Davis. Jean was close at his heels.

The pirates preyed on shifting political alliances and wars as the US severed diplomatic relations with Spain, and Saint-Domingue offered a steady stream of refugees. It was pirate business as usual, much to the chagrin of Governor Claiborne. The picture became more complicated when the US and Great Britain went to war with each other, on June 18, 1812. When General James Wilkinson arrived to take command of the defence of New Orleans and the Gulf coast on July 9, the Laffite brothers noticed new opportunities for pirate profits.

Basking in the glory of the US's newest state of Louisiana, Governor William C.C. Claiborne did not fancy being embarrassed by the Laffites. But they were slippery in every way. Patriots they were not. They considered themselves Frenchmen first, and Claiborne feared they would join sides with the British. Cagey as ever, the Laffites had their island havens, first Barataria, then Cat Island. They knew every nook and cranny of the bayou and the Gulf. This was no easy feat, considering the murky, alligator-infested waters framed with jungle flora, mosquitoes, low-hanging moss, and tall marsh grass, not to mention quicksand. Sometimes the pirates entered New Orleans with legal goods, then loaded up contraband to sail out. They took the chance that port authorities would not bother checking them.

Jean undermined New Orleans so thoroughly that rumours began to fly that he had once been a general in Napoleon's army. Meanwhile, fed up and embarrassed to the hilt with Jean Laffite's shenanigans and the apathy of New Orleans residents, Claiborne offered a $500 reward for Laffite. The next day, residents found a notice about a $1,000 reward posted at the Exchange Coffee House for anyone who would deliver Governor Claiborne to Cat Island. The reward offer had a signature: "Laffite." Just in case no one grasped his sense of humour, Jean Laffite pointed out in a corner of the paper that he was joking.

The tide turned at 10:00 a.m. on September 3, 1814, when an unknown warship dared to pass between Grand Terre and Grand Isle. Jean Laffite decided to investigate. He found Captain Nicholas Lockyear, commander of the *HMS Sophie*, who declared he wanted an audience with Jean Laffite. Jean feigned ignorance, hid his identity and talked Lockyear into coming to Grand Terre to deliver a package in his possession.

When all was exposed, Lockyear handed Laffite a packet addressed to the pirate. Inside was a letter from Lieutenant Colonel Edward Nicolls, commander of the British forces operating out of Florida, that was in essence an invitation to Laffite to join the British forces against the Americans. Lockyear wanted Jean to spread the call to rebellion against the US in New Orleans. The British hoped to walk right into a city that would welcome them with open arms.

Jean stalled for time, and wrote a letter asking for 15 days to organise everything. But as he weighed his options, he realised he was better off throwing his support behind the Americans, because the Gulf Coast still needed illegal slaves, and slavery had been outlawed by the British. Jean set his plan in motion. This could be the bargaining chip he needed to free his brother Pierre, who was being held in New Orleans.

So Jean Laffite suddenly, conveniently decided to be an American patriot. His pretence proved convincing. His deal was simple: drop all the charges against my brother Pierre and me, and my pirates will defend Barataria if the British attack. That sounded like a good deal, considering Barataria consisted of three islands: Grand Terre, Grand Isle, and Cheniere Caminada. Laffite did not volunteer to defend New Orleans or to be part of the US army.

He returned to his pirate post a happy man, but not for long. Claiborne had answered Jean's offer by sending a ship to attack his island. Jean escaped. While he and Claiborne continued their feud, General Andrew Jackson marched across the Gulf Coast towards New Orleans. The war had not been going well for the US. On August 24, the British had seized Washington and burnt the White House. The US government decided it needed all the help it could get – including help from pirates – so it would offer pardons for the pirates' assistance. The Laffite brothers (Pierre had been freed) came out of hiding (probably in Baton Rouge) and entered New Orleans, no later than December 22. They made a beeline for Andrew Jackson, who handed them a safe-conduct pass signed by a judge and a marshal. No one expected to stuff Jean into a uniform or give him a formal title, but they did not underestimate his value. He had the backing of the creole community, and his knowledge of the interior routes of Louisiana and the route from

Barataria to New Orleans proved important, along with his knowledge of the geography of the area in general.

On December 16, Jackson had declared martial law, and the British attacked, just outside New Orleans. Jean Laffite had only about two per cent of Jackson's forces. No one knows his exact whereabouts during the Battle of New Orleans, so historians question his actual contribution to Jackson's stand, but it was enough to elevate him to a legendary position in the battle, and it was sufficient for President James Madison to honour his agreement for clemency, on the recommendation of Jackson. Laffite's service was enough for Claiborne to pave the way for a pardon. In the end, Jean Laffite's main contribution to the Battle of New Orleans comes from what he did not do: join forces with the British.

The Laffite brothers became privateers again after the battle. But, the good life in Barataria behind them, the brothers abandoned their escapades in New Orleans. On August 21, 1821, Pierre Laffite died in the Yucatán peninsula of Mexico, in a tiny village called Yalahau. He might have been ill and unable to defend himself when Miguel Molas – a pirate from Spain who had migrated to Mexico – and his men found him. The last sound and sight of this slave-smuggling pirate would have been thousands of pink flamingoes filling the lagoon. He was buried in a Franciscan convent that had been attacked by pirates through the ages.

Jean Laffite headed south and became a privateer for Venezuelan leader Simón Bolívar. Wounded in a battle with General Francisco de Paula Santander from the United Provinces of New Granada (Colombia), Laffite died at 41 on February 5, 1823. His crew buried him at sea off the Gulf of Honduras.

But Jean Laffite's story kept surfacing in American folklore. Forever immortalised as a dashing pirate who helped to save New Orleans – no matter how much of a stretch of the imagination that was – Jean Laffite still possesses a romantic image. Hollywood helped boost it by casting Clark Gable, known best for his portrayal of Rhett Butler in Margaret Mitchell's *Gone with the Wind*, as Laffite on the Lux radio soap opera *The Buccaneers* in 1938. The Clark Gable image stuck, and more than 200 years after the Battle of New Orleans, it is impossible to separate the man from the myth.

Chapter 14
OLIVER PERRY:
"We have met the enemy..."

Canada had proved impenetrable. Ethan Allen and his Green Mountain Boys from Vermont tried during the Revolutionary War, but had suffered an embarrassing defeat. American plans to take Canada resurfaced again before the War of 1812, when the US plotted three separate invasions. Now, 2,500 men marched through dense wilderness in Dayton, Ohio, as they advanced towards the Canadian border. Elsewhere, they struggled to cross the Niagara River, five miles north of the Niagara Falls, but failed. They tried to take Fort Malden, near the mouth of the Detroit River, but on August 16, 1812, the British, Canadians and Indians forced the Americans into a humiliating surrender. The Americans tried to cross the St Lawrence River and capture Montreal, but suffered a stinging defeat that reminded them of their previous Revolutionary War blunder.

"For two long weeks the British pounded the beleaguered American outpost, and during that period one pitched battle was fought when 1,200 American soldiers sallied against the British artillery; of the attacking force, more than half were killed, wounded, or captured," wrote naval historian Gerald Altoff.

The British eventually backed off and sailed back to Amherstburg, but they would not give up. Again and again they challenged the forces at the border. As they badgered the Americans, President James Monroe realised that there was only one way to put a stop to the war: to secure the waterways of the Great Lakes that bordered Canada and the US.

The decision would unexpectedly change the course of American history and usher in one of America's greatest naval heroes: Oliver Perry. Who could have known what role Perry's enemy, the British, would play in his life, or, for that matter, what part the West Indian island of Trinidad would play, long after the bitter battle of Lake Erie?

When the time had come to choose a commander for the Lake Erie squadron, the US government picked 27-year-old Master Commandant Oliver Hazard Perry, who had been named for his paternal grandmother's father, Oliver Hazard, and an uncle, Oliver Hazard Perry, who had vanished at sea just before Perry was born.

He brought a wealth of experience to the job, though he was quite young for the task. The quick-tempered, strong-willed, and determined Perry had begun his career at sea at 13. It was not all smooth sailing. Under his command, the *Revenge* was damaged when it struck a reef along the New England coast in 1811. Perry blamed the pilot, who had promised he could navigate the ship in foul weather. By the time Perry married 20-year-old Elizabeth Champlin Mason at Newport, Rhode Island, he was out of work because of the *Revenge* fiasco. He longed to return to the sea, but all his correspondence to the government went unanswered.

Finally, a summons came: "You are the very person I want for a particular service where you may gain honour for yourself and reputation for your country," wrote Isaac Chauncey, who then commanded naval operations on the Great Lakes. So on March 26, 1813, Perry arrived at Erie, a small outpost of 400 people. The good news was the abundance of wood to build ships. The bad news:

Perry was now in the middle of the wilderness trying to build a flotilla. He commanded about 60 officers – and tried to figure out how to protect the ships as they were built.

At the same time, the US was on the move on the Great Lakes. As it geared up for another attack on Canada, Perry arrived at Fort Niagara, and helped to capture Fort George, at the northern end of the Niagara River, a strategic point on the Great Lakes. Perry still needed sailors. But by June 18, he commanded 11 vessels. With a motley crew of untrained seamen (between ten and 20 per cent of whom were black), Perry pressed on; still desperate for a crew, he opened a recruiting station in Pennsylvania. Always wary of British ships patrolling the area, he worked at a feverish pace to build his squadron.

On September 10, 1813, the long-awaited cry came: "Sail ho!" Perry planned to hunt down the enemy. About 116 men – a fifth of his sailors – were too ill to report for duty. Perry set sail in the *Lawrence*, named for a friend who had perished in battle. First the *Niagara* left Put-in-Bay. The *Lawrence* followed. They knew their enemy, Robert Heriot Barclay, lay in wait on the *Detroit*, and he was a formidable foe. Barclay had been in Lord Horatio Nelson's fleet at the Battle of Trafalgar, and later an injury had led to his losing an arm. Desperate for officers, the British, locked in war with France under Napoleon, had sent Barclay to Lake Erie.

The *Niagara* and the *Lawrence* skirted Gibraltar Island. A southwest wind gave Barclay the edge, but Perry had a bold plan: to sail west of Rattlesnake Island, giving the Americans the larboard or port side. Perry and his sailors fought for position on the lake for three hours, but could not win that fight. A light wind blew unpredictably, making the impending battle a precarious one. Perry ordered Sailing Master William V. Taylor to wear ship (turn with the wind). He had already been warned that he was sailing into the enemy's plan: the British would have the advantage in such a move. "I don't care," Perry said. "To windward or to leeward, they shall fight today." He had his crew spread sand over the deck so that the men would not slip when water splashed onboard – or when blood spilled from their wounds.

Then the wind suddenly shifted, propelling Perry's ships towards the British. Barclay waited. Perry realised Barclay's flagship was not in the centre of the squadron, but loomed ahead, in the second slot in the line. Perry grabbed his speaking trumpet to talk with Captain Henry B. Brevoort, a former army captain and commander of the *Niagara*. The shifting wind now favoured the Americans, but the light breeze meant the ships could only slowly creep towards each other. Ready for battle and worried that his men would become demoralised by the wait, Perry had a large blue banner hoisted to the topmast of the *Lawrence*. The white letters read "DON'T GIVE UP THE SHIP." They were the same words his friend Captain James Lawrence had spoken before he was mortally wounded on June 1, 1813, while the *Chesapeake* duelled with the British frigate *Shannon* off Cape Ann, Massachusetts. Perry's sailors had a long time to think about gunfire, cannonballs, flying splinters and sinking ships in battle.

Altoff said:

> At 11.45 am a bugle sounded on the Detroit and a band began to play 'Rule Britannia.' Then, a gun blast. The battle of Lake Erie began and the Lawrence did not fare well. British roundshot

and grapeshot created iron projectiles and wood splinters and men fell at an alarming rate. By 14.30, the Lawrence was a floating helpless wreck: sails were pockmarked and hung limply in tattered strips; rigging trailed from her masts and yards like tangled kite string hanging from a tree; bulwarks were riddled with jagged holes and planking was shredded; the gun deck was littered with gear tossed about in utter chaos... and the wholesale butchery left the American flagship's gun deck strewn from bow to stern with dead, dying, and bleeding crewmen—four out of every five men fit for duty had been either killed or wounded.

There was no way to fight on, and that is when Perry made the decision: he had the "DON'T GIVE UP THE SHIP" flag lowered from the *Lawrence*. Private Hosea Sergeant, a farmer and seaman from Maine, handed it to him. Perry put Lieutenant Yarnall in command of the battered, defenceless *Lawrence*. A small boat protected during the battle was pulled alongside the ship. Clutching his flag, Perry jumped into the rowing boat and the oarsmen pulled towards the *Niagara*, so far miraculously free of damage. She sailed towards the British ships, which bombarded her mercilessly, but somehow she managed to damage the *Detroit* and *Queen Charlotte* more than they damaged her. The ships began to drift apart. Perry manoeuvred his ship through the debris-laden sea and chased the British ships.

Silence...

"Grabbing his hat as a makeshift writing table, Perry hastily scribbled a note to William Henry Harrison. Written in pencil on the back of an old envelope, the commodore's message read: 'Dear General: We have met the enemy and they are ours...'" said Altoff.

He comments:

The decisive United States naval victory on Lake Erie on September 10, 1813, spawned several significant developments that either affected the outcome of the War of 1812 or directly influenced America's ability to continue the struggle. Oliver Hazard Perry's victory crushed British naval strength on Lake Erie, secured control of the lake, and enabled Harrison's troops to be transported simply and efficiently to the Canadian mainland.

Perry sailed away a hero, and will always be remembered for his part in the War of 1812. But few people know the story of his untimely death, and how he is remembered over 200 years later.

At 10:00 a.m. on a bright, sizzling-hot day, April 4, 2014 – 212 years after the war that made Perry famous – US Ambassador Beatrice Welters stepped up to the podium in a makeshift tent outside Tranquillity Primary School, Port of Spain, Trinidad. The occasion was the rededication of the Oliver Hazard Perry Gateway at Lapeyrouse Cemetery, where Perry had once been laid to rest.

"Oliver Perry," she said, "is among the most celebrated American naval heroes, and several cities and counties across the US are named after Commodore Perry. He also lends his name to the US Navy's Oliver Perry Class Frigate."

This was a grand, red-carpet event. Police cleared the way for the Trinidad and Tobago Regiment Band to parade up and down the empty street, which was cordoned off. US naval officers in pristine white uniforms and sailor caps stood with their hands clasped behind their backs.

Most of the curious onlookers had no idea of Perry's connection to Trinidad.

The War of 1812 had ended in 1815, and in 1819, President James Monroe had dispatched Perry to Venezuela to speak to Simón Bolívar about piracy in the Caribbean region. Venezuela's sticky, mosquito-infested jungles were a far cry from the cool, temperate climate of North America where Perry had made his name. By the time negotiations ended, most of the men on Perry's ship were sick with yellow fever.

On August 15, 1819, Perry too complained of feeling "heaviness in the head". A fever and great back pain followed. Perry could not work. Bloodletting did not help. His symptoms worsened, his eyes turned yellow. By midnight on August 22, Perry clung to life. He could not sleep, and he was delirious. He was given opium to ease the pain. He desperately wanted to make it to Port of Spain, but there was little wind to propel the ship forward.

Perry dictated his will and bid his seamen farewell. After a successful mission to the Orinoco River, Venezuela, he died on board the US schooner *Nonsuch* at 3:30 p.m. on August 23, 1819 – his 34th birthday. The crew wanted to take his body back to the US, but the surgeons said it was not feasible to transport it in the heat. They felt he should be buried in Trinidad, a British colony. They laid Perry's body in a leaden casket encased in a mahogany coffin. The Americans asked Sir Ralph Woodford, the governor of Trinidad, for permission to bury Perry, and Woodford agreed, even though Perry was an American war hero who had defeated the British at Lake Erie. At 4:00 p.m. on August 24, 1819, the crew took Perry's body off the *John Adams* and two small American boats escorted his remains ashore.

"All of the officers and 120 seamen, everyone who could be spared to accompany the commander on his final journey, travelled in boats rowed with measured strokes as minute guns commenced firing from the flagship," wrote Perry's biographer David Skaggs. A hearse bearing Perry proceeded down the wharf. The procession included officers and men of the *John Adams* and *Nonsuch*, local citizens, and the governor.

The Americans realised how unusual it was for a British representative to participate. Historian and journalist Louis Homer wrote in the *Trinidad Express* of Woodford:

> He was still presiding over the placement of black US marines who had fought at Chesapeake in the US, on the side of Britain. After Britain lost the war, that country had the responsibility to find homes for the marines. They were sent to Trinidad in batches and settled in Moruga, where they became known as Merikins.

The procession made its way to Lapeyrouse Cemetery, where the chaplain read the solemn petition from the Book of Common Prayer and some onlookers in the crowd were moved to tears. His death came far from home, but Perry was not without many of his countrymen. Even the British respected him. Officers and men of the 41st Regiment of Foot, who had been assigned to Trinidad after the war, had heard of Perry and admired him, and came to his simple burial ceremony.

"Perry's burial in Lapeyrouse was of historical significance," wrote Homer many years later. "It was the first such burial in Trinidad, but due to a strained wartime relationship between the US and Britain over the War of 1812, it prevented him from receiving a military burial in Trinidad."

Devastated by the news, Betsy Perry kept a private memorial at her home on Touro Street in Newport, Connecticut.

In 1826, the US government brought Perry's body home on the USS *Lexington* for re-interment in Newport, Rhode

Island. By 1866, the relationship between Britain and the US had improved, and when Arthur Hamilton Gordon was appointed governor of Trinidad, he collaborated with members of the Town Council to erect a monument at Lapeyrouse in honour of Perry, where his body had entered the cemetery. The monument consisted of two columns, 15 feet apart, and was adorned with historical details concerning the incident. The metal gate was decorated with the silver-gilt coats of arms of Britain and the US. The Perry Memorial Gateway was opened on April 11, 1870, in the presence of the governor and Port of Spain Mayor John Bell-Smythe.

Neither the US nor Trinidad and Tobago forgot the historical significance of Perry's burial. Today, there are monuments to Perry in the US states of Ohio, Pennsylvania, New York, and Illinois. And from 1870 until 2000, a contingent of US naval officers came to Trinidad annually on August 23 to clean the columns and polish the brass epitaph. Eventually, vandals stripped the monuments, but they were restored, and the wall on the northern, Tragarete Road side of Lapeyrouse Cemetery bears a plaque at the Perry Gateway.

In life, Oliver Hazard Perry conquered the enemy; in death, he brought his country and the enemy together in a symbolic act of peace that took place on the island of Trinidad.

Chapter 15

WILLIAM ALEXANDER LEIDESDORFF:
All That Glitters is Not Gold

William Alexander Leidesdorff lived a charmed life. Nothing, it seemed, could go wrong for the handsome young man with dark, mesmerising eyes and an engaging personality. He was born in 1810 in the Danish West Indies, where his father, Alexander Leidesdorff, a Danish planter, had abandoned Leidesdorff's light-skinned mulatto mother, Anna Marie Sparks, in St Croix, but Leidesdorff caught the attention of an English plantation owner, who took care of the young boy and sponsored his education.

Through his father, William Leidesdorff had Danish citizenship, but when he became a young man, the Englishman who cared for him sent him to New Orleans to live with the planter's brother, so that Leidesdorff could become a cotton merchant. Leidesdorff made a favourable impression, mastering the mercantile business with ease, and building a reputation as an astute businessman. Somehow both of the brothers who served as Leidesdorff's mentors suddenly died, just months apart, and Leidesdorff inherited their New Orleans estate.

He settled into New Orleans life, managing his estate well. Once again, Leidesdorff's engaging personality came to his rescue, and he began courting a well-positioned woman named Hortense, who boasted an impeccable lineage that earned her family membership in New Orleans' high society. They even claimed ancestral ties to King Louis XIV of France.

It was a far cry from Leidesdorff's ancestry, which defied social convention. A murky mixture of history and legend shows Leidesdorff could not charm his way through this phase of his life. As the story goes, on the eve of his wedding, Leidesdorff's conscience got the better of him and he confessed his true background to Hortense. Her family could not condone her marriage to a mixed-race man, and when the wedding was cancelled, a devastated Leidesdorff packed up his life and turned his back on New Orleans. Broken-hearted, embarrassed, and unaccustomed to rejection, Leidesdorff, who had conducted his life as a confident, amiable, and successful man, bought two schooners, the *West* and *Julia Ann,* and sold his personal effects in New Orleans.

Hortense fell ill soon after their broken engagement and asked a priest to honour her dying wish: she wanted Leidesdorff to have the small gold crucifix she wore, as a symbol of her love.

Leidesdorff took to the seas, spending time in New York and Hawaii. In 1841, he landed in the small, undeveloped settlement of Yerba Buena, California, which then belonged to Mexico. It was nothing more than marshes, muddy streets, saloons, and a few makeshift homes, but Leidesdorff saw something more: a trading town.

Journalist Cindy Hu wrote:

> Leidesdorff opened a mercantile business and developed a profitable export-import trade route between Yerba Buena and Honolulu. He sold hides and tallow, California's principal exports during that era. From the proceeds of his business Leidesdorff began to build his empire. He purchased a lot at the corner of Clay and Kearny Streets that later became the site of the city's first hotel; built the town's first cargo warehouse; opened a general store; became a shipbuilder; and established a lumberyard.

A businessman to the core, Leidesdorff forfeited his American citizenship and became a Mexican citizen so that he could get 35,000 acres of land in the Sacramento Valley from Mexico; in 1844 Governor Manuel Micheltorena confirmed his land grant of 35,000 acres on the American River. Leidesdorff's ranch, Río de Los Americanos, was near the spot where James Marshall would discover gold in January 1848. But apparently citizenship was just a piece of paper for Leidesdorff, because he remained a loyal American who secretly supported the Americans eyeing the west coast. In 1845, Consul Thomas Oliver Larkin appointed him Vice Consul to Mexico. In this capacity, Leidesdorff gave aid to John C. Fremont and the Americans who raised the Bear flag in the historic rebellion at Sonoma in 1846.

In 1844, there had been about a dozen houses in Leidesdorff's town. By 1846, there were about 200 people; by April the following year, there were 79 buildings and the permanent population was 459. On January 30, 1846, an ordinance from Chief Magistrate Washington A. Barlett appeared in the *California Star*. It changed the name of Yerba Buena.

> Whereas, the local name of Yerba Buena, as applied to the settlement or town of San Francisco, is unknown beyond the district; and has been applied from the local name of the cove, on which the town is built: Therefore to prevent confusion and mistakes in public documents and that the town may have the advantage of the name given on the public map.
>
> It is hereby ordained, that the name of San Francisco shall hereafter be used in all official communications and public documents, or records appertaining to the town.
>
> *Washington Bartlett, Chief Magistrate*

Determined to see the area grow, Leidesdorff bought a steamship later called the *Sitka,* built as a pleasure boat for the officers of the Russian Fur Company. It was brought down to San Francisco in October 1847, and became the first steam-powered vessel to enter San Francisco Bay. By November 28, the *Sitka* began carrying goods and transporting passengers as far as Monterey, California. Wrecked in a gale that swept through San Francisco, the *Sitka* was saved, carried inland by oxen, rechristened the *Rainbow,* and worked the Sacramento River.

Leidesdorff's popularity seemed to grow with his business, and he became known for his entertaining. He owned the largest estate in town – euphemistically called the "Cottage" and situated on what is now the corner of California and Montgomery Streets, near the waterfront.

For those who knew and dealt with him, Leidesdorff was an interesting and lively character. According to one of California's early historians and ethnologist Hubert Howe Bancroft, Leidesdorff was "intelligent, fairly well educated, speaking several languages, enterprising, public-spirited and honourable, but somewhat obscured by quick temper, jealousy and a tendency to quarrel."

History records a string of Leidesdorff firsts: member of the first town council; the first treasurer; served on the town's first school board and helped plan and build the first public school; and as mentioned, the town's first hotel, the City Hotel. He organised the first official horse race ever held in California, in a meadow near Mission Dolores.

Even an astute businessman and visionary like Leidesdorff could never have envisioned the population explosion that was about to hit San Francisco courtesy of the Gold Rush. It was about to become a booming city.

The gold rush began on January 24, 1848, when James W. Marshall discovered a gold nugget while constructing a sawmill for John Sutter, a Sacramento agriculturalist. News of Marshall's discovery brought thousands of immigrants to California from elsewhere in the US and from other countries.

The large influx of "forty-niners", as the gold prospectors were known, caused California's population to increase dramatically. San Francisco's grew from 1,000 in 1848 to over 20,000 by 1850. California's overall population growth was so swift that it was incorporated into the Union as the 31st state in 1850 – just two years after the US had acquired it from Mexico under the Treaty of Guadalupe-Hidalgo, which ended the Mexican-American War. In addition to massive emigration from the eastern US, the California gold rush attracted fortune-seekers from China, Germany, Chile, Mexico, Ireland, Turkey, and France, making it easy to forget the Danish West Indian who had built San Francisco.

Leidesdorff did not witness the changes that the Gold Rush would bring. He died at the age of 38, probably of typhoid fever.

A weekly newspaper carried his obituary.

May 24, 1848, *Californian*

DIED. In this town, on Thursday last, of brain fever. Capt William A. Liedesdorff late US Vice Consul for this port. Dying in the Roman Catholic faith, he was buried on Friday last in the Mission Church of Dolores, near this place. A large and respectable procession of the citizens followed the hearse from the late residence of the deceased to the place of interment. The flags at the barracks and of the shipping in port were displayed at half mast during the day, and as the procession moved from town minute guns were fired from the barracks.

He was educated in the city of Flensburg,
Denmark. He early entered the merchant service
of the United States, and was for some years well
known as a ship master in the ports of New York
and New Orleans. He arrived on this coast in the
year 1841, master of the schooner *Julian*.

A tombstone marks Leidesdorff's burial site in the
floor of the chapel. He left no will bequeathing his estate,
which was valued at $1.5 million, and he never married.
His mother, Anna Maria Spark, eventually inherited his
estate, although she was chiselled out of most of the
money by army captain Joseph Folsom. Today, a plaque,
dedicated in 1988, rests at the corner of Leidesdorff and
Sacramento Streets, honouring the man who envisioned
San Francisco as a great city.

Leidesdorff is said to have been the first African
American millionaire. But although his *Sitka* took
prospectors up the river to pan for gold, Leidesdorff
missed out on the gold rush that buried his name and his
invaluable contribution to building the city. He probably
never thought about gold, other than the gold cross his
fiancée had left him when she died. San Francisco would
grow into one of the most beloved and romanticised
cities in the US. In 1953, more than a century after the
Danish West Indian's death, singer Tony Bennett would
croon a popular song, "I Left My Heart in San Francisco."
But Liedesdorff, the West Indian who founded San
Francisco, had left his heart in New Orleans.

Chapter 16

THE INVISIBLE WEST INDIANS OF THE PANAMA CANAL

In 1850, Dr Edward Cullen, an Irish physician and member of the Royal Geographical Society, confidently claimed he knew of a route from the Caribbean Sea to the Pacific Ocean. His claim piqued the interest of England, France, Colombia (then called New Granada), and the US enough for them to organise an exploratory expedition to Central America, that narrow strip of land connecting North and South America.

No one doubted Cullen, because of a book published in 1849 by an Irish adventurer who had also declared that he had "crossed and recrossed [the territory Cullen described] several times and by several tracks," and that only "three or four miles of deep cutting" would be necessary for a ship canal the entire distance, wrote newspaper editor and historian Joel Tyler Headley. "Aroused by this report – which proved to be a mere fiction – Sir Charles Fox and other English capitalists took up the subject, and sent out Mr Gisborne, a civil engineer, to survey the route. He pretended to do so and also published a book mapping down the route, and declaring that it was only '30 miles between tidal effects' and the 'summit level 150 feet,'" wrote Headley.

In 1854, this great fiction persuaded an English company to invest millions of dollars in an exploratory adventure.

When one of the ships in the expedition, the *Cyane*, reached Caledonia Bay, in what is now the country of

Panama, a restless and eager US navy lieutenant, Isaac Strain, could not contain his excitement. The route of the expedition was to begin in Caledonia Bay and end in Darién Harbour; it had not been passed over since 1788.

Strain was part of the Darién Exploring Expedition of 1854. Expecting to run right into Cullen's trail, he and 27 other men decided not to wait for the remaining members of the expedition to arrive. Instead, they headed for the jungle. They got hopelessly lost and tricked by Amerindians; hungry enough to eat live toads; and foolish enough to try a palm nut that burned the enamel off their teeth. The jungle devoured them. Seven men in Cullen's party died; the rest, stunned and emaciated, eventually stumbled out of the forest.

The disaster seemed to be a rehearsal for the horrors that would forever be associated with the building of the Panama Canal, in what was one of the most formidable and least known areas of the world. This also proved to be one most inhospitable, a geographical force to be reckoned with, a nightmare that popped up from the ocean millions of years ago.

"Underwater volcanic activity and plate tectonics had been throwing up islands that eventually emerged above the sea and continued to grow from geological convulsions," wrote Olive Senior in *Dying to Better Themselves: West Indians and the Building of the Panama Canal*.

> Massive amounts of sediment from North and South America filled the gaps between the islands, and about three million years ago, the Isthmus of Panama assumed its present form.

> ...The geologic upheavals had also thrown up a formidable mountain range that combined with

equatorial heat to create what was considered the wettest place on earth, the rain supporting festering jungles and feeding volatile rivers like the Chagres.

If exploring the area proved to be such a nightmare, who in the world would be able to build this canal? It took five years to complete a railway across the isthmus, started in 1850, and that effort cost countless lives.

But, desperate for a faster sea route from New York and the eastern seaboard to San Francisco and the west coast of the US – especially after the California Gold Rush of 1848 – the US focused more and more on the idea of creating a sea passage through Central America. The 13,000-mile voyage around South America took months. If there was a passage through somewhere like Panama – the narrowest point – it would be only 5,200 miles.

But the Americans were not always focused on Panama. They clung to the notion of cutting a watery pathway across Nicaragua for quite some time. Between 1870 and 1875, US President Ulysses S. Grant sent exploratory expeditions to Central America to find the right spot for a canal. He must have felt no other task could be as daunting as winning the US Civil War for the North.

If the Americans' desperation to halve the sea route had permitted them to reflect on others' previous experiences, they would have learned sobering stories from old letters and leather-bound journals about the "broiling heat and sudden blinding rains, vermin-infested native huts, epidemics of dysentery...and the blue-black Panama muck," wrote David McCullough in *The Path Between the Seas: The Creation of the Panama Canal*.

"Panama had been known as a pesthole since the earliest Spanish settlements. But the horror stories to come out of Panama as the railroad was being pushed ahead mile by mile quite surpassed anything imaginable. The cost paid in human life for the minuscule bit of track was of the kind people associated with dark, barbaric times," said McCullough.

Senior writes, "The difficulty in throwing up just 47.6 miles of rail across such inhospitable terrain would make the Panama Railroad infamous, contributing to the legendary 'dead worker for every tie' railroad-construction story."

With such horrific conditions, it might seem puzzling that West Indians would go to Panama to work on the railroad and later the canal, but Senior explains,

> The opening of work on the isthmus coincided with a period of severe economic depression in the British West Indies. The decline of the sugar plantation is a contributing factor. Then a new, devastating disease came to the west in the 19th century: cholera. Add to this the Gold Rush in California, the promise of good wages for people with no jobs and probably above all, the adventure of a new start.

> ...By 1884, Colón was being called 'the new Jamaica.' For most of the construction period, Jamaicans outnumbered not just all other nationalities there, but they almost swamped the native population as well.

Nobody knows, or probably cared, exactly how many people died in that railroad venture. The railway was merely a prelude to a larger obsession – a canal. Nothing would stand in the way – not even the fact that the isthmus of Panama was then part of New Granada (Colombia) and Bogotá was one of the most inaccessible capitals of the world.

The French persevered and got permission to build a canal across the isthmus. In 1879, an international congress convened in Paris to choose the route, and work began in 1881. Throughout both the building of the Panama Railroad in the 1850s and the French excavation 30 years later, workers from Jamaica were recruited heavily. Boatloads of them arrived as unskilled labourers. In 1881, French recruiter Charles Gadpaille ran advertisements throughout the island, offering wages much higher than average. The campaign showed the "Colón Man", a Jamaican who had supposedly gone to work in Panama, returning to his home country rich and prosperous.

In fact, West Indians earned US$0.10 an hour and the work was treacherous. During the eight-year French excavation period, of the more than 20,000 workers who died, most were West Indians. Strikes proved fruitless, as there were always more men eager to take the jobs.

Every step of the way proved to be a reminder of the horrific geography of the area. Take, for instance, the decision to go through Manzanillo Island. "The engineers could not have chosen an unhealthier spot to plant a railroad than the one-square-mile Manzanillo Island," said Senior.

> Here were poison apples with "caustic milky sap. The latter can cause serious burns, blisters and even blindness and many a pirate or castaway sailor died from eating the attractive 'apples,' fruit of the 'poison tree.' The native Indians used manchineel to tip their poisoned arrows."

Building the canal was even worse than building the railroad. The French attempt to build a canal would be led by the world-famous Ferdinand de Lesseps, described by McCullough as "charming, persuasive, and indomitable". But the Panama Canal would end up defeating the French. Their canal was not built, and de Lesseps was accused of mismanagement. The West Indians who survived the disaster were abandoned when the French quit the project; the Jamaican government paid to bring them home.

When the Americans began work on a canal in 1904, labour once again came from all over the world – 97 countries. But the unskilled workers wielding picks and shovels were nearly all black, mostly from Barbados this time. Not forgetting the horrors of the French venture, the Jamaican government prevented the Americans from recruiting in Jamaica, and imposed a tax on anyone who still wanted to work on the canal.

So this time only skilled Jamaican men who could afford the tax went to Panama. There were 7,500 workers from the French West Indian islands of Martinique and Guadeloupe, and nearly 20,000 from Barbados. They worked for ten cents an hour, ten hours a day, six days a week. Skilled white workers from the US got paid in gold; black people were paid in silver.

In that 50-mile stretch of land from coast to coast, those West Indian labourers, now working for the Americans, faced deadly coral snakes with bites that attacked the nervous system and ten-foot mapana snakes that caused internal bleeding before organs shut down. They faced a rainy season from May to November that kept them drenched in a steamy climate. They battled smallpox, pneumonia, typhoid, dysentery, hookworm, cutaneous infections, bubonic plague, yellow fever, and malaria. In 1906 alone, 80 per cent of the total workforce was hospitalised. West Indians had the toughest and most

dangerous jobs: slicing paths through the jungle, digging trenches, cutting brush, carrying lumber, carrying away debris, and the worst job of all: dynamiting.

Yet the Americans complained about the quality of their work, calling West Indians lazy and saying they could not swing a pickaxe properly, perhaps because nearly all had a history of cane farming and no experience of the type of work they were expected to perform. Supervisors in charge of the West Indian workers told reporters, "The West Indian's every movement is slow and bulging; every small object a subject of debate; anything at all a sufficient excuse for all hands to stop work," McCullough wrote. The workers were exhausted, overworked and underfed, on a high-starch, low-protein diet of rice and yams. Still, the Americans recruited eager Barbadians at their office in Trafalgar Square in Bridgetown. "The police had to be on hand to keep the crowds in order," said McCullough.

Over time, the American opinion of West Indian workers softened. "The West Indian, while slow, has learned many of the trades and many of them have developed into first-class construction men," American army officer Robert Wood wrote in an official report. "The bulk of the building work on the Canal has been done by West Indian carpenters, masons and painters...."

From March to the end of 1905, 34 Americans died on the project, compared with 362 Barbadians, 197 Jamaicans, 68 Martiniquans, 29 St Lucians, and 27 Grenadians. They died from railroad accidents attributed to alcoholism, dysentery, suicide, syphilis, and tuberculosis; however, most black people died of pneumonia. In the first ten months of 1906, 390 employees had died of viral pneumonia, and 375 were black. Malaria was the second cause of death, claiming 186 lives; 174 were West Indians who had not been exposed to the disease in Barbados. Malaria still claimed lives because it was impossible to drain all stagnant areas. US President Theodore "Teddy" Roosevelt had been appalled at conditions when he visited a Panama hospital. He pointed out the cooking sheds, with muddy floors and unclean pots; the need for better hygiene and better housing.

But the newspapers covering the Panama Canal project painted a brighter picture, which was downright untruthful. About 30,000 labourers from the West Indies did most of the work, but they were not featured in the newspapers that provided rosy updates for Americans.

"In the United States the public had little if any conception of the part played in Panama by 'pioneers' who were neither American nor white or how very small numerically the white American force was by contrast. To judge by many published accounts, the whole enormous black underside of the caste system simply did not exist," said McCullough.

Visiting politicians were "amazed, even astounded, at the degree to which the entire system, not simply the construction, depended on black labour." On the canal site, employers gathered statistics on men who died in explosions or were crushed to death, but no obituaries appeared in the papers, no weddings, social affairs, or births of black children. It was as though the tens of thousands of black people on whom the canal depended did not exist.

As bad as things were, West Indian workers continued to earn respect. McCullough quotes chief engineer John Stevens as saying he "never knew such law-abiding people and the records show the crime rate, as well as the incidence of alcoholism and venereal disease, among the black employees have been abnormally low throughout the construction years."

In the end, West Indian workers were said to be "generally speaking soft-spoken, courteous, sober and very religious." Most importantly, they persevered.

When the first ship passed through the Panama Canal on August 15, 1914, no one gave a thought to how many West Indian lives had been lost to accomplish that impossible dream. The Atlantic and the Pacific Ocean no longer symbolised the great divide, thanks to the workers from islands in the Caribbean. The US had its canal, and it changed the course of US history, making two distant shores feel a whole lot closer.

Chapter 17
HAZEL SCOTT:
A Class Act

At a time when Hollywood had decided black women could only play dowdy maids, Hazel Scott played the most glamorous role of all: herself. Dripping in diamond earrings and bracelets, wrapped in fluffy fur coats or sporting shimmering strapless gowns, she sidestepped the accepted prejudice of the day and negotiated a hefty contract under which she would only be introduced on the big screen as Hazel Scott.

This meant she had to play her real-life role of pianist, but Scott already knew how to turn a role upside down. She had been doing that as a popular working musician in Harlem before Hollywood came knocking. Scott's world of music in the 1930s meant there were two choices for a pianist: prim and proper classical music, or swinging jazz. Scott found a way to make the classics sizzle while giving jazz her own special touch of class.

In the film *Takin' a Chance*, she strides onto the scene followed by an entourage of black and white men in top hats. Dressed in a dark, sparkling ballgown for her "audition," she sits at a piano.

"How's the piano, Hazel?" the manager asks.

"I guess it will hold up," she answers nonchalantly as her fingers glide effortlessly over the keys.

In *Rhapsody in Blue*, the audience follows patrons through the fancy wrought-iron doors into a club where Scott, in a fitted white gown with spaghetti straps, sings a sultry tune in French and English. She gazes off into the distance as though she is lost in the music, then stands up to introduce the great American composer George Gershwin, who is visiting Paris. Gershwin looks entranced as she breaks into his songs. The movie is corny, but Scott is regal. Close-ups of her many diamond bracelets reveal hands moving so fast they are a blur.

"I've got rhythm, I've got my man, who could ask for anything more?" she sings, and then finishes with a little shimmy.

Hazel Scott had talent, pizzazz and class all rolled up into a neat little package, with talent always at the top of the list. Witness *Black and White are Beautiful*, where Scott plays two pianos at the same time, and manages not to make it look like a gimmick.

There were other film performances: *I Dood It*, directed by Vincente Minnelli and featuring Lena Horne, or *The Heat's On*, starring Mae West. The heat was on indeed. The fiery, outspoken Scott was playing a US Women's Army Corps (WAC) sergeant. That suited her fine, but she protested when other black actresses in the movie had to wear aprons. To add insult to injury, the director felt the aprons needed to look dirty. Scott thought that was preposterous, not to mention stereotypically prejudiced.

"No woman would see her sweetheart off to war wearing a dirty apron," she insisted before she went on a three-day strike. She won the battle, but lost the war. The producers scratched the apron scene altogether – and Hazel got the boot. She shrugged it all off.

"I've been brash all my life, and it's gotten me into a lot of trouble. But at the same time, speaking out has sustained me and given meaning to my life," she said.

Actually, she was not brash her entire life. Born in Port of Spain, Trinidad, on June 11, 1920, Hazel Scott was a shy child who blossomed into a poised woman with unshakable confidence because she had a strong grandmother, Margaret, with Venezuelan roots, and an equally strong mother, Alma. In fact, her grandmother was a bit too conservative and strong for Hazel's liking; and her father, Thomas, a British-educated scholar with a flair for languages, was not a stable figure in her life.

Hazel idolised her mother, a concert pianist who had to give up her dream because her wrists were too weak. Her mother taught piano in Port of Spain, but that wouldn't last. On June 11, 1924, Alma and Hazel boarded the *Maraval* and headed for New York to join Margaret, who was already living there with another daughter. Margaret worked as a maid while Alma tried to reinvent herself musically – she taught herself the saxophone.

In 1928, she took Hazel to an audition for the prestigious Juilliard School of Music. Eight-year-old Hazel had no chance, because the minimum age was 16, but a professor heard her jazzing up some classics and took her under his wing for private lessons.

By this time, the Scotts – sans Thomas – had become part of the brownstone West Indian scene, with Alma maintaining the regal air of her Trinidadian upbringing. She joined an all-girls band. Hazel had already proved to be a child prodigy, rearranging her bedtime lullabies even before primary school. Hazel's childhood home always seemed to be filled with music and musicians, among them Fats Waller, Art Tatum, and Lester Young, who boosted both her confidence and her talent.

On a winter night in 1939, blues singer Ida Cox was supposed to sing at the Café Society, New York City's first integrated nightclub. When she fell ill, the club's impresario panicked. Singer Billie Holiday said, "Hire Hazel Scott."

Puzzled, the impresario, Barney Josephon, asked, "Who's that?"

He soon found out when 19-year-old Scott, dressed in her signature strapless ballgown, took her place at the piano. She gave them some straight Bach, Liszt, and Rachmaninoff – and then turned them upside down and inside out with some jazz rhythms. Scott was a hit at the Café Society (advertised as the "wrong place for the right people"), and she soon became a headliner.

Scott hung around musicians whom most mothers might have scorned, and she rose to the occasion when need be with grace, elegance, and a flirty innocence that transcended the oppressive sadness associated with women like Holiday, who went the route of the blues. She was fiercely independent and she had a style all her own.

One day, *Time* magazine would write, "...where others murder the classics, Hazel Scott merely commits arson. Strange notes creep in, the melody is tortured with hints of boogie-woogie, until finally, happily, Hazel Scott surrenders to her worse nature and beats the keyboard into a rack of bones."

By the age of 22, Scott was famous.

"She loved the limelight, and it loved her back. She had her hands insured by Lloyds of London, fell in love with expensive fur coats, and had all of her jewellery – diamonds mostly – custom-made by the celebrated jeweller Harry Winston," wrote biographer Karen Chilton.

Scott's independent streak and her beauty caught the eye of someone in the audience: a young Harlem preacher, Adam Clayton Powell Jr. Scott knew he was 12 years her senior, married and a well-known womaniser, but he pursued her relentlessly, and she succumbed to his charm, marrying him in August 1945. Journalist Mike

Wallace, who would become famous on the CBS TV magazine *60 Minutes*, commented on the pair, who were the talk of the town and later the entire country: "They were stars, not only in the black world but the white world. That was extraordinary."

Powell had taken over as minister of the Abyssinian Baptist Church in Harlem from his father. In 1941, he became the first African American to win a seat on the New York City Council, and in 1945 he became the first African American from New York to be elected to the House of Representatives.

He had met Scott turning the classics into jazzy tunes that popped. Her repertoire included some of her own compositions, like "Hazel's Boogie Woogie" and "Blues in B Flat". She had already begun to cut popular records like *Swinging the Classics*, and he was quite aware of the attention her signature style garnered among music critics. None of this fame or flamboyance could be considered good or welcome news among his congregation. By all accounts, Scott and her husband had a passionate and stormy marriage. Initially, she made sacrifices, setting aside her jazz for a more dignified classical career, which suited the image of a preacher or politician's wife. But the marriage did not last. Scott moved to Paris for a time, but she could not escape her husband's legal and political woes, including an indictment for tax evasion in 1958.

She fought depression and attempted suicide twice, but pulled herself together for the sake of her child, Adam Clayton Powell III. She remembered her mother, her roots and her music, and rallied to put her musical career back on track. Scott always spoke respectfully of her husband, even though his money troubles caused her great distress, both emotionally and financially. On April 4, 1972, Powell died from cancer in Miami. Scott went to his funeral, even though he had remarried.

Near the end of her own life – all too brief – Hazel Scott enjoyed her grandchildren. She had an offer to be a headliner once again, in a job on her own terms. She kept a diary, and she had wanted to write her memoirs. When she died of pancreatic cancer on October 2, 1981, Dizzy Gillespie was at her side, playing a soft trumpet solo of one of her favourite songs, "Alone Together". She was 61.

The New York Times wrote that:

> Although jazz was her forte, she was also accomplished in politics, dramatic acting and classical music. To these endeavours she brought a certain swinging style that marked her life from its earliest days through last August, when she performed at the Milford Plaza Hotel despite the fact she knew she was dying.

The newspaper reminded readers that in December 1940, when Scott had made her piano debut at Carnegie Hall, she began by playing Liszt's "Hungarian Rhapsody No 2", in a conventional style. Then, to the relief of her fans, she switched the tempo to her own modern-jazz interpretation. "It was witty, daring, modern, but never irreverent," wrote a critic reviewing the performance. "Liszt would have been delighted."

John Wilson, jazz critic of *The New York Times*, once wrote,

> She can be a musical chameleon, but her changes are not just on the surface. Miss Scott has an unusual ability to get into her material, to find the right interpretive qualities, whether she's singing a ballad or a blues or making her piano jump.

She had honed her skills in the most unusual circumstances, with a mother who never fitted the traditional mould. She had appeared before the House Un-American Activities Committee to defend her appearances and performances at rallies and fundraisers for various groups and causes. All the newspapers captured highlights of her brilliant life.

What some of them forgot to mention was that Hazel Scott was one of the first people of colour to host a show on US national television. It was remarkable for that time. Scott, a Trini to the core, never played around when it came to fame.

Chapter 18

MARCUS GARVEY:
The Black Star Line

As Marcus Garvey stood on the deck of the SS *Saramacca* in New Orleans on December 3, 1927, few people realised just how much the Jamaican-born pan-Africanist, businessman and motivational speaker had shaken up mainstream America. Decades ahead of the Civil Rights and Black Power movements that would irrevocably alter the US through the '60s and '70s, Garvey had stirred up a hornet's nest in Harlem. He refused to kowtow to racists and their prejudices throughout the US, and that stung.

An unremarkable-looking man leaning on a cane, and dressed in a three-piece linen suit and fedora hat, Garvey had been hounded by the Federal Bureau of Investigation (FBI), tossed in jail a few times, and was finally being thrown out of the US, but it was all too late. He had stirred up feelings of rebellion that would lie dormant for half a century, then rise to new, unprecedented levels under black leaders of the future, including the West Indian-born civil-rights organiser Stokely Carmichael. Rastafarians would one day hail Garvey as a prophet, and Jamaican reggae singers would honour him in song. Disenchanted Caribbean youths would view him as a symbol of power and pride and embrace his anti-Establishment philosophy.

In his life, Marcus Mosiah Garvey Jr never lacked confidence. Born in St Ann's Bay, Jamaica, on August 17, 1887, Garvey often seemed to live in his own world.

His dreams of political and economic freedom for blacks everywhere served him well in times of trouble, and Garvey saw plenty of trouble in his life. He lived through suffering and destruction and the everyday hardships of poor people trying to make ends meet in Kingston – especially after the devastating earthquake of January 14, 1907, which left his family homeless.

His father, Malchus Mosiah, a self-educated master mason, had a fierce pride and a strict sense of discipline. Garvey's mother had been the daughter of peasant farmers, and she worked as a domestic servant. Marcus Garvey could never please his "intolerant and punitive" father, as Colin Grant describes Garvey Senior in the biography *Negro with a Hat*. Malchus Garvey's cruelty was unimaginable. His idea of character-building included leaving his young son for several hours in an underground vault he had been digging to bury a wealthy landowner's child.

Garvey would not follow in his father's footsteps, and instead learned the printing business. But in 1910, he left Jamaica and sailed to Costa Rica. There, he became a timekeeper, an overseer of sorts, for banana-planation workers. He appears to have experienced great discomfort with this job, which served as a reinvention of the slavedriver. Garvey left after only a few months and worked his way through Panama, Honduras, Ecuador, Colombia, and Venezuela. Eventually, he headed for Europe. His peregrinations would shape his visions of unification in the future.

Garvey was a different and more worldly man when he returned to Jamaica in 1914 after a two-year sojourn in Europe, only to set sail once again in 1916. His new destination: New York City. By then, Garvey considered himself an orator. In Jamaica he had not been taken seriously, but nothing could ever shake his vision of a new world for black people. Garvey was 29, and at a turning point in his life. He tried his hand at printing handbills and organising lectures, and wasted no time organising his own first public lecture in Harlem.

"There, with startling chutzpah, the unknown race leader with a following of zero hurried...to seek out the biggest name in black American life: W.E.B. Du Bois, the solitary black board member of the NAACP [National Association for the Advancement of Colored People]," wrote Grant. On May 9, 1916, Garvey took the stage in Harlem for the first time. Du Bois had declined his invitation, but Garvey shook off the slight.

That night turned out to be nothing like what Garvey had envisioned. Standing there on stage, he did not appear to be a person who would attract much attention. At five foot seven, he could not be considered statuesque.

"He had a broad chest, an overall stocky build, and a head that was slightly too large for the rest of his body; he did not have the kind of stature that would make him stand out from the crowd. Garvey's eyes, though, were what people most often commented on...They were very dark, almost black but sparkly and intelligent," said Grant.

Garvey paced, "mounted the platform shaking like a leaf, and after struggling to make himself heard above the heckles and whistles, fell off the stage," said Grant. But, always the optimist, Garvey wrote home "upbeat" about the experience of his first speech. He conveniently left out the embarrassing parts. Then he headed for the South, steeped in prejudice that manifested itself in lynchings, an ugly combination of torture that included the mutilation, castration, burning, branding, and hanging of blacks at the hands of a white mob.

By the time Garvey returned to Harlem, he had honed a speaking style that combined his Jamaican accent and "a style of speech that reminded Southern migrants of the forceful preachers in their 'shouting chuches' back home," wrote Grant.

The West Indian community – mostly Jamaicans, Trinidadians and Virgin Islanders (many of whom had come from working on the Panama Canal) – gravitated towards Garvey. They had never bought the notion that they were second-class citizens because of their race. They had come from colonial societies based on class as well as race, and many of them were skilled labourers. So West Indians "turned out in their hundreds; the men uniformly in their straw boaters, and women carrying parasols spilling off the pavement and onto Lenox Avenue, blocking traffic to hear Garvey's doctrine of self-help. Their numbers would soon be swollen by curious, impoverished African Americans: the bellboys, janitors, and maids who had made the great trek from the South," Grant summed up.

Other black followers too began to find Garvey's sense of pageantry attractive. It provided upliftment and unprecedented visibility for a race that had spent much of its history in the US equating invisibility with safety. "Don't rock the boat" had been the unofficial motto before Garvey. But the end of the First World War had compounded economic problems for African Americans as millions of men came home and competed for jobs. Disillusioned and desperate for work, black Americans flocked more and more to Garvey.

When a race riot erupted in East St Louis on July 2, 1917, Garvey gave a speech at Lafayette Hall in Harlem entitled "The Conspiracy of the East St Louis Riots". He now knew exactly which direction he was going with his Universal Negro Improvement Association (UNIA). Garvey would inject the UNIA with great pomp and circumstance. He doled out frivolous but important-sounding titles, and charged a $1 tax for membership in the UNIA. He sold stock in various businesses, including the shipping empire he envisioned, with its Black Star Line.

By the time Amy Ashwood, his future wife, joined Garvey in New York, he was on the Federal Bureau of Investigation's (FBI's) radar. The first issue of his newspaper *The Negro World* came out on August 17, 1918; by 1919, the authorities were confiscating it. It was banned in Belize, seized in numerous British West Indian territories and deemed seditious in Trinidad.

Garvey told his followers:

> We have to build ships, railroads, banks, factories and plants of all kinds. To compete with the white man means that we must be equipped to take care of ourselves 100 per cent. America must be made safe for the Negro by the Negro becoming an industrial and political power; the West Indies must be dominated by Negroes because they form 98 per cent of the population; Africa must be restored to the Negro as the haven of refuge when we need maternal shelter; the world must be made safe for the race.

For Garvey, the Black Star Line symbolised that independence. It would offer first-class accommodation to black people at three-quarters of the price they paid on other ships. He planned to hire an all-black crew. But as Garvey's popularity grew, so did his troubles.

On September 17, 1919, the UNIA paid a deposit on its first ship: the SS *Yarmouth*, a former coal boat that had served in the First World War. The ship was in bad shape and worth about $15,000, but Garvey paid $165,000 for it, and thought himself quite lucky when Captain Joshua Cockburn came forward to be its captain. He was one of the few black sailors who held a maritime master's certificate. The charming Cockburn was not the most competent of men, and he sabotaged Garvey at every turn, personally profiting from purchases. Now, it seemed Garvey was becoming a victim of his own optimism. He trusted some shady people who worked for him.

Garvey's world was about to explode. On October 14, a part-time vendor of the *Negro World*, George Tyler, who had bought about $25 worth of bonds in Garvey's Universal Restaurant, walked into the UNIA's brownstone office on 135th Street. Tyler intended to sell his shares, but had no proof of his purchase. When he did not get through, Tyler cocked his .38-calibre pistol and began to kick down doors. He spotted Garvey, shot and missed. Garvey ducked. The second shot grazed his temple and two bullets hit his legs. Shielded by Amy Ashwood and another secretary, Mary Clarke Roach, Garvey lay in agony on the floor while the switchboard operator grabbed the gun and UNIA members who were in the office chased Tyler, who was nabbed by a passing police officer.

George Tyler committed suicide in jail, and Garvey forged ahead as though nothing had happened. He married Amy Ashwood on Christmas day, 1919, and his plentiful plans kept rolling along.

On January 17, 1920, the SS *Yarmouth* sailed out of New York loaded with whisky and headed for Havana, Cuba, just after Prohibition went into effect. The dilapidated *Yarmouth* encountered many problems on its first and subsequent journeys, but that did not stop people from turning out at every port in the Caribbean and South America to witness Garvey's history-making ship venture.

Back at home, Garvey's state of bliss had eroded. After three months of marriage, his wife was seeking an annulment. He marched on, setting the date of his first international conference of the Negro Peoples of the World for August 1, 1920, the anniversary of the date when slaves had been emancipated in the Caribbean. A massive parade with a national flag of red, black and green ushered in his call for Negro unity throughout the world. He rode through the parade in a convertible. Dressed in robes and a plumed bicornate helmet, he looked regal to his followers, an estimated 25,000 of whom attended the parade.

Singing "Onward, Christian Soldiers" and the anthems of the UNIA and Black Star Lines, the crowd watched Garvey step to the podium, take a scented handkerchief from his pocket, inhale deeply and then speak:

> Wheresoever I go, whether is it England, France or Germany, I am told, 'This is a white man's country.'... wheresoever I travel throughout the United States of America, I am made to understand that I am a 'nigger.' If the Englishman claims England as his native habitat, and the Frenchman claims France, the time has come for 400 million Negroes to claim Africa as their native land....

Garvey looked the crowd in the eye and asked them if they believed in the dream. They stood and roared in approval.

In January 1922, Garvey was charged with mail fraud, on the ground that the UNIA was soliciting the purchase of stocks in a ship it had not yet bought. Released on bail, he dusted off his troubles and ploughed on. A few months afterwards, Garvey married Amy Jacques (formerly a close friend of his first wife), and then his see-saw ride of ups and downs took a new turn. The UNIA appeared to be unravelling with the advent of a rival organisation: the Universal Negro Alliance. In addition, the UNIA had suffered from so much pilfering and mismanagement, courtesy of Garvey's trusted employees, that it could no longer pay its rent. The federal government was after Garvey for mail fraud, and he was sent to prison for five years. Supporters worked to get him pardoned, but the fiasco ended with Garvey's deportation.

Now, the only bright spot in Garvey's life appeared to be his marriage to Amy Jacques and the birth of two sons, Marcus and Julius Winston. But his personal life was unravelling too.

The flamboyant Garvey disappeared from the public eye, and ended up in England. There, he had the misfortune of reading his own obituaries as he lay alone in a cold and draughty house in West Kensington, London, where he was recovering from a stroke. His secretary had brought him the news of his own demise, based on rumours started by the Trinidadian pan-Africanist George Padmore, the *Chicago Defender*'s London correspondent. The obituary was not kind.

Garvey was lonely and agitated, as is anyone sick, and his problems were compounded by the loss of his public image; the loss of his dreams for a mass movement of united blacks; and the personal loss of his wife, who had taken his two children and left him two years before, in 1938.

If Garvey had any chance of recovering from his stroke, the brutal analysis of his life's work spread out bitterly and cruelly in the newspaper before him prevented his rallying. He suffered another stroke two weeks later, on June 10, 1940. This one proved fatal.

The *New York Times* reported his death on June 11:

> Marcus Garvey, West Indian Negro, who once set himself up as 'Emperor of the Kingdom of Africa' in New York's Harlem and later appeared before the League of Nations as representative of 'the black peoples of the world,' died here yesterday.

The article described Garvey as a "short, stout, ebony-coloured firebrand who styled himself a 'world-famous orator.'"

In other places too, the article appeared to poke fun at Garvey.

> Where Father Divine of a later day created 'angels' and 'archangels' among the coloured population of Harlem, Garvey in his time sprinkled the area with princes and princesses, barons, knights, viscounts, earls and dukes, and kept for himself for a time the comparatively humble designation of 'Sir Provisional President of Africa.' There was no evidence that he had ever set foot on that continent.

The *Defender* filed a much kinder story:

> Endowed with a dynamic personality, with unmatched oratorical gift, Garvey was easily the most colourful figure to have appeared in America since Frederick Douglass and Booker T. Washington....

In time, those who attacked him – including the Trinidadian writer C.L.R. James – would have a change of heart. The charismatic and controversial Garvey, with his unshakable confidence and belief in a Back-to-Africa movement, would end up inspiring American Black Power and the Rastafarian movement in Jamaica. He would bridge the US and the Caribbean in unimaginable ways, leaving his detractors with as many questions as doubts: was he a naïve idealist who stumbled into trouble with mismanaged dreams, or was he a careless crook who defrauded black people of money for his Black Star Line?

Marcus Garvey, a portly man with cherubic cheeks, "the Negro with a hat", as his biographer described him, turned out to be a star that burned brighter in death than in life. He would be one of the most unlikely and enigmatic heroes to emerge from the Caribbean: an icon who in hindsight seemed to be light years ahead of black people in the US and the Caribbean when it came to a fundamental feature of the Black Power Movement: black pride. He dared to dream big – as only a West Indian from a small Caribbean island could.

Chapter 19

FIDEL CASTRO:
An American Obsession

They had barely survived a treacherous voyage from Mexico four days earlier, landing on December 2, 1956. Exhausted, famished, and shocked by the harrowing journey on the *Granma*, Fidel Castro and his band of 81 rebels found themselves scrambling for their lives after their yacht crashed ashore, leaving them shipwrecked revolutionaries just off Los Cayuelos, in the southwest corner of Cuba.

They knew they had to skirt an area patrolled by Cuban President Fulgencio Batista's soldiers. Fidel and his motley group saw the fighter planes dip low above the sugar cane. Automatic rifles snapped and stuttered a staccato rhythm, and the revolutionaries scattered, crawling on their hands and knees like babies, in slow motion, through the cane.

With the sun like a spotlight directly overhead, the situation looked bleak, if not impossible, to the 30-year-old Castro and his men. The attack was relentless. They were surrounded. Bombs dropped from the sky, and Castro, dressed in olive-green army fatigues, covered his six-foot frame with dry sugar cane leaves to hide. He whistled softly and two of his men made their way to him.

"We are winning," he whispered.

Universo, who had lost his boots in the scramble, and Faustino, who had lost his gun, stared at him silently. They only had two guns.

Cautiously, pulling down sugar cane stalks to suck and licking the dew off leaves in the morning, the three awaited their fate. Castro could not stop mumbling under his breath. He planned his revolution, but slept with his pistol under his head so that he could shoot himself if Batista's men discovered him.

When they were certain the soldiers had passed, they made their move. Two weeks later they met up with Fidel's younger brother Raúl, who had five guns. Now there were seven.

"And that's when I said, 'Now we can win this war,'" said Castro. "I remember[ed] a phrase by Carlos Manuel de Céspedes, who, replying to the pessimists when he was in a similar situation and had only twelve men, said, 'We still have twelve men! That's enough to win Cuba's independence.' All it takes is ten per cent of the civilian population, maybe only five per cent, to provide the base for a guerrilla war."

Castro knew that with only 147 poorly armed men, Céspedes, a planter, had declared Cuba's independence from Spain in 1868. Céspedes had failed, but he started the Ten Years' War, which would result in Cuba's independence.

Castro would find their doctor and comrade Ernesto "Che" Guevara, an Argentine whom they had met in Mexico. Then they had to get to the Sierra Maestra, so they could begin a guerrilla war. As a young man, Castro had been a mountain climber; as a child, he had known and, you could say, "studied" the poor people who lived there.

But few people would have bet on him. Many of Batista's soldiers could hardly perceive him as a real threat to Cuba and its American-controlled puppet president.

For a time, Castro seemed little more than a bombastic, bungling revolutionary, ill fitted for the job because of his background. His father, Ángel María Bautista Castro y Argiz, an immigrant from Spain, had worked hard to lease land from the United Fruit Company, then grew cane and worked his way up to become a landowner with his own sugar plantation.

Fidel Castro was born on August 13, 1926 or 1927 (the records are unclear, but Castro said 1926). He had a privileged childhood, but he did not feel aristocratic, because his father had not been born into money, and his mother's family was poor. Castro attended prestigious private schools and went to Havana University's Law School in 1945. Here, he discovered a world of politics and a world of corruption, with Havana at the centre.

In December 1946, Vito Genovese arrived early for a Mafia "conference" in Havana. Lucky Luciano, who had recently been deported from the US, had surfaced there, and the mobsters congregating for their "conference" wanted to turn the entire Caribbean into the "greatest gambling operation the world had ever seen". Gangster Meyer Lansky planned to create his own version of Monte Carlo from the Isle of Pines, the penal colony where Castro would later be held as a political prisoner. Cuba was America's playground. On February 11, 1947, singer Frank Sinatra came to visit Luciano with a suitcase stuffed with $2 million. Havana was heating up, and Castro was learning about Marxism as Cuba deported Luciano.

In 1950, Castro had graduated with a doctor of law, social science and diplomatic law. His first stab at a revolution turned out to be a comedy of errors that would go down in history as the 26 of July Movement. In 1953, he devised a plan to attack the Moncado army barracks in Santiago de Cuba, during carnival celebrations, with about 160 men, all dressed in army sergeants' uniforms they had made. The ambitious rebels would only be able to recognise each other by the street shoes they would wear.

On their way, one car made a wrong turn. Another got a flat tyre. Thrown off by a foot patrol outside the barracks, the entire plan went awry and had to be scrapped. The cars took off to the sound of sirens screeching for help, and the rebels headed for the mountains and eluded capture until fatigue got the better of them and they went to sleep in a deserted shack, where Batista's men spotted them.

An empathetic Lieutenant Pedro Manuel Sarria saved their lives from the angry soldiers who wanted to shoot them on the spot. Sarria kept repeating to his men, "Don't shoot. You can't kill ideas." He did not return them to the Moncada Barracks, where they would certainly have been executed. Miraculously, Castro ended up in court instead of in front of a firing squad, and made that courtroom his stage, garnering the sympathy of all those who hated the callous and blatantly corrupt Batista. Insufficiently concerned by Castro's charisma and convictions, the court slapped him with a 15-year sentence on the Isle of Pines.

There, Castro spent his time in solitary confinement, plotting. This was where he formed his Rebel Army. He wrote letters – always double-spaced: the real messages were written between the lines, with invisible ink made from lemon juice. He smuggled messages to fellow conspirators in mashed potatoes and cigars.

Fidel Castro most certainly was not a joke.

"He had the inner certainty of triumph that only visionaries feel when the odds are impossibly and virtually mathematically arrayed against them," wrote Castro biographer Tad Szulc.

Meanwhile, American investments in Cuba continued to grow. After the Second World War and into the 1950s, US business investments rose from $142 million to $952 million. From 1952 to 1959, a stark contrast developed in Havana between abject poverty and obscene wealth, with large hotels, casinos, decadent nightclubs, and posh tourist resorts. Hunger, high infant mortality, poor schools, and poor medical facilities accompanied corruption, prostitution, and gambling.

Castro recognised American exploitation for what it was – neocolonialism – and he fought his revolution to end that vicious cycle of corruption. On January 8, 1959, he rode triumphantly into Havana. Just 32 years old, he had pulled off his revolution.

Castro was heading down a socialist road, even if he was not declaring it out loud. The idealism expressed in his revolution vanished with the public trials of his enemies. The second shock wave came with agrarian reform. Castro would shake the economic foundations of Cuba by confiscating companies and corporations that were privately owned. This did not make the US happy. Americans had owned the best land and the most lucrative businesses, including nightclubs.

As Castro's government became entrenched, a flood of Cubans migrated to the US, changing the demographics of the state of Florida, especially Miami. Between 1959 and 1962, Castro estimates more than 270,000 Cubans went to the US: doctors, engineers, lawyers, professors, and technical personnel. By 1965, almost 300,000 people had left.

The American government knew Castro had to go; and the place for him to go, a Cuban community in exile decided, was the Bay of Pigs. President John F. Kennedy had inherited a secret Central Intelligence Agency (CIA) plan from former President Dwight D. Eisenhower on how to dispose of Castro.

On April 15, eight World War II B-26 bombers disguised as Cuban air force planes flew from Nicaragua to bomb Cuban airfields. They missed their targets, and Castro's airforce survived. Someone took photos exposing the planes as US planes, and Kennedy cancelled a second airstrike. On April 17, 1961, 1,400 exiles landed in the Bay of Pigs, on Cuba's swampy, mosquito-infested south coast, battered by rain. José Miró Cardona led the anti-Castro exiles. Castro's army reacted swiftly, sinking two escort ships, and destroyed half the exiles' air support. On April 19, six unmarked American fighter planes headed for Cuba to support the invasion effort. Forgetting the time difference, they arrived an hour late to bomb their targets. The Cuban army shot them down. Almost 1,200 Cuban invaders surrendered. About 100 had been killed. Castro freed the refugees after negotiating with Attorney General Robert F. Kennedy for $53 million worth of baby food and medicine.

President Kennedy still felt Castro had to go; he never made a secret of that plan, boldly outlined years later on the Kennedy Library website: "Determined to make up for the failed invasion, the administration initiated Operation Mongoose – a plan to sabotage and destabilise the Cuban government and economy. The plan included the possibility of assassinating Castro."

It had taken Castro two years after taking power to announce formally what the US and everyone else had guessed: he was a Marxist/Leninist. This only reinforced the risks of which the US had always been aware: Cuba, with its communist-leaning dictator, was just 90 miles from Florida. The Soviet Union bought the sugar the US would not buy, gave Cuba a low-interest loan and agreed to sell it oil below market prices. The US was terrified, and was about to be terrorised further by a Caribbean island.

Senator Edward Kennedy wrote in his autobiography, *True Compass:*

> Since the end of World War II, the focus of American anxieties and the source of the Cold War had been the prospect of globally ambitious communism, emanating chiefly from the Soviet Union. Thus it was that a Caribbean island of only 42,000 square miles proved the crucible in the early 1960s of America's reckoning with the communist threat, and with the prospect of nuclear war. As a Soviet

proxy, Cuba came to enmesh itself in my brother's administration, and his destiny.

Castro was about to make the world shudder with fear, and caused President Kennedy the biggest crisis of his career, by agreeing to let Soviet leader Nikita Khrushchev place intermediate-range nuclear missiles in Cuba. On October 16, Kennedy pondered over reconnaissance photos that the military experts said clearly showed the Russians were feverishly constructing missile installations there. Secretary of State Robert McNamara favoured a blockade. Other advisers to the President advocated all-out war.

President Kennedy informed the American people about their plight on October 22, 1962.

"A series of offensive missile sites is now in preparation on that imprisoned island. The purpose of these bases can be none other than to provide a nuclear strike capability in the western hemisphere," he said. Kennedy told Americans Cuban missiles could strike as far north as Hudson Bay, Canada, and as far south as Lima, Peru. "Neither the United States of America nor the world community of nations can tolerate deliberate deception and offensive threats on the part of any nation, large or small."

Kennedy imposed a naval blockade. He dashed off a letter to Khrushchev asking him to observe the quarantine legally established by a vote of the Organization of American States (OAS).

"Neither side wanted war over Cuba...but it was possible that either side could take a step that – for reasons of 'security' or 'pride' or 'face' – would require a response by the other side," wrote Attorney General Robert Kennedy.

The quarantine went into effect, but the President soon learned Russian ships were heading towards Cuba. At 7:00 a.m. on Friday, October 26, the US had stopped and boarded a vessel: the *Marucla*, an American-built Liberty ship, Panamanian-owned, registered from Lebanon and bound for Cuba under a Soviet charter from the Baltic port of Riga.

Expecting the worst, Castro wrote: "Dear Comrade Khrushchev, from an analysis of the situation and the reports in our possession, I consider that the aggression is almost imminent within the next 24 or 72 hours...You can rest assured that we will firmly and resolutely resist attack, whatever it may be."

Robert Kennedy commented: "Each hour the situation grew steadily more serious. The feeling grew that a direct military confrontation between the two great nuclear powers was inevitable."

The CIA had never felt the blockade would work, and was considering contingency plans. Also on that Friday morning President Kennedy ordered a crash course on Cuban government so the US would be prepared to invade and occupy Cuba.

"We are going to have to face the fact that if we do invade, by the time we go to these [missile] sites, after a very bloody fight, they will be pointed at us," he told his advisers.

On Saturday, October 27, the ships neared the 500-mile barrier imposed by the Americans.

"We either had to intercept [the ships] or announce we were withdrawing," said Robert Kennedy. "Shortly after 10, McNamara announced two Russian ships, the *Gagarin* and the *Komiles*, were within a few miles of our quarantine. Then came the disturbing navy report that a

Russian submarine had moved into position between the two ships...Was the world on the brink of a holocaust?... [The President's] hand went up to his face and covered his mouth. He opened and closed his fist. His face seemed drawn, his eyes painted, almost grey."

Each agonising moment brought more questions and a sense of dread.

At 10:25 a.m., a messenger announced, "Mr President, we have a preliminary report which seems to indicate that some of the Russian ships have stopped dead in the water."

"No ships will be stopped or intercepted," said the President. "If the ships have orders to turn around, we want to give them every opportunity to do so."

The Russian tanker the *Bucharest* reached the barrier, identified itself to a naval ship and was allowed to pass, with an American escort. Tension was mounting.

"The whole world was becoming more and more alarmed," noted Robert Kennedy.

President Kennedy sent low-flying flights apiece over Cuba to take more pictures. They showed work on the missile sites was proceeding at an "extraordinarily rapid pace".

Then an East German passenger ship with 1,500 people aboard arrived on the scene. Not wanting to risk an incident that might kill innocent civilians, the president allowed it to pass.

Every step of the way, Kennedy and Khrushchev had been exchanging long letters. The latest from Khrushchev scolded: "The actions of the USA with regard to Cuba are outright banditry...or the folly of degenerate imperialism. The US is pushing mankind to the abyss of a world missile-nuclear war."

Kennedy replied strongly: "In early September I indicated very plainly that the United States would regard any shipment of offensive weapons as presenting the gravest issues."

Also on October 27, the president learned that Major Rudolf Anderson Jr, one of the two Air Force pilots who had carried out the original U2 reconnaissance flights, had been shot down. This pushed the hawks into further cries for stronger action and armed conflict. Kennedy held off and responded to Khrushchev's October 26 letter, which expressed a desire to find a solution.

He wrote, "You wish to ensure the security of your country and this is understandable. But Cuba, too, wants the same thing: all countries want to maintain their security."

Kennedy told his Executive Committee Khrushchev was seeking a compromise.

"He's offered this deal that he will withdraw the bases in Cuba for assurance that we don't intend to invade."

It seemed to be taking an eternity, but the two sides appeared to be heading for an agreement to remove Soviet weapons from Cuba and lift the American blockade. On October 28, Khrushchev finally decided to withdraw the missiles.

"The crisis abated, but it did not end. Tensions between the United States and the Soviet Union quickly mounted again over several residual issues," wrote Peter Kornbluh, director of the Cuba Documentation Project at the National Security Archive in Washington, and project director Laurence Chang.

For one thing, Castro refused to allow missile-site inspections of any kind and would not back down. So the crisis ended, but the tension between Cuba and the US never did. In October that year, the world had been on the brink of total annihilation because of Cuba; a bitter, covert battle continued, and the obsession with isolating Cuba and obliterating Castro lasted for decades.

The 1990s would see Cuba floundering as the Soviet Union left the island to fend for itself. As the Soviet Union broke apart, Russia, the nucleus of the Communist bloc, had no use for Cuba in its foreign policy. The Cold War was over, and Cuba was on its own. But the US embargo continued; so did Castro's reputation as the stubborn revolutionary frozen in time, with the isolated, cash-strapped Cuba summed up in images of Chevrolets from the 1950s, along with faded, crumbling buildings that once symbolised colonialist and neo-colonialist values and exploitation.

But despite all its hardships, Cuba, Castro said, eradicated illiteracy, offered free education to every Cuban child, and state support for citizens 17–30 to pursue education, from preschool through a doctorate, special schools to support the arts, and special schools for the mentally and physically handicapped. He introduced radio-based language programmes geared towards teaching people to read and write in Creole, Portuguese, French, English, and Spanish. Castro's Cuba achieved a dramatic drop in infant mortality from 60 per 1,000 live births to about 4.63 (the reported figure for 2015), and an increase in life expectancy of about 15 years. Medical care is unprecedented, and there are more than 20 medical schools, one of which caters mainly for foreign students.

Castro survived 11 US presidents, from Dwight D. Eisenhower to Barack Obama – the only one to entertain the idea of ending the embargo on Cuba. At 12:01

p.m. Eastern Standard Time on December 17, 2014, Obama released a statement from the White House.

"Today, the United States of America is changing its relationship with the people of Cuba. In the most significant changes in our policy in more than fifty years, we will end an outdated approach that, for decades, has failed to advance our interests, and instead we will begin to normalise relations between our two countries," he said.

So on August 14, 2015, the US flag could be seen flying above the American embassy in Havana, for the first time since 1961. Secretary of State John Kerry became the first to visit Cuba in 70 years.

Jon Sopel of the BBC wrote: "The handing over of the flag by three old men who, 54 years ago, as young marines, took it down; the US army band striking up the national anthem; the Stars and Stripes hoisted once more. Twice I saw John Kerry wipe his eye."

There is no doubt that Castro's legacy will loom large over the future.

"Few men have known the glory of entering the pages of both history and legend while they are still alive. Fidel is one of them," said Ignacio Ramonet, who collaborated with Castro on a *Spoken Autobiography*.

Castro had been a thorn in the side of the US from the time his revolution succeeded. Slippery and elusive, stubborn and determined to see Cuba a totally independent nation, he became one of the longest-surviving leaders in the world before he turned his power over to his brother Raúl in 2008. In those 50 years, while he created a whole new Cuba, with world-class education and medicine, harsh political conditions prevailed.

Castro did not transform Cuba into a paradise, but he did ensure Cuba was a force to be reckoned with. He will be remembered for snuffing out neocolonialism and forcing the US to think of Cuba as a place that refused to be America's playground. And a large part of his legacy will undoubtedly be the memory of the Cuban Missile Crisis that made a Caribbean island a big-time player between the world's two superpowers.

Fidel Castro died on November 25, 2016.

Chapter 20
STOKELY CARMICHAEL:
Stoking the Fires of the Civil Rights Movement

Two guards stood on a platform and two on the floor, where they scanned a crowd of over 1,000 mostly "negro" adults and youths who had paid $2 a ticket to hear a speech in the United Packinghouse Workers Hall at South Wabash, Chicago on a sticky July night in 1966. It was 8:45 p.m. Entertainer Dick Gregory was there, but he had not come to entertain the crowd. A spy from the Federal Bureau of Investigation (FBI) lurked in the shadows.

Everyone had come to hear Stokely Carmichael, a Trinidadian immigrant known for his charm, wit and searing devotion to the Civil Rights Movement. The crowd cheered, and members of the audience sometimes shouted "Black Power! Black Power!"

When he came on stage, Carmichael spoke in a bold, confident voice with a slight Trini accent:

> If we got what we deserved for working and sweating, we'd run the country. We work hard – the white man has us pick his cotton for $3 a day, wash his dishes, dig his ditches, be porters in his banks and run his elevators for him – and all we get is a hard way to go. They oppose us because we're black, and we're going to use our colour to get out of the trick bag they put us in. You've got to be proud of being black.

The FBI agent working that night also noted: "Carmichael first used that slogan (about being proud to be black) in Mississippi and it has become widely –

and controversially – associated with Carmichael and the organisation he heads."

Carmichael praised Black Muslim leader Elijah Muhammad as a true Muslim – not Black Muslims "as labelled by the white man", and this troubled the FBI. After his meeting on Friday, July 29, 1966, the *Chicago Sun Times* noted Carmichael had met for half an hour with Martin Luther King, Jr.

If charisma had been a crime, the FBI would have investigated Stokely Carmichael for that too. There is no doubt about it: Carmichael had swagger at a time when black people in the US were now standing up for their rights, and although he entered the Civil Rights Movement after many protesting students had already been knocked off dime-store lunch counters, he became a defining face of the movement: outspoken, fearless, and like the symbol of the black panther that he created while serving on the Student Non-Violent Coordinating Committee (SNCC) in the South.

Barely a month after his selection, Carmichael, then just 25, raised the call for black power, thereby signalling a crucial juncture in the civil-rights struggle. Increasingly uncomfortable with King's resolute nonviolence, he sensed a shift among some younger blacks in the direction of black separatism. Many were listening sympathetically to the urgings of Malcolm X, who had been assassinated the previous year, that the struggle should be carried out "by any means necessary."

> "When I first heard about the Negroes sitting in at lunch counters down South," he told Gordon Parks in *Life* magazine in 1967, "I thought they were just a bunch of publicity hounds. But one night when I saw those young kids on TV, getting back up on the lunch-counter stools after being knocked off

them, sugar in their eyes, ketchup in their hair –
well, something happened to me. Suddenly I was
burning."

Stokely Carmichael held American people under his spell.
In 1966, it was difficult to deny his charm and conviction,
which transcended the rough and raucous image of the
intimidating Black Panther party (later formed in Oakland,
California) that rallied around him. The US government
considered him no less of a threat than the Black Panthers.
Carmichael had a fat file of FBI memos.

UNITED STATES GOVERNMENT MEMORANDUM
August 10, 1966
To: Mr Tolson
From CD DeLoach
Subject: Stokely Carmichael

Marvin Watson called me from the White House at 2
pm today. He stated the President was very concerned
about the activities of Stokely Carmichael...Watson
stated that the President would like to be reassured
that the FBI has good coverage on Carmichael. I told
him we had excellent sources within this group. The
President would like to have, <u>at least several times a
week,</u> a memorandum on the activities of Carmichael
and his group.

Stokely Carmichael kept the FBI hopping. He was first
arrested for trespassing by the Jackson, Mississippi Police
Department in 1961. He stopped counting the number of
arrests at 32. The FBI questioned his citizenship and his
West Indian roots, stating in a letter on August 2, 1966
from Chicago, Illinois that: "This area [the West Indies]
is a stepping stone for the Communists to infiltrate into
the Western Hemisphere to promote unrest here in the
States."

Carmichael would not be intimidated, but continued his crusade.

> The Southern Negro...has been shamed into distrusting his own capacity to grow and lead and articulate. He has been shamed from birth by his skin, his poverty, his ignorance and even his speech. Whom does he see on television? Who gets projected in politics?

His enemies wrote letters to the FBI.

> How in the world can the FBI allow a person who comes from another part of the world, a non-American, be head of this organisation [the SNCC] and travel thru (sic) the states on lecture tours... The pendulum is swinging too far in the wrong direction.

(The name on this letter, written by a former Peace Corps trainee from Maine, is obliterated in Carmichael's FBI file.)

Carmichael had appeared on the FBI's radar on August 21, 1964. In a memorandum to FBI Director J. Edgar Hoover, an investigator pointed out that Carmichael, then living in Washington, DC, had participated in civil-rights demonstrations and had been affiliated with the SNCC. He duly noted that Carmichael was born in Port of Spain, Trinidad, British West Indies on June 29, 1941, and was a "B" student who graduated from Howard University in 1964, with a BA in philosophy. The FBI noted Carmichael was six foot one and weighed 165 pounds.

The willowy student protester appeared again in an FBI file on July 6, 1966, when the FBI took note of Carmichael's election to the Emergency Civil Liberties Committee (ECLC) – "...whose avowed purpose is to abolish the House Committee on Un-American Activities and discredit the FBI." The FBI stated that ECLC actually operated as a front "for the Communist Party".

The FBI also noted that on June 19, 1966, a panel of CBS newsmen and other reporters had grilled Carmichael on the CBS news show *Face the Nation*. Carmichael boldly stated that he did not oppose violence, even as a member of SNCC (pronounced "Snick"). He opposed black people's fighting in Viet Nam when they did not have freedom at home, and he clarified his statement that all courthouses in Mississippi should be burnt down, with his usual dramatic flair.

"I meant it literally – not figuratively," he said.

"By this he claimed the old 'redneck sheriffs' in Mississippi should be cleaned out," his FBI file says.

Carmichael's 284-page FBI file, often featuring thick black strokes to block out certain information, consistently noted his fiery rhetoric.

> Our country does not run on reason: it is run on violence. That's the reality of how things are done here. It is to my benefit to get the Negro out on the streets to stop the machine, which is keeping me from my rights. Whether they do it by marching or singing or dancing or fighting is irrelevant.

The July 13, 1966 entry states, "Our files also reflect that Carmichael is the founder and director of the Black Panther Party."

As his biographer, historian Peniel E. Joseph, wrote:

> Stokely Carmichael's belief that black political power resided in the will and political self-determination of local people helped to create the original Black Panther Party. For Carmichael, the Panthers offered the best vehicle for promoting radical democracy in Alabama. Unbeknownst to him, the Panthers would, in many ways, become one of the most enduring elements of his legacy... The Black Panther concept would travel from the heart of Dixie to the Bay Area in a dizzying

reinvention that refocused the snarling animal from a defensive posture to one of revolutionary foreboding.

Carmichael had carried the heated protests brewing in American universities to the Deep South where simmering unrest was now surfacing. Both were a form of education for Carmichael, who had rejected scholarships from several white universities, before he had entered Howard, in Washington, in 1960. According to Joseph:

> In a remarkably short time, Carmichael became a leader among equals. His knack for turning competitors into friends made him an effortless politician, one whose gift for mimicry could soothe a wounded ego and whose words could alternately flatter, tease, cajole, and admonish. Carmichael's ability to simultaneously project an aura of bold confidence, reckless nerve, and laid-back cool made him something of a phenomenon on campus.

By the end of his freshman year, he had joined the Freedom Rides of the Congress of Racial Equality, hazardous bus trips by blacks and whites that challenged segregated interstate travel in the South. The Freedom Riders often met with violence, and at their destinations Carmichael and the others were arrested and jailed, the first incarcerations he experienced. One early arrest brought him a particularly harsh 49-day sentence in Parchman Penitentiary in Mississippi. Historian David Oshinsky describes modern-day Parchman as the "quintessential penal farm, the closest thing to slavery that survived the Civil War. Its story covers the panorama of race and punishment in the darkest corner of the South."

It is unimaginable to think what Parchman was like before the Civil Rights movement. But Carmichael did not cower in the horrifying conditions. While there, he made his presence known.

"One of the memorable scenes from Parchman," Oshinsky said, "involved a tall, reed-thin Howard University student named Stokely Carmichael being dragged along the cell-block floor on his mattress, singing, 'I'm Gonna Tell God How You Treat Me.'"

It was "'Freedom Summer' in the year and SNCC...was sending hundreds of black and white volunteers to the South to teach, set up clinics and register disenfranchised black Southerners."

He organised the all-black Lowndes County Freedom Organization, which, to fulfil a state requirement that all parties must have a logo, took a black panther as its symbol. It was later adopted by the Black Panther Party that developed in Oakland, California, and in 1966 Carmichael was chosen as chairman of SNCC, replacing John Lewis, a hardworking integrationist who was to become a Congressman from Georgia.

In Lowndes County, Alabama, Carmichael helped raise the number of registered black voters from 70 to 2,600, 300 more than registered whites. He thrived in the southern, rural United States. Identifying with their poverty, he did not hide the struggles he had gone through when his comfortably middle-class family from Trinidad ended up poor in the US, where eight of them lived in three rooms in a run-down area of New York City.

On October 29, 1966, Carmichael spoke to a crowd of 14,000 people at the University of California's Greek Theater in Berkeley.

"Thank you very much. It's a privilege and an honour to be in the white intellectual ghetto of the West," he said.

The audience laughed. Carmichael often disarmed his audience with a joke before his hard-hitting rhetoric.

"We are engaged in a psychological struggle in this country," he told his audience. "And that is whether or not black people have the right to use the words they want to use without white people giving their sanction to it."

The crowd applauded.

> And that we maintain whether they like it or not, we gonna use the word[s] 'Black Power' and let them address themselves to that...We have taken all the myths of [this] country and we found them to be nothing but downright lies. The country told us that if we worked hard we would succeed, and if that were true we would own this country lock, stock and barrel.

The crowd applauded.

"If we had said 'negro power,' nobody would get scared."

The crowd laughed.

"Everybody would support it. If we said, 'Power for coloured people,' everybody'd be for that. But it is the word 'black' that bothers people in this country, and that's their problem, not mine."

No one could inject a provocative argument with a wry sense of humour like Stokely Carmichael.

> I maintain that every civil-rights bill in this country was passed for white people, not for black people. For example, I am black. I know that. I also know that while I am black, I am a human being. Therefore I have the right to go into any public place. White people didn't know that. Every time I tried to go into a public place they stopped me. So many boys had to write a bill to tell that white man, 'He's a human being; don't stop him.'

> That bill was for the white man, not for me. I knew I could vote all the time and that it wasn't a privilege, but my right. Every time I tried I was shot, killed or jailed, beaten or economically deprived. So somebody had to write a bill to tell white people, 'When a black man comes to vote, don't bother him.' That bill was for white people....

Carmichael is remembered as a unique voice in the Civil Rights Movement because of his West Indian roots.

"Though his active participation in the struggle for civil rights lasted barely a decade, he was a charismatic figure in a turbulent time, when real violence and rhetoric escalated on both sides of the colour line," *The New York Times* wrote.

Carmichael never forgot the time he spent at 54 Oxford Street, at the foot of 42 steps, in the city of Port of Spain – a working-class African neighbourhood, he remembered. His house, built by his father, had movable walls for entertaining. Steelbands played. Carmichael could be considered a true Caribbean man, with family from Antigua, Montserrat, the Panama Canal, Tobago and Barbados.

He felt the injustice in America as he arrived when his father, respected in Trinidad for his craft, struggled to find suitable work and make decent wages. But Carmichael always saw the bigger picture, and it transcended black and white, the Civil Rights Movement, the US and the Caribbean.

When the Civil Rights Movement wound down, Carmichael changed his name to Kwame Ture, reinvented himself as a pan-Africanist and moved to Guinea, where he dedicated his life to African unity. Unlike the two martyred leaders, Martin Luther King Jr and Malcolm X, Carmichael survived and redefined himself. Like his predecessor Marcus Garvey, Kwame Ture knew the importance of self-confidence and black pride. He knew social movements were not abstract entities. They were made up of individuals, and that individuality was of paramount importance.

Kwame Ture died of prostate cancer in faraway Conakry, Guinea, on November 15, 1998. He was 57 years old.

Chapter 21
SIDNEY POITIER:
The Big Picture

He had been scanning the ads in the *Amsterdam News*, searching for a job as a dishwasher, but when he finally gave up and tossed the newspaper into the trash, an unusual notice caught his eye: "Actors Wanted". There on the corner of 125th Street and Seventh Avenue in New York City, that chance discovery, in a newspaper he could barely read, would end up changing Sidney Poitier's life and the course of cinema history.

Poitier headed for the American Negro Theatre in Harlem, a few blocks away from where he had bought the newspaper. The young man from the West Indies knew little about this place where he struggled to make a living except for the prejudice he experienced on a level he had not known in the Bahamas, where he had grown up.

Dreaming of a better life, Poitier approached the director of the theatre and read some lines. When he finished, the director shouted, "Go on, get out of here. Stop wasting people's time. Why don't you go out and get yourself a job as a dishwasher or something? You can't read, you can't talk, you're no actor."

Poitier never forgot that director who showed him the door. It was that image of himself as a dishwasher in the director's eyes that made him think about his life. He had not told the director he had been looking for a job as a dishwasher, so Poitier figured if that was how people perceived him, then he had a problem.

This humiliating experience, Poitier said, is what motivated him. He would practise reading, and work on polishing the edges off his Bahamian accent, just so he could prove a point about his self-worth. Succeed he would – far beyond his wildest dreams. In the future, Sidney Poitier would be one of Hollywood's most respected and beloved actors. His career as an iconoclast who would redefine the role of black people in Hollywood would be a far cry from his humble West Indian beginnings.

Poitier's parents, who most likely had Haitian roots, were poor tomato farmers on Cat Island in the Bahamas, and they had no inkling their son would grow up to be one of the world's most famous movie stars, who would crush the stereotypical image of black actors as tap dancers, buffoons, slaves, and dim-witted sidekicks. His parents did not think he would survive his birth in Miami, where they had travelled on a sailing boat to sell the tomatoes they grew. There, Sidney, born prematurely, did not look like he had a chance. Expecting the worst, his father brought a shoebox to bury his son. Much to their surprise, the baby survived.

The family – with Sidney in tow – returned home to Cat Island, a place with no running water or electricity in the house, no cars, and of course, it goes without saying, no movie theatres. But Sidney Poitier would always recall his life on Cat Island as idyllic and free of prejudice.

"I didn't think about the colour of my skin. Not any more than I would have bothered to wonder why the sand was white or the sky was blue," Poitier wrote in his memoir, *The Measure of a Man*. This changed somewhat when the family migrated to Nassau, but the prejudice he experienced there was not anywhere on the level of what he met when he migrated to the US.

By the time Poitier's perseverance paid off and he got his foot in the door of the American Negro Theatre, he was, by his own admission, "more of an observer than most. I was from a black culture in the Caribbean, but it was wonderful being a part of the black culture of New York. The Harlem that I knew for fourteen years was an amazing place – a fabled destination well known in African-American communities throughout the country."

He would have met many Caribbean immigrants. "About 125,000 citizens of Harlem hailed from the West Indies. Poitier was both inside and outside the West Indian milieu," wrote his biographer Aram Goudsouzian. Ironically, his West Indian roots, which barred his initial entry into acting, would become a critical force in his life, providing charisma and a confidence that insulated him and isolated him from the barrage of prejudice that most African Americans had experienced from the day they were born.

Soon, it became clear Poitier possessed something alluring: a poise and dignity that freed him to explore roles that had never existed before.

He received only fourth billing in his first movie, a black-and-white 1950 film entitled *No Way Out*. He played a doctor confronting both disease and prejudice in a slum, and Poitier, only 23 years old, made his presence known. In 1955, he played a defiant student in *Blackboard Jungle* with Glen Ford. By May 1957, that low-budget film had grossed over US$8 million. In 1958, Poitier continued to climb the ladder of success, starring as an escaped convict with Tony Curtis in *The Defiant Ones*. This role enraged critics, who pounded Poitier for a scene near the end of the movie where he bailed on his own chance for freedom to save Curtis, who could not make it to the train that could lead to their escape. Poitier defended his role as a portrayal elevating friendship and caring over racism.

In *Cry, the Beloved Country*, based on the famous anti-apartheid novel of 1948 by South African writer Alan Paton, Poitier played Msimangu, a young South African priest. After his success in that movie, Poitier returned home to the Bahamas for the first time in eight years "and came very much back down to earth," he wrote in his memoir.

Not all of Poitier's roles were hits, but his string of successes far outweighed those few movies that failed.

He turned to Broadway to play Walter Lee Younger, a black man struggling with the American dream, in *A Raisin in the Sun*, by the young black playwright Lorraine Hansberry. Poitier then turned the character into a resounding success when it became a movie in 1961. Once again, he took a role that could have been solely about race and elevated it into one that transcended race and became the struggle of everyman, questioning his dreams and values.

Then came the defining moment of Poitier's career: an Oscar nomination for Best Actor in *Lilies of the Field*, a low-budget, black-and-white film based on a novel by William E Barrett. Poitier's character, Homer Smith, a black drifter helping out some nuns who dream of building a chapel in the desert, proved an astounding success. The relationship between Smith and the nuns goes beyond race to capture the pure joy of achieving a seemingly impossible goal.

At the 1964 Academy Awards, Poitier tried to hide his nerves. "He drummed his fingers. Sweat rolled down his forehead," said Goudsouzian. The competition for the

Best Actor award was keen: Paul Newman for *Hud*; Rex Harrison for *Cleopatra*; Albert Finney for *Tom Jones*; and Richard Harris for *This Sporting Life*.

"We're in the adrenalin section. It's knee-knocking hour here, and I won't delay any more," actor Jack Lemmon said, as he introduced the previous year's winner for Best Actress, Anne Bancroft, to name the best actor. Dressed like a goddess in long white gloves and a white gown, Bancroft read the nominees' names and the audience cheered for Poitier. When she announced him as the winner, the orchestra broke into a jubilant version of the spiritual "Amen," which was featured in the film.

Dressed impeccably in a tuxedo and bow tie, Sidney Poitier beamed a wide smile and bounded to the stage.

"Because it is a long journey to this moment..." he began.

He had made Hollywood history as the first black man to receive the Academy Award for Best Actor. (Hattie McDaniel had won an Oscar for a supporting role in *Gone with the Wind* in 1940.)

There would be no Oscar curse for Sidney Poitier. His body of work would bring more success and cause great debate in American society. In 1965, *A Patch of Blue*, the story of a black man who befriends a blind girl, proved another controversial and groundbreaking film, as Poitier continued to irk some critics, who pointed out that he never had a love interest. Audiences did not mind. They continued to be mesmerised by Poitier films.

In 1967, Poitier answered his critics when he starred in his most daring and controversial film to date: *Guess Who's Coming to Dinner*, the story of the successful Dr John Prentice, who comes to meet the family of the white woman he wants to marry. The film, which also starred Katharine Hepburn and Spencer Tracey as his prospective in-laws, sparked a debate about interracial marriage, at a time when such marriages were still illegal in some southern states.

That year, Poitier owned Hollywood. He starred in two other movies, *In the Heat of the Night* and *To Sir with Love*, based on the memoirs of Guyanese writer E.R. Brathwaite. Each movie was groundbreaking in its own way. *In the Heat of the Night* gave Poitier the chance to break into a new genre, as he played Virgil Tibbs, a Philadelphia homicide detective drawn into a murder case in the Deep South, seething with prejudice. Tibbs, a no-nonsense cop who cannot be intimidated, has to overcome the prejudices of everyone in town – including the sheriff. The film won the Oscar for Best Picture. Poitier stunned audiences when his character slapped a white man in the face.

In *To Sir with Love,* Poitier left an indelible mark on one of Hollywood's favourite types of movies: the volatile classroom that examines the values and educational process of a generation. In this movie, a black Guyanese teacher enlightens poor white students in London. The three movies chalked up the biggest box-office draws for 1967.

Through all his fame Poitier never forgot Cat Island. In his second memoir, *Life Beyond Measure: Letters to My Great-Granddaughter*, Poitier recalled the island where life centred on the "fundamental questions of life, survival and death. They made houses of palm leaves and tree trunks; exchanged fish for land crabs, worked the sea 'in respectful ways.' Some owned shops that sold dry goods, tobacco, fishhooks and lobster pots," he wrote.

He remembered Nassau as the place where he discovered ice cream, marvelling at the treat like the young boy featured in Jamaican writer Olive Senior's short story "The Boy Who Loved Ice Cream" from *Summer Lightning*. Here was also the place where he had discovered movies. Poitier was ten when his family had made that move to Nassau; ten when he saw his first movie.

Looking back on his life, Poitier wrote, "One of my few advantages in weathering the storms ahead was that, even by age 15, I had a core of knowledge that was going to travel with me – a sense of who I was, regardless of what the world chose to say to me."

He had left school at 12 to go to work at a construction job to help the family. His family had sent him to Florida to live with a brother because they were afraid he would get into trouble in the Bahamas. Stunned at the prejudice that was normal in the southern US, Poitier had left

Florida and travelled to New York at 16. He had only $15 to his name. In 1943, he headed for Harlem, slept on a rooftop, worked as a dishwasher and joined the army. He had no idea what direction his life would take.

"So I arrived in America with nowhere to turn except to those values that life had implanted in me. That was the only ground that I could stand on."

He would earn Hollywood's respect and become a box-office hit. Film producer and director Stanley Kramer once called Poitier "the only actor I've ever worked with who has the range of Marlon Brando – from pathos to great power."

"For over a decade, from the late 1950s to the late 1960s, Poitier was Hollywood's lone icon of racial enlightenment; no other black actor consistently won leading roles in major motion pictures," said Goudsouzian.

That success and fame stood for the values of freedom, dignity, and equality taking shape in the civil-rights movement, which he actively supported.

"The civil-rights movement had shaped the contours of Poitier's career," Goudsouzian added.

He marched, he spoke out for civil rights, and he personified the dignity of black America on screen, never accepting roles that he considered condescending or stereotypical. Poitier's films managed to push the envelope and go beyond racial issues to become human issues. Few actors have had such a memorable body of long-lasting work that consistently addressed the social questions of the day while laying a foundation for other actors to prove creativity has no boundaries – racial or otherwise. The boy from Cat Island who had never seen himself in a mirror until he was ten became one of the most recognised faces in motion pictures.

Chapter 22

SHIRLEY CHISHOLM:
A Barbadian in the House

Shirley Chisholm had a collection of anecdotes that she told in interviews to demonstrate how she often fought prejudice in the US House of Representatives with her wry sense of humour. This petite, soft-spoken politician could stop an opponent in his tracks with her well-placed antics and clever quips.

"There was one gentleman who sat near the aisle on the floor [of the House of Representatives]," she said in an interview featured in the Visionary Project. "Every day I came from my office to the House, he coughed so badly. I turned to a representative from Washington one day, and said, 'Why doesn't someone do something for that poor man? He sounds like he has TB.'"

The representative from Washington said, "Shirley, every time he sees you coming through, he starts coughing and when you get right in front of him, he spits in his handkerchief. That is his way of spitting in your face.'"

"I went out," said Chisholm, "and bought a man's handkerchief. I came in [to the House of Representatives] the next day. He started to cough. I synchronised when he would pull the handkerchief out and I pulled the one I bought out of my pocket and spit in it just before he could spit. I said, 'Beat you to it today.'"

"The newspapermen in the balcony almost toppled over with laughter. The speaker had to beat that gavel and yell, 'Order in the House,'" laughed Chisholm.

That surly, prejudiced congressman never spit into his handkerchief again when Chisholm entered the House of Representatives.

When Chisholm was elected in 1968, there were 435 members in the House: 417 white males, ten women, nine blacks. She was the first and only black woman. It was a long, difficult and lonely road for this pioneering politician.

"For the first two to three months, I was miserable. The gentlemen did not pay me any mind at all. When I would go to the lunchroom to eat, they would not sit at the same table as I did because I (am) a black woman...I always took *The New York Times* and read it because no one would sit with me," Chisholm said in an interview for the Visionary Project.

Chisholm quickly proved that she was her own woman. She refused a position on the House Agricultural Committee because she felt it was irrelevant to the needs of her constituency in Brooklyn. Her constituents were 70 per cent black and Puerto Rican, and the rest white: Jewish, Polish, Ukranian, and Italian.

"Speaking for them at this moment in history is a great responsibility because they have been unrepresented and ignored for so long and their needs are so many and so urgent," she said in her autobiography, *Unbought and Unbossed.*

Chisholm developed a reputation as a fierce and fearless individualist who did not engage in political platitudes or empty rhetoric. She sought solutions for the plight of the poor.

> I do what my conscience tells me to do. The easiest thing for anyone to do is to label you. I am not concerned about labels. I'm concerned about what

my behaviour and actions indicate to the blacks
and to the whites in this country. I see myself as a
potential reconciler on the American scene.

Her staff described her as "warm, kind, hardworking
and independent. She stands up to the system," they
said.

Shirley Chisholm's family was like the one Barbadian
writer Paule Marshall wrote about in *Brown Girl,
Brownstones.* Like the immigrant family in that novel,
Chisholm's family, the St Hills, migrated from Barbados
looking for a new life and work in Brooklyn in the early
1920s. Chisholm's father, Charles St Hill, came from
British Guiana (Guyana), but had grown up in Cuba and
Barbados. Her mother, Ruby Seale, was from Barbados.
In Brooklyn, her father worked in a bakery; her mother
did sewing. Shirley Anita St Hill was born in Brooklyn,
New York, on November 30, 1924.

Shirley's mother and father had two dreams: getting a
good education for their children and buying a house – in
that order. Desperate to get ahead, they sent Shirley and
her two sisters to Barbados to live on their grandma's
farm.

"It is important to notice that they never questioned
they had to do these things; Barbadians are like that.
They are bright, thrifty, ambitious people," said Chisholm.
"So early in 1928 a diminutive young black woman sailed
out of New York Harbour on an old steamer named the
Vulcania with her three little girls...and ten trunks full of
food and clothing bound for Barbados."

Her Barbadian grandmother was a "stately woman
with a stentorian voice. She was one of the few people of
authority I would never dare to defy." But her house was
furnished "with the two necessities: warmth and love".

It was a simple life, with goats, sheep, ducks, pigs, chickens in the yard, and an outhouse. She grew up eating yams, sweet potatoes, pumpkins, cassava, and breadfruit. Her uncle Lincoln was a writer on the Bridgetown newspaper. At four, Shirley's grandmother put her in school, something unheard of in the US, where even in the '60s children began school at six. The school was a white wooden building with one room containing seven classes separated by blackboards and benches.

> When all seven classes were at work, 125 children reading aloud, spelling, reciting history or arithmetic, it was like a Tower of Babel," wrote Chisholm. "Years later I would know what an important gift my parents had given me by seeing to it that I had my early education in the strict, traditional British-style schools of Barbados. If I speak and write easily now, that early education is the main reason. Schooling is important on the islands.

She learned to read at five, and was way ahead of her peers in school when she returned to the US in 1934, at ten. But she knew British and West Indian history, not American history, and so she was put in a lower class than she expected.

Once back in New York, Chisholm learned her father was a Garveyite. He was proud that the Jamaican-born Marcus Garvey, leader of a back-to-Africa movement, was a West Indian, and he felt Americans had a lot to learn about treating the races equally. At home, Chisholm's family was always West Indian, firmly planted in its Barbadian roots. Her father dressed up and attended Marcus Garvey's meetings, and took Shirley with him.

"There I heard my first black nationalist oratory – talk of race pride and the need for unity."

Chisholm got several university scholarships, but ended up attending Brooklyn College because the family could not afford to send her to university outside the city. There, 98 per cent of the students were white. Without the protection of her West Indian home, Chisholm really learned about the plight of black people in the US.

When she was a senior in university, her hairdresser, Cleo Skeete, told her about Wesley McD Holder, a black man from British Guiana who had been working on the *Amsterdam News* in Washington, DC, before coming to New York to organise movements to elect black candidates to represent black districts. He was the "shrewdest, toughest, most hard-working, black political animal working in New York," and Chisholm said meeting him changed her life. She became part of Holder's political movement and was even elected a director of the Democratic Club and a board member of the Stuyvesant Community Center.

She left the Bedford-Stuyvesant Political League in 1958 and married Conrad Chisholm, a "stocky, quiet, handsome Jamaican". After earning her degree in early childhood education, Chisholm enrolled in night classes for a master's degree in education at Columbia University, because she was sure it would be her life's work.

But politics continued to tug at her. Along with five other people, Chisholm formed a new organisation, the Unity Democratic Club, to do what the Bedford-Stuyvesant Political League had never managed to do: "Take over the entire Seventeenth Assembly District political organisation and boot out the failing, but still potent white machine."

Chisholm said their organisation "made a lot of noise" for the mayor to appoint more Negroes and Puerto

Ricans to jobs. At one meeting, 75-year-old former first lady Eleanor Roosevelt showed up. The Unity Democratic Club became Chisholm's stepping stone to city, state and national politics. In Albany, she learned just how slowly political wheels turn and just how much bureaucracy weighs down politics.

She shook national American politics when she dared to run for president in 1972. Practical and pragmatic, she had no illusions about winning. She announced her candidacy by saying, on June 4, 1972:

> I am a candidate for the Presidency of the United States. I make that statement proudly, in the full knowledge that, as a black person and as a female person, I do not have a chance of actually gaining that office in this election year. I make that statement seriously, knowing that my candidacy itself can change the face and future of American politics – that it will be important to the needs and hopes of every one of you – even though, in the conventional sense, I will not win.

In the article "The Ticket that Might Have Been" in *Ms* magazine, feminist Gloria Steinem noted, "Senator Hubert Humphrey was amazed by the showing Chisholm made in the Florida primary, and said often that, with a little money and organisation, 'She might have defeated us all.'" Steinem wrote:

> All over the country, there are people who will never be quite the same: farm women in Michigan who were inspired to work in a political campaign for the first time; Black Panthers in California who registered to vote, and encouraged other members of the black community to vote, too; children changed by the sight of a black woman saying, 'I want to be President'; radical feminists who found this campaign...a possible way of changing the patriarchal system; and student or professional or

'blue-collar' men who were simply impressed with a political figure who told the truth as she saw it, no matter what the cost.

Osborn Elliott, editor of *Newsweek*, wrote,

I do believe the Chisholm campaign effectively raised the national consciousness on the issues of blacks and women. But what comes to mind when I think of her candidacy is the convention. The absolutely top moment, the epitome of those days in Miami, was her speech before the Black Caucus. The audience was rocking in the aisles. I remember her explaining why she had chosen to run, and using a phrase over and over again. Something like, 'I did this because I had the courage to do it. I did this because I had the guts to do it.

What may have been most remarkable about that presidential run was that Chisholm's was approved by Alabama Governor George Wallace, who was also running for President in 1972. Wallace, a sworn segregationist, had tried to block the integration of the University of Alabama on June 11, 1963 by standing in the doorway of the administration building. President Kennedy had to send federal troops to stop him.

"For some strange reason, George Wallace liked me," said Chisholm. She visited him after he was shot in an assassination attempt during that presidential election campaign. People in her district criticised her for visiting him. But as always, her conscience was her guide. "I said, 'This is not the way we do this.' I had to lecture to them and tell them, 'I wouldn't like this to happen to anyone.'"

After the national election, Chisholm returned to the House of Representatives, where she represented New York's 12th Congressional District, including parts of Brooklyn, for seven terms, from 1969 to 1983. She had been elected time and time again because of her involvement in the Bedford-Stuyvesant district, with its political legacy of open-mindedness, dating back to its Dutch West Indian roots and Governor Peter Stuyvesant.

Shirley Chisholm died on New Year's Day, 2005. By her own admission, her West Indian experiences and values had defined her as a woman of courage and conviction. Her legacy lives on through the many early childhood education centres that dot New York City. Her portrait hangs in the Brooklyn Borough Hall and in the portrait gallery of the US House of Representatives, as a reminder of her contribution to civil and women's rights.

In November 2015, US President Barack Obama announced the recipients of the Presidential Medal of Freedom, the nation's highest civilian honour, presented to individuals who have made especially meritorious contributions to the security or national interests of the US, to world peace, or to cultural or other significant public or private endeavours. When the awards were presented at the White House, Shirley Chisholm received a posthumous award.

Chapter 23
ROBERTO CLEMENTE:
Faith, Hope and Charity

Roberto Clemente felt he had two strikes against him: he was black and Puerto Rican, at a time in the US when being either one translated into an insurmountable obstacle. But Clemente, one of baseball's most famous (yet paradoxically overlooked) players, would not accept striking out, either on the baseball field or in real life. Clemente would not bow to prejudice, and he would not accept suffering at any level in the Caribbean or in Latin America. In his short life, Clemente, a determined visionary, quietly created a legacy that ensured his place as a hero and a legend in sports history. There is one quality that Clemente possessed which went beyond his accomplishments as an athlete and redefined American sports in an unexpected way.

Born on August 18, 1934, the youngest of four sons, Clemente lived with his family of eight in the El Comandante section of Río Piedras, about ten miles southeast of San Juan, the capital of Puerto Rico. By the time he was five, he spent any money that came his way on rubber balls that he threw against the wall of the house to practise catching. It was a simple and memorable life, though limited by hardship, which fed Clemente's determination and compassion.

"I was so happy," Clemente said in one of his last interviews with United Press International, "because my father and my mother...used to get together at night, and we used to sit down and make jokes, and...eat whatever we had to eat. And this is what was wonderful to me. I grew up with people who really had to struggle to eat."

As a boy, Clemente often accompanied his father to the sugar mill where his dad worked as a foreman. First, Clemente woke up at 6:00 a.m. to deliver milk, earning about 31 cents a month. In school, he became a track star and a baseball player. He became obsessed with baseball. He squeezed a rubber ball to build up his throwing arm.

"While in high school, Clemente signed a $60-a-month contract to play professional baseball. He also received a $5,000 bonus and a new glove to play for Santurce, a professional team in the Puerto Rican league. Clemente, then 18, hit an impressive .356 in the winter of 1952–53," said sports writer Larry Schwartz.

Clemente faced unforeseen obstacles in the major leagues. First, in 1954, the Brooklyn Dodgers had grabbed him in the draft and tried to hide him on an AAA farm team in Montreal. They even put a pinch hitter in the first inning to replace him so the opposition wouldn't see Clemente, but Clemente's talent could not be hidden. The Pittsburgh Pirates drafted him the following year.

"He wasn't an instant hit. In the beginning, he batted .255 with five homers [home runs] in 124 games. The next year he hit .311. Two years later, he recorded 22 assists, tops among outfielders," said Schwartz, of ESPN. "He had a wicked right arm. From right field, he unleashed lasers."

Always serious, Clemente could rarely be seen smiling or celebrating after games with his teammates. He was a man with a mission, both on and off the field. He always felt there was no time to waste in life. He met Vera Zabala, the woman who would become his wife, when she worked in the Banco Gubernamental de Fomento in San Juan. One day he just showed up at her workplace to take her to lunch. The other bank staff watched in awe as they left. Clemente went home and told his mother he had found the girl he was going to marry. The first time he visited Vera at her home, he brought pictures of houses to buy and a diamond engagement ring.

"He wanted to marry quickly because he had to get to spring training very soon," said Vera. "He planned everything fast, because he used to always say, 'I'm going to die young.'"

They married on November 14, 1964. He settled into his baseball career and headed for all of those records, but Clemente constantly seemed to battle pain. He suffered through malaria and excruciating back pains caused by a road accident that happened when he visited his brother in Puerto Rico and a drunk driver struck his car. That could have ended his career, but Clemente fought on.

Still, he could hardly be described as stoic. He constantly grumbled about pain, and that the baseball world often overlooked his accomplishments. He complained he did not receive the recognition he deserved: in 1960, he thought he should have won the National League's Most Valuable Player award, but he didn't. *Sports Illustrated* ran a full-page image of all the physical complaints Clemente mentioned. "People saw him as a hypochondriac, always complaining of injuries," said a UPI report. "I'm fed up with the guy," Dr Joseph Finegold, the team physician, said when Clemente flew off to Puerto Rico for treatment by his personal physician. "If he comes to me for help again, I'm going to tell him to go back down to Puerto Rico."

Clemente still played baseball at a high level in spite of his injuries. Eventually, no one and nothing could deny him his place in baseball history. He spent 18 years with the Pirates, where he gained a reputation for his blistering throws and reliable batting. He won 12 consecutive Gold Glove awards as a top outfielder in baseball's National League (NL), tying the record set by Willie Mays. He also led the NL in batting four times (1961, 1964–65, and 1967) and he hit .300 or better 13 times (in 12 of his last 13 seasons). He was the National League's Most Valuable Player (MVP) in 1966 and the World Series MVP in 1971, when he hit an unbelievable .414. He had a lifetime batting average of .317 with 1,305 runs batted in 2,433 games played.

Baseball fans can never forget that warm day, blanketed in haze, when Clemente propelled the Pirates into their first World Series in 35 years. It was 1971 and a crowd of 36,684 cheered on the Pirates, who were the underdogs. Clemente dribbled a grounder to the right of the mound. Billy "Moose" Skowron scooped up the ball, and this should have been the third out of the inning, had James Coates covered first base, but Skowron did not beat Clemente to the bag. Clemente got an infield hit that enabled Gino Cimoli to score the second run of the inning. Clemente's teammates all agreed he was the most valuable player in the series.

But Clemente is known for something even bigger than his contribution to winning that World Series. When it came time for the interviews, Clemente spoke in Spanish – quite possibly the first time that had happened in baseball or even US sports.

In the last weekend of the 1972 season, Clemente got his 3,000th hit, in the last regular season game he ever played. He made history as the first Latino player and only the 11th player in baseball history to achieve 3,000 hits. Clemente would help his team earn two World Series titles, and was named Most Valuable Player in one World Series. He finally felt at peace. As the accolades piled up, and he received the attention he rightfully reserved, he said, near the end of his career, "My greatest satisfaction comes from helping to erase the old opinion about Latin Americans and blacks."

In Pittsburgh, historian Robert Ruck explained, "You were black or you were white in Pittsburgh. You weren't Latin. You weren't Puerto Rican.

"On the other hand, I suspect that both black and white Pittsburghers had a hard time understanding Clemente. They had little experience with people from Latin America, with Latin American culture, with that sense of Latin pride. The black community saw him, and physically he was black to them, but not culturally."

When he was not playing baseball for the Pittsburgh Pirates, Clemente had always returned to Puerto Rico to play winter baseball and hold clinics for young players. He spent time with his family, and he was always involved in charity work. His team was so proud of Clemente's life off the field, it still records these achievements on the team's website. Life for Clemente was never just about baseball. His humanitarian spirit prevailed. It took no holidays.

So while most people cheered in the New Year at parties around the US, Clemente busied himself loading a DC-7 with 16,000 pounds of supplies for Nicaraguans, who had just experienced a devastating earthquake. Hearing that emergency supplies had been stolen by greedy people who did not give them to the survivors who needed them, Clemente decided to make the trip himself, to ensure they were delivered safely. He said goodbye to Vera on the tarmac; she remembered he looked sad. Something did not look right with the wheels of the plane. But Clemente was determined to go on this humanitarian mission, and chose to ignore dire warnings that the plane had been overloaded. On that New Year's Eve, 1972, as it took off, the plane "bobbed and bucked and wheezed asthmatically for air. Moments later, the engines burst into flames, and the DC-7 pitched into the sea off San Juan (Puerto Rico)," in the words of a documentary on Clemente, PBS Experience.

When Roberto Clemente died, Puerto Rico declared a three-day mourning period. Many of the Pittsburgh Pirates flew to Puerto Rico. The Baseball Writers Association of America held a special election, waiving the mandatory five-year waiting period for Clemente to be inducted into the Hall of Fame. On August 6, 1973, he was posthumously inducted at Cooperstown, New York, the first Hispanic elected to this shrine. In memory of Clemente, player and humanitarian, in 1973 the Pirates wore uniform patches with his number, 21, on them.

"The baseball world did not need time and distance to remember the vivid images of Clemente's contributions to baseball. The images were strong and striking and they would remain for decades," said Schwartz. "At the plate he would stretch and coil like a large cat and lightning bolts would sizzle off his bat. In the field, he ran down the uncatchable with unfurled throws of pristine poetry."

People remembered how Clemente had been neglected, and how he had been considered part of the first big Latino wave of baseball players. Charley Feeney, a reporter at the *Pittsburgh Post-Gazette,* recalled how he was told when he was on his way to work in Pittsburgh, "You're going to a town that might have the best player in baseball, and nobody knows it." On the television documentary *Sports Century*, baseball player Hank Aaron explained, "If you don't play in a big city, people don't even think you play baseball."

They remembered Clemente's boldness and his love for Puerto Rican culture and his family: "He had the audacity to speak in Spanish on national English TV."

Historian Robert Ruck once said, "Clemente is the first athlete to transcend both race and nation and culture. He's also not defined by commercialism. It's about pride, it's about doing what he believes is right. It's about loyalty."

Many organisations still honour Clemente's memory and his work. Major League baseball gives the Roberto Clemente Award to current players who exemplify his commitment to community and helping others. Bard College's Clemente Course in the Humanities offers free courses to thousands of economically and educationally disadvantaged people in American cities. In Puerto Rico, Clemente's family helps support a sports complex that teaches and inspires hundreds of thousands of youths annually, and in Pittsburgh, they founded the Roberto Clemente Foundation to help disadvantaged young people.

Roberto Clemente was not the most graceful or the most powerful baseball player of his time. He didn't look quite right at the plate, with his unconventional stance and endless rituals of bat-swinging and foot-tapping; but his playing matched his personality: it was all heart – on and off the field.

The world remembers Clemente as an athlete with a social conscience that loomed large over the sports world. He was a man of integrity, and proud of his Spanish/ Puerto Rican roots. He set the marker high for American athletes to stand for something bigger. In many ways, he established the standard by which all American athletes are measured off the field through community service.

Roberto Clemente was just 38 when he died. His body was never recovered. All that was found was a single sock.

Chapter 24
EUZHAN PALCY:
Making Waves in Hollywood

The story of an Afrikaner schoolteacher who has a rude awakening when he realises his beloved country, South Africa, is not the great place he had imagined had to be a movie-maker's nightmare. A white South African's plight in apartheid South Africa is not supposed to evoke pity or challenge viewers to understand ideas perceived by the world as evil. In the wrong hands, the movie *A Dry White Season*, based on the novel by South African writer André Brink, could have been a disaster.

But Martiniquan director Euzhan Palcy took on the challenge of creating a hero and martyr out of an Afrikaner in the throes of apartheid. Staying true to the book, she created a compelling story that rises above race to become a story of courage and integrity, capturing an ordinary individual standing up for what is right against a corrupt, totalitarian government. At only 34, Palcy co-wrote the screenplay for the film. When she signed up as director, she made cinematic history as the first woman of colour to direct a major Hollywood studio film.

A Dry White Season, released in 1989, featured a respected cast, including well-known Hollywood actors Donald Sutherland, Susan Sarandon, Zakes Mokae, and the iconic Marlon Brando. Even with all that talent, sceptics must have wondered if Palcy was naïve, foolhardy, out of her league, or simply able to see something no one else could see: something that she could relate to in her native Martinique.

Euzhan Palcy and her five siblings were the children of a pineapple-factory worker and his wife, who lived in the small town of Gros Morne. By the time she was 14, Palcy knew she wanted to make movies. As a child she had lived in the dream world of the cinema, but she also noticed the stories around her. She knew the world of sugar plantations captured in the 1950 novel *Rue Cases Nègres (Black Shack Alley)* by Joseph Zobel, and she turned it into a feature film in 1983.

Palcy must have been guided partly by nostalgia when she wrote the screenplay for Zobel's novel while she was a film student in Paris. Her work, sensitive, and striking a deep chord of empathy, while exposing historical travesties of justice, impressed French director François Truffaut. From him, she learned about structuring a screenplay. He confided in her his hatred for injustice, which he recognised in the screenplay of the Zobel story.

Rue Cases Nègres became the first film ever made in Martinique; Palcy was only 25 when she filmed this story about a grandmother who sacrifices everything to give her grandson the opportunity to rise above the tradition of the cane fields. Unlike *A Dry White Season, Rue Cases Nègres* produced a sense of pride in all involved from the moment it was conceptualised as a film. In Martinique, people were so excited when Palcy returned to make the film, with a grant from the French Government, that they wanted to help in whatever little way they could.

"I found people, people from the streets, people who knew the novel, and had such respect for it because it is our history, and they said, 'Ok, we don't have a lot of money, but we can give some money, an envelope with a small cheque,'" said Palcy.

The film received 14 international awards and ran for over two years in Paris. It became a Caribbean classic.

This undoubtedly gave Palcy confidence and the experience she needed when it would be time to face a challenge like *A Dry White Season*. It took almost seven years to raise enough money to complete this controversial movie. Palcy received death threats once her name became associated with it, but she never lost sight of how she would capture the life of dedicated schoolteacher Ben du Toit (played by Donald Sutherland).

The film would portray du Toit as a man who had always taken pride in his teaching and his country, and who appears to be honestly unaware of the horrors of the apartheid system. Palcy exposes something no one wants to face: the complexity of all political and social situations that we demand be reduced to a simple case of right or wrong. She shows that fine line between knowing and not knowing: that leap to an understanding that certain people are always duped by a government. There comes a point when du Toit can no longer trust in his government. He cannot believe the lies any longer.

Ben du Toit succeeds in driving home the message that people cannot be judged because of their colour. His patriotism initially clouds his judgment and his assessment of his country, but when he becomes aware of the problems and the hideous side of his government, there is no turning back. The jolting realisation of apartheid in South Africa during the late 1970s comes when his gardener's son is brutally beaten up by the police at a demonstration by black schoolchildren. Wrestling with his own conscience and sense of justice, du Toit realises that the country he loves is hopelessly flawed.

With great tension and grit, Palcy showed the political conflict that develops in du Toit's own home. Even the most blatant social and political injustices cannot be grasped by some members of the family. Ben du Toit and his son Johan are on the same page, partly because of what they learn about apartheid from Melanie Bruwer (played by Susan Sarandon), but du Toit's wife, Susan (South African actor Janet Suzman) and their daughter Suzette hold steadfastly to the comfort zone their ignorance provides.

A Dry White Season came dangerously close to never being made. While Palcy struggled to raise money for it, Hollywood released Richard Attenborough's film *Cry Freedom*, the story of South African freedom fighter Steve Biko, told from the viewpoint of a white South African journalist, Donald Woods. There was doubt as to whether Hollywood could absorb and market two films about apartheid. When MGM agreed to produce *A Dry White Season*, Palcy approached the legendary actor Marlon Brando, who had retired. He must have liked what he saw in the script, and Palcy must have done an excellent job in selling her film to him, because he took the role.

It soon became clear Palcy could make this movie palatable by juxtaposing the stories of the white family with the black janitor and his son to create a solid theme of good men who believe in justice that transcends colour.

The late Roger Ebert, one of the most respected movie critics in Hollywood, gave *A Dry White Season* four stars.

He got the message: "When you are safe and well-off, and life has fallen into a soothing routine, there is a tendency to look the other way when trouble happens – especially if it hasn't happened to you," Ebert wrote.

Ebert asked whether Americans would understand the scope of events in South Africa:

> I wonder what the average American reader makes of the headlines. How does he picture South Africa? What does he think life is like there? Does he see these marches in the same context as American freedom marches? Does he ask how six million whites can get away with ruling twenty-four million Africans?

Then a chain of events is set into motion that leads Ben du Toit into a fundamental difference with the entire structure of his society. The movie follows him step by step, as he sees things he can hardly believe, and begins to suspect the unthinkable – that the boy and his father have been ground up inside the justice system and spit out as 'suicides.'

Ebert exposed how the South African political system fails everyone and musters up sympathy for du Toit.

> After her husband is reported dead, the gardener's widow no longer has a legal right to stay in her house and must be deported to a 'homeland' she has never seen, from where it will be impossible to lodge a legal protest. As a respected white man, he is allowed access to the system until it becomes obvious that he is asking the wrong questions and adopting the wrong attitude. Then he is ostracised. He loses his job.

The schoolteacher spirals downward into a political and social abyss from which there is no return.

Finally, Ebert concluded, *A Dry White Season* is a powerfully serious movie, "but the director, Euzhan Palcy, provides a break in the middle, almost as Shakespeare used to bring on pantomime before returning to the deaths of kings...."

This is the part filled by Marlon Brando, who had not appeared in a film since 1980. Brando hears an appeal against the finding that one of the dead had committed suicide.

"The Brando character knows the appeal is useless, that his courtroom appearance will be a charade, and yet he goes ahead with it anyway – using irony and sarcasm to make his points, even though the outcome is hopeless," wrote Ebert, while in Brando's character we see "a lawyer with a brilliant mind, who uses it cynically and comically because that is his form of protest.

By now, Palcy has convincingly shown that du Toit is hopelessly trapped in a web of deceit and dire circumstances that he can never escape. He wants to choose his family, but his conscience won't allow him to forget the injustice that surrounds him. Palcy does not spare the viewer the physical torture of black South Africans or the hateful stalking of du Toit.

"Here," Ebert concluded, "is also an effective, emotional, angry, subtle movie." Calling Palcy "a gifted filmmaker," Ebert spoke of her Martiniquan roots and said,

> with a larger budget and stars in the cast, she still has the same eye for character detail. This movie isn't just a plot, trotted out to manipulate us, but the painful examination of one man's change of conscience. For years he has been blind, perhaps willingly. But once he sees, he cannot deny what he feels is right.

The New York Times wrote,

> *A Dry White Season*, which opens today at Loews New York Twin and other theatres, is no less

predictable than its predecessors, but its frankness and sincerity matter more than its fundamental bluntness. Miss Palcy, whose graceful Sugar Cane Alley [Rue Case Nègres], shown in New York City in 1984, offered a moving glimpse of class and racial tensions in her native Martinique, depicts a similarly broad cross-section of South African life, replete with the kinds of contrasts that in other hands – say, those of Sir Richard Attenborough – could seem dangerously pat.

Brando received an Academy Award nomination for Best Supporting Actor in *A Dry White Season*, and Palcy, a West Indian filmmaker, made history with a seemingly impossible movie to make. She pulled off her cinematic coup because of a sensitivity and understanding that can be traced to her West Indian roots.

Chapter 25

BOB MARLEY:
"Rastaman Vibration"

What was he thinking when he boarded that plane for London? Was Bob Marley pondering the meaning of life after he had come within inches of being assassinated on December 3, 1976, as he stood in his kitchen juggling a grapefruit someone had just brought for him?

The vision must have crossed his mind of the gunmen who had brazenly walked up the steps of his home at 56 Hope Road, Kingston, Jamaica, which he had bought from music producer Chris Blackwell. Although his home resembled the remnants of a plantation house, with its curving drive meandering towards the colonnaded front door, the mango tree looming large in the front yard, Marley had expected it to be his ticket out of the ghetto – not because he no longer identified with the people there, but because the ghetto was an endless round of crime and constant police harassment.

He had fashioned a "free-living, free-loving, sanctuary...constantly alive with activity, from the never-ending games of soccer on the front lawn to the endless preparation of salt-free Rasta food in the kitchen..." wrote British journalist Vivien Goldman. And the dream had all come crashing down around him, 13 years after the formation of the Wailers, on that December day when Marley's bombastic manager entered the kitchen, demanding, "Give me a juice, nah!" and three – or was it four? – gunmen following close behind him, lost in the crowd that mingled at the house, opened fire like buffalo soldiers or something out of a cowboy movie or, as Marley's friend Goldman chronicled, "like Jimmy Cliff in *The Harder They Come*."

"Even though this was the moment Marley had been dreading, when the shock came, he froze. Everything went into slow motion. He felt something push him, and he fell down," said Goldman. Manager Don Taylor, who had a lifetime of street smarts garnered from working in the "volatile bars and brothels of the Kingston waterfront, pushed Marley – the gunmen's target" – out of their range so that the bullet grazed his arm instead of his heart.

Did Marley remember the anger he felt when two police officers escorted him down the steps where the gunmen had just fled? "He didn't look shaken or fearful. The Tuff Gong was angry," wrote Goldman in the British newspaper *The Guardian*.

A newsflash on the attempted assassination raised one question in everyone's mind: did someone not want Marley to sing in the concert scheduled for December 5? As he climbed the steps to the plane, did Marley see himself climbing the steps to that stage at the National Heroes Park in Kingston? Did the plane's groaning engines drown out the memory of how that crowd of 80,000 people had roared when he appeared on stage? Did it erase that surreal image of his summoning two political enemies onstage – the People's National Party's (PNP) leader Michael Manley and the Jamaica Labour Party (JLP) leader Edward Seaga – and then holding their arms in the air?

How far back did the images go? Perhaps to Nine Mile, where Marley grew up with a beloved grandfather, Omeriah Malcolm, and a dreamy teenage mother,

Cedella, who spun an unlikely love story about marriage to a middle-aged Briton, only to learn from a passing relative that her "long-estranged husband – lordly white Captain Norval Sinclair Marley, deceiver, heartbreaker and reptile – had now added bigamy to his many sins, getting married under her very nose to a light-skinned woman who had installed herself at his residence," as Timothy White wrote in his biography of Marley, *Catch a Fire*.

Did the memories raised by his near-death experience include his early days in Trenchtown, when he lived in a small room at the back of Clement "Coxsone" Dodd's music studio, a room that Marley believed was haunted; or did he focus on the meeting with producer Chris Blackwell in 1972, when The Wailers were in London, planning to be the opening act for Johnny Nash, with his hit song "I Can See Clearly Now"? When that gig did not work out, the broke and broken Wailers decided to visit Blackwell, who had been warned about the ganja-smoking trio, but still gave them £4,000 to make a record. Did this flight to London trigger the memory of that trip when he returned to Jamaica after that meeting with Blackwell to make *Catch a Fire*?

Now, after everything that had happened, Bob Marley was in self-imposed exile, going back to England to work on the album that would be known as *Exodus*, released in 1977. The songs "Natural Mystic," originally recorded with Lee "Scratch" Perry in 1975, and "One Love", originally recorded at Dodd's Studio One somewhere between 1963 and 1966, would serve as musical bookends for the album, which would capture Marley's Rastafarian philosophy, but transcend religion to capture his spirituality. Chastising the Establishment and its politics, Marley sings about the "natural mystic flowing through the air...This could be the first trumpet, it might as well be the last. Things are not the way they used to be."

In "So Much Things to Say," Marley addresses guilt and consciousness, reminding listeners, "Don't forget where you stand in the struggle." In his song, the "downpressor" suffers from his own negativity. "Woe to the downpressor, they'll eat the bread of sorrow...."

In the middle of the album comes the title track, "Exodus": a bold, pounding reggae rhythm leads the "movement of Jah people – so we're going to walk through the roads of creation...Open your eyes and look within/Are you satisfied with the life you're living?/ We know where we're going/We know where we're from/ We're leaving Babylon."

There's "Jamming" and "Waiting in Vain", before Marley croons another, simply divine love song, "Turn Your Lights Down Low" – rumoured to have been written not for his wife, Rita, but for the former Miss World Cindy Breakspeare, mother of one of Marley's many children, Damian Robert Nesta Marley – "Junior Gong".

By the end of the album, Marley seems to have reconciled himself to the events that led him into self-exile from Jamaica. With a song of hope, "Three Little Birds," who bring the message "Don't worry 'bout a thing/ 'cause every little thing gonna be all right," and "One Love," with its message of peace, Marley concludes the musical journey of his life.

Exodus made it perfectly clear that Bob Marley, the first and only real musical superstar to emerge from a third-world country, was rising to a new philosophical and musical level. The assassination attempt would not change or constrain his life. He would continue to look outward to the world with a message of spiritual awareness. Marley, who sang reggae songs filled with biblical allusions that crossed over pop boundary lines, became bigger than life. His discipline and devotion to music had paid off. Through his music, Marley elevated the religion of Rastafarianism to a level of respect that had previously eluded this faith born in Jamaica. "Rasta was the last thing you wanted your children involved with. People said it turned its followers worthless..." Rita recalled.

In those moments of world fame, did he remember the early days, as Rita did, when the Wailers passed her house on the way to Dodd's Studio One on Brentford Road in Kingston? Rita had called him "Robbie" back then. Marley, Peter Tosh, and Bunny Wailer spent most of their time in Studio One, meeting at 9:00 or 10:00 a.m. (early for musicians, who usually work through the night). They would get a patty or coco bread and a sweet drink, or Bunny would cook a soup. Lee "Scratch" Perry, who climbed from being a cleaner to auditioning talent, had dubbed the trio Bob Marley and the Wailers.

Who would have guessed how far Marley's music would take him? At midnight on April 18, 1980, Marley witnessed Zimbabwe becoming a free country and had led the nation in song. The Rufaro Stadium in Salisbury, the capital of Zimbabwe, roared. The flag of Rhodesia came down and the new red, green, gold, and black of Zimbabwe now flew from the flagpole.

But, Marcia Griffith, a member of the I-Threes, Marley's backup singers, said:

> There was this strange sensation...and we felt we were going to die." The wind had shifted, and tear gas floated from the crowded streets into the stadium. Marley sang, "Every man has a right to

decide his own destiny." The crowd pushed towards the stadium and spilled over the walls. "When the freedom fighters heard his voice outside, they pushed ahead.

Marley broke into "Positive Vibration" and "I Shot the Sheriff" and finally "Zimbabwe". On that stage, he must have recalled Marcus Garvey blazing a trail from Jamaica to Africa with his Back to Africa movement. As the African people fought police spraying them with tear gas and beating them with batons, the vision that Marley had of a strong, black Africa rooted in its own independence must have been shattered forever. He had witnessed black men turning on black men on the eve of an African nation's independence. He had spoken so often of the violence in Jamaica and how wrong it was for black people to turn against each other – and here was the same problem in Africa.

The pain Marley must have felt as he gazed into the darkness filled with screams could only be matched by the throbbing pain in his bandaged toe. He could no longer hide the truth from himself or others. Wearing shoes was terribly painful, but the alternative was worse. For over a year doctors had wanted to amputate the toe, which showed signs of cancer. Marley refused. Rumour had it that he did not want the surgery because it violated his Rastafarian religion. Rastafarians do not believe in cutting off hair, let alone a toe. But his wife Rita said Marley feared cutting off his toe would affect his balance and make it hard for him to perform on stage.

So Marley would not live to see the full impact of his singing career on Rastafarianism and the international music scene. At 36, he died of cancer, on May 11, 1981, long before *Time* Magazine named *Exodus* the album of the century, in 1999.

But the vision of Bob Marley, dreadlocks flying, remains the face of reggae music. "On stage, with his Medusa locks spiralling outward from his head in wild abandon, he was a wraith... preaching timeless truths of God," wrote Roger Steffens, who is well known for his reggae archives. Marley sold more than 20 million records in his career. "No Woman No Cry" ranked at 37 of *Rolling Stone's* 500 greatest songs of all time. In 1994, he was posthumously inducted into the Rock and Roll Hall of Fame. Marley seems to be everywhere, a haunting, handsome image of hope and rebellion.

In *Long Way Gone: Memoirs of a Boy Soldier*, Ishmael Beah speaks about how Marley's music helped him to deal with the horrors of being a boy soldier in Sierra Leone.

The Havasupai Indians, who live at the bottom of the Grand Canyon, call Bob Marley "one of their own," wrote Steffens. In Nepal, there are people who worship Marley as a reincarnation of the Hindu deity Vishnu. In Addis Ababa, some people believe he is a modern reincarnation of the ancient Ethiopian church composer the Holy Yared. On a mountainside above Lima, Peru, the words "Bob Marley is King" have been carved into a mountainside.

In *Making Waves,* Peruvian writer Mario Vargas Llosa speaks of the shock he felt when, in 1975, at 16, his son came home from boarding school in England as a Rastafarian. Thirty years after he made his initial assessment of Rastafarianism, Vargas Llosa visited Nine Mile, where Marley was born, and Trench Town, and wrote:

> ...on the sad streets of Trench Town, or amid the poverty and neglect of the villages of the parish of St Ann, the faith that for my son and his friends was doubtless a passing fashion, a fickle extravagance of privileged youth, seemed to me a moving bid for a spiritual life, a bid against moral disintegration and human injustice. I ask forgiveness of the Rastas for what I once thought about them, and along with my admiration for their music, I proclaim my respect for the ideas and beliefs of Bob Marley.

Sociologist Jason Toynbee writes that Bob Marley "is probably the best known secular figure in the contemporary period. Cumulative record sales in the US up to 2005 were 16.5 million albums. RIAA has the album *Legend* rated as 15th in top 100 certified albums."

No one questions why Bob Marley's music became or remained so popular. "Rebel music, Babylon, freedom, rights, justice – all these terms from Bob Marley's lyrics assume a local, de-racialised meaning," wrote historian Arnold Toynbee. "The struggle of the Trench Town ghetto is a universal story." His music represents:

> A resource of hope, a significant means through which people can begin to work out common interests and develop cross-cultural connections. In particular, Bob's lyrics depend so much on allegory and allusion that they can take on quite specific local meanings.

Marley's use of allegory also allowed his music to be listened to on many levels, so that people could appreciate a simple message or reach for a more intellectual meaning. Biblical allusions infuse a sense of spirituality and universality into his songs.

> Bob Marley is probably the most enduringly influential popular songwriter of the twentieth century, worldwide. He is also one of the most beloved songwriters among mass audiences...and Marley's face has taken on an iconic status,

wrote professor of English Gregory Stephens.

The memory of Marley continuously surfaces in pop culture. In October 2015, *A Brief History of Seven Killings* by Jamaican writer Marlon James won the Man Booker Prize for fiction. It is a novel about the assassination attempt on "the Singer" – Bob Marley.

Marley was a study in contrasts, a study of mixtures: half black and half white; a boy from rural Jamaica and a teenager from the inner-city ghetto; a man who looked inward to his Jamaican religious roots and outward to his African ancestry. He wrote soft romantic songs and hard-hitting political and social commentary. His popularity goes beyond marijuana-smoking youth trying to drown their teenage angst in a foggy high. His music transcends colour, class, race and country. In Marley, everyone sees a part of himself that hopes for a better world.

Chapter 26

KOOL HERC:
Trenchtown Rocks Hip Hop

It was 1973, the year that Tony Orlando and Dawn topped the American Billboard charts, crooning the love song "Tie a Yellow Ribbon Round the Old Oak Tree." Jim Croce took the number two spot with the more melodious than malicious "Bad, Bad Leroy Brown". Roberta Flack sang the dreamy, romantic "Killing Me Softly with His Song," with its haunting story about a lonely woman who hears her life unfolding through a young singer's lyrics, and Paul McCartney surfaced from the fragmented Beatles with "My Love" as Elton John climbed the charts with the pop hit "Crocodile Rock". It was an era, journalist Steven Kurutz says, "when disco was king".

Nothing, it seemed, could rock the musical boat floating on a flat, calm sea until a couple of West Indian teenagers from New York cooked up an idea for a party. Like all teenage girls, Cindy Campbell dreamed of returning to high school and making her own fashion statement. She wanted to stand out from the crowd. Campbell had her eye on some boutiques on Delancey Street, ten miles from Manhattan's Lower East Side, where she could buy uptown clothes for a Bronx-based girl. She roped her parents into her plan.

Campbell was an enterprising teen with a desire to buy her threads with the money she could earn from throwing a party. With her parents' help, she booked the first-floor recreation room of the 100-unit apartment building where the Campbells lived: at 1520 Sedgwick Avenue in the Bronx, just two miles from Yankee Stadium and near the crossroads where the Cross-Bronx Expressway leads the way to Manhattan.

Then Campbell hired her towering, muscular 16-year-old brother, Clive, known as Hercules in the neighbourhood, to play the music. They made invitations on index cards and invited friends and neighbours. Campbell knew she had something special with her brother's deejaying skills. She had heard him experimenting around the house, and had seen him hanging around DJs in Kingston, Jamaica, where he had been born and raised. His eclectic tastes had come from their father, who collected reggae, American jazz, gospel, and country music.

On August 13, 1973, Cindy celebrated her birthday and the birth of DJ Kool Herc. The emerging hip-hop movement now had a crucial part of its culture: deejaying, which joined graffiti, breakdance, and rap as a cultural force that would redefine music. Wherever he went, Kool Herc pumped up a party with James Brown grunting and yelling, "Stomp your feet!" Then he cut to an extended sassy Latin beat. He elevated the audience with rhythm tracks that made dancers shout and raise their hands in an ecstatic anticipation of lyrics that just might not ever come. It all had a very Jamaican feel.

Hip-hop journalist Jeff Chang explains:

> Along with his immigrant friend Coke La Rock, Clive distinguished their crew from the disco DJs by translating the Kingstonian vibe of sound-system DJs like Count Machuki, King Stitt, U-Roy and Big Youth for the Bronxites. Herc hooked up his [microphones] to a Space Echo box...They set off their dances by giving shout-outs and dropping little rhymes. They developed their own slang.

Four decades later, when the UK *Guardian* recounted the history of R&B and hip-hop music, journalist Angus Batey would write the story of Cindy's dream and Clive's musical innovation. It became the first in a series on 50 key events that defined R&B and hip hop.

Batey recalled the simple, almost primitive beginning of a multi-million-dollar music business, from Campbell's hand-drawn flyer to the spray-can slogans plastered all over the Bronx advertising the "Back to School Jam," for which boys paid 50 cents to enter; girls paid 25.

"No one had heard of DJ Kool Herc before that night: the next day, he was famous across the Bronx. Soon, he would be hailed as the architect of an entirely new music," wrote Batey.

It was all unexpected, but not totally unpredictable.

"When I started deejaying back in the early '70s, it was just something that we were doing for fun," Kool Herc told Batey. "I came from the people's choice, from the street. If the people like you, they will support you, and your work will speak for itself."

And Kool Herc's music spoke volumes. His playlist was an eclectic mix of rhythms that propelled the emerging DJ into the role of musical iconoclast. He did not really care what was the in thing to play. He went for a groove: a dance groove juxtaposing Jimmy Castor Bunch and James Brown with English sounds from Babe Ruth and the Edgar Winter Group's "Frankenstein".

As Kool Herc grew as a DJ, his sound became bigger and bolder. By 1974, he had moved into Bronx clubs, where he decided one night to spin the percussion breakdown from two copies of the same record one after another, effectively replaying the break and extending it. "When I extended the break, people were ecstatic, because that was the best part of the record to dance to, and they were trippin' off it," he said in the interview with Batey.

He hooked on to his Jamaican musical roots, which led him to experiment with heavy, downbeat musical tracks dominated by the rhythm and the bass. And he found a way to blast music louder by rewiring the sound system. Thanks to his mammoth sound system, partygoers could feel the music pounding inside them. Hip-hop historians like Chang point out: "DJ Kool Herc spent his earliest childhood years in the same Second Street yard that had produced Bob Marley."

Kool Herc is proud of that link to Marley. "Them said nothing good ever come outta Trenchtown, [Jamaica]. Well, hip hop came out of Trenchtown."

By the mid-70s, Kool Herc, Afrika Bambaataa (who had Jamaican and Barbadian roots) and Grandmaster Flash became the three names called as innovators of the music that would define hip-hop culture. According to Kool Herc:

> To me, hip hop says, 'Come as you are. We are a family.' It ain't about security. It ain't about bling-bling. It ain't about how much your gun can shoot. It ain't about $200 sneakers. It is not about me being better than you or you being better than me. It's about you and me, connecting one to one. That's why it has universal appeal.

He had come a long way since the bitter-cold winter of 1967, when he arrived in New York at 13. He fell into American culture as a break dancer with an ever-growing interest in music that suited the emerging hip-hop culture. He kept searching for records that no one else owned. He knew that music must have a sense of roots and he wanted a rough and edgy sound that suited the dance needs of teens who were not into a pop scene – something that would offer a tough sense of individuality, as well as an escape from the gangs that terrorised the area. This was a place where people needed to use their imagination to recreate a better life.

Dub music lent itself to all those qualities, and so did something else: the merry-go-round.

"Every Jamaican record has a dub side to it," Kool Herc told Batey, "so I just tried to apply that. As the years went along, I'm watchin' people, waiting for this particular break in...the rhythm section. One night, I was waiting for the record to play out. [I thought,] 'Maybe there are dancers waiting for this particular break. I could have a couple more records [with] the same break in it – I wonder how it [would] be if I put them all together?' and I told them: 'I'm going to try something new tonight. I'm going to call it a merry-go-round.'"

In his first merry-go-round Kool Herc mixed sections of James Brown's "Give It Up or Turn It Loose" into Michael Viner's "Bongo Rock" and back out into Babe Ruth's "The Mexican."

The audience went wild.

"The part of his set he came to call 'the merry-go-round' was one of the key creative decisions of 20th-century music. This created the concept of...breakbeats, and then sampling and digital music-production technology, as well as more or less every kind of loop-based composition technique," wrote Batey.

"With the merry-go-round, Kool Herc played two copies of the same record, back-cueing a record to the beginning of the break as the other reached the end, extending a five-second breakdown into a five-minute loop of fury," explained Chang.

The merry-go-round became the blueprint for hip hop. Some historians trace the development of breakdancing to the African martial-arts form capoeira, brought to America by slaves a century before. But it took people like Kool Herc, searching for a new identity and reaching back to their African roots, to give it a modern twist. The sound became the heartbeat of the hip-hop party scene, and it led to a new style of dancing as well. Herc was known for throwing all-night parties and invariably present at a Kool Herc party during the mid-'70s were young dancers (called b-boys), the early incarnations of the breakdancers of the '80s.

Nothing, it seemed could stop Kool Herc until everything came to a screeching halt in 1977. In the Bronx, danger seemed to lurk around every corner, and he had no special talisman to ward it off. One night, a fight broke out at the Sparkle, where he was scheduled to play. Mike-with-the-Lights had a scuffle with someone at the door. Kool Herc stepped in and felt a knife stab him three times in the side. He raised a bloodied hand to block his face, and the attacker stabbed him in his raised palm. After that night, Kool Herc faded from the hip hop scene.

Today, people break down hip-hop culture into four essential elements: deejaying, b-boying, emceeing, and graffiti, but Kool Herc thinks hip hop culture is about much more than that: "The way you walk, the way you talk, the way you look, the way you communicate. Back in my era, we had James Brown and civil rights and Black Power," he said in an interview with Chang.

"When Kool Herc first came on the scene, he stayed ahead of the other DJs with the power of his sound system. Bambaataa changed the game with his programming genius," said Chang.

Looking back, you could say Kool Herc helped to develop a different type of turf war in New York: a war between the musical generals. Kool Herc had his own army of DJs, dancers and rappers who became known as the Herculords. He worked down in the trenches to create a powerful new sound that elevated the ghetto from a powder keg filled with doom and destruction and scorned by society. He made rebellion cool on a whole new level – but this time, white American culture would actually look up to what was coming out of the ghetto. Kool Herc made hip hop cool.

Chapter 27
JANELLE COMMISSIONG:
Stealing the Show

On the balmy night of July 16, in the Dominican Republic, a horse-drawn cart stopped in front of the President's Palace, and the reigning Miss Universe of 1976, Rina Messinger, strolled down the steps. Wearing a flowing white gown and tiara, the Israeli beauty queen took the coachman's hand and climbed into the carriage. The coachman, dressed in a top hat and jacket far too warm for a Caribbean night, conjured up a picture-perfect scene from Spanish colonial history. This was the setting for the world's most famous beauty contest.

"Miss Universe was in its heyday in 1977; an over-the-top confection of a beauty pageant that simultaneously took a certain amount of moral high ground," wrote English hairstylist Vidal Sassoon in his autobiography. Sassoon was one of the judges that year.

No one expected any startling change on pageant night in 1977; no one expected that this could possibly be the night that the pageant would break with tradition. And that tradition was basically a very western European and American vision of the wholesome girl: blonde or brunette, and fair-skinned. Since 1952, when Armi Kuusela, Miss Finland, claimed her crown, all the winners had fitted the same mould. In twenty-five years, no one dreamed a woman of colour could win the competition – not even Janelle Commissiong, the petite, dimpled Trinidadian who had mesmerised photographers with her presence and pizzazz in the week leading up to the competition. But competitions always bring some form of hope.

"It was more than just gorgeous girls; it was about culture," said Sassoon. "Televised globally each year, millions of people tuned in worldwide, praying that the representative from their country would win. There was always much interest in the girl who became Miss Universe, and all of us judges took our responsibilities quite seriously."

Those judges included Argentine-American actress Linda Cristal; former Miss Universe Marisol Malaret; film producer Howard W. Koch; flamenco guitarist Armando Bermudez; photojournalist and filmmaker Gordon Parks (who had recently directed the popular movie *Shaft*); Grammy Award-winning singer Dionne Warwick; fashion designers Oscar de la Renta and Roberto Cavalli; the head of Wilhelmina Models, Wilhelmina Cooper; and film producer Robert Evans.

A carnival atmosphere prevailed in Santo Domingo, with masqueraders dancing through the streets. They eventually threaded their way through the audience and to the stage of the competition hall as viewers around the world settled down to watch the show. As the camera tracked Rina Messinger following the carnival procession, the salsa music of the marine band and the presidential band of the Dominican Republic ushered in the first brigade of the Dominican army, dressed like Roman soldiers. When master of ceremonies Bob Barker and 80 contestants took the stage, it seemed clear that tradition reigned.

The world had no clue that this would turn out to be a pivotal moment in the definition of beauty. Change would come in this year, the year that the diet drink Slim Fast hit the market and *Annie Hall,* a Woody Allen movie starring Diane Keaton as the nervous, scatterbrained love interest of a supernerd, was the movie of the year.

American television perpetuated a stereotyped image of beauty. Valerie Bertinelli, Jacqueline Bisset, and Kate Jackson represented high-energy brunettes with bouncy waves in their hair, while Charo, Farrah Fawcett, Cheryl Ladd, Dolly Parton, and Suzanne Somers headed up the blonde contingent of big names on TV.

In music, Diana Ross and disco queen Donna Summer found their place in the mix without rocking any boats. The top television show proved to be Laverne and Shirley, about two hilarious friends who portrayed the monogrammed-sweater era of the 60s. Laverne and Shirley was a spinoff from another popular show, Happy Days, which featured actor-director Ron Howard as a nerdy teenager. Three's Company featured a lucky John Ritter living with two beautiful women – one blonde and one brunette – and Charlie's Angels made crime-solving a pretty predicament. All in the Family tackled prejudice in a humorous manner, while MASH pitted Hot Lips Houlihan against male-chauvinist American doctors practising in the Korean War. The hard-hitting 60 Minutes was the only show that broke the norm.

On this night, the world was about to meet Janelle "Penny" Commissiong, a 24-year-old fashion buyer, who had lived in New York for nearly a decade. Born in Port of Spain, she had grown up with her grandparents, joined her mother in New York at the age of 13 and recently returned to Trinidad to live. Something about her had caught the photographers' attention that week. It could have been the sultry voice, the deep dimples, the striking brown eyes or the hearty laugh. She had an uncanny ability to exude grace and confidence. Whatever it was, the photographers noticed Commissiong and awarded Miss Trinidad and Tobago the Miss Photogenic prize before the pageant.

This, Miss Trinidad and Tobago thought, was the consolation prize: a sure sign that the show would end with business as usual. But the five-foot-five beauty had a winning smile and undeniable poise. Looking regal in her shimering Carnival costume and stately in the bathing-suit competition, Commissiong commanded attention. Her confidence rose as the competition was whittled down to the semifinalists: Scotland, Trinidad and Tobago, the US, Germany, Venezuela, Austria, Spain, Argentina, Nicaragua, Colombia, Holland, the Dominican Republic. Commissiong was the only person of colour among the 12.

In the swimsuit competition, where all the contestants wore identical one-piece bathing suits and a sombrero, the narrator revealed that Miss Trinidad and Tobago had said she had never had an embarrassing moment in her life. In the evening-gown segment, Commissiong was elegant and relaxed in her gold dress.

At the end of the preliminary sections, the judges had narrowed the group to five finalists: Miss Germany, Miss Scotland, Miss Austria, Miss Trinidad and Tobago, and Miss Colombia.

And then there were two: Miss Austria and Miss Trinidad and Tobago. With a broad smile and a generous offering of good luck to her rival, Janelle Commissiong waited for the results without a trace of anxiety. When the results came, she gave a little leap for joy. She did not stop jumping for the night. Later, when all the lights had been switched off, Miss Trinidad and Tobago and Miss Barbados celebrated together.

"We jumped up and down on the bed," Penny Commissiong-Chow laughs as she reminisces about the contest.

She was unaware of the judges' reactions. It had been a momentous night for them too. Sassoon wrote: "When it came to the final judging, something dynamic happened that thrilled us all: Janelle Commissiong, a ravishing girl from the Caribbean, took the crown...Dionne Warwick was out of her mind with joy. Gordon Parks...turned to me and asked, 'Why did it take so long for this to happen?'"

Commissiong has many fond memories of that night.

"I remember the simple things: walking on stage past the guy who was singing, and feeling the vibe was so good and positive; the host, Bob Barker [famous for the *Price is Right* game show] saying when I walked past him, 'They sure love you, little one'; watching the tape after the pageant and seeing women of colour gathering around me and sobbing. I remember Miss Liberia sobbing. And then there was the memory of Miss Barbados and me jumping up on the bed and laughing after the pageant. We were like kids.

"I remember all of that more than the actual moment of being crowned. It wasn't about me winning. It was about the victory. It was about opening a door."

Commissiong never felt the crown created any burdensome responsibility.

> Responsibility dictates behaviour, and winning never dictated how I lived my life. It is an event in my life, I guess because I didn't come out of the beauty-queen culture – I went into it from a business point of view, because I had just returned to Trinidad to start a business, and I thought the pageant would be good publicity. That was the only reason I was really there.

Never afraid of being her own person or speaking her mind, Commissiong took on the official chaperone provided by the Miss Universe pageant during her reign. When their personalities clashed and her chaperone said, "Don't think that you're the most beautiful [woman in the world]," Commissiong fired back, "The company you work for told me that I am." When Commissiong had had enough, she phoned the Miss Universe vice president to issue an ultimatum, but was told the chaperone had just resigned.

Commissiong returned to an appreciative Trinidad and Tobago and was awarded the nation's highest honour, the Trinity Cross, in 1977. The following year, she crowned her successor, Miss South Africa, Margaret Gardiner. Racially speaking, Gardiner did not represent the majority of South Africans; but the colour barrier in the pageant had been broken, and this would not be forgotten.

After her reign as Miss Universe, Janelle Commissiong headed home to Trinidad and Tobago to live. She married Brian Bowen, the founder of Bowen Marine, a pleasure-boat manufacturing company. She was in New York, at the Fashion Institute of Technology (FIT), where she had gone to finish the fashion degree she had started before she returned home in 1976, when she received the news that her husband had died in a hit-and-run accident while riding his bicycle. Two days after the funeral, she walked into Bowen Marine with the news that she would run her late husband's business.

"I wanted to continue what Brian had spent his life developing," she said in an interview with the *Trinidad Express*. "I felt I had nothing to lose."

She knew nothing about the boat-building business and she received little backing. The bank withdrew the company's overdraft, and the accountant, who had initially seemed supportive, told her she really was not needed in the business.

"I had to learn that business one day at a time," she remembers.

Once again, she fought her way through uncharted territory and persevered, even though there was visible resentment of a woman in the exclusive men's club of boat-building. Nor was she content with merely running the business. She wanted to take it in new directions.

"She increased the brand's visibility, expanding to markets up the island chain as far as Puerto Rico," wrote the *Express*.

Commissiong eventually sold Bowen Marine in 2004, and married for a second time to businessman Alwin Chow, also adopting a daughter, Sasha. She never allowed the title of beauty queen to define her, and she never dwelt on the past.

"Nothing at this stage bothers me, because I know my life, and I know who I am. I know when I'm not comfortable with myself and when I have to do work. I'm completely comfortable in my skin," she said. "I laugh off the emphasis on the physical. I come from a family with tremendously great genes. I can't take the credit."

Looking back on her time as Miss Universe, Commissiong remembers all the people who turned out to see her when she made official visits around the world. She remembers a woman running after her motorcade to give her an African carving; a necklace presented to her by an American Indian tribe in Oklahoma; and a special welcome from aborigines in Perth, Australia.

"I think [my becoming Miss Universe] meant something to people of colour across the world, at a time when one, mainly Caucasian, standard of beauty was presented to all of us," she said.

Miss Trinidad and Tobago, with her mixed African and Spanish/Venezuelan heritage, had ushered in a new standard of beauty that did not depend on race.

Chapter 28

OSCAR DE LA RENTA:
The Man Who Dressed First Ladies

It was, on a small scale, a collision between the New World and the old, fashion's version of the Columbian Exchange. This time the explorer was 18-year-old Oscar de la Renta, who ventured from his home in the Dominican Republic to study art at the Academy of San Fernando in Madrid, Spain. He had no idea that his experiment with abstract art would lead to a legendary place in fashion history that he would design for himself.

After Francesca Lodge, the wife of John David Lodge, the US Ambassador to Spain, spotted some of de la Renta's dreamy and dramatic dress sketches, she commissioned him to design a debutante gown for her daughter, Beatrice. The dress, which perfectly combined fun and fashion, sported a strapless, plunging V-neck with a fitted bodice that melted into two layers of puffy ballgown glamour. It made the cover of *Life* magazine, and de la Renta's fashion boat was launched.

Well, not quite. First he embarked on an apprenticeship with Cristóbal Balenciaga, Spain's most famous designer of the era.

"I was picking pins off the floor," de la Renta joked in interviews about this period of his career.

Perhaps, but he also had time to dance with the glamorous American actress Ava Gardner and other famous women as he brought his New-World charm to the Old World. De la Renta's life would be filled with prominent, stylish women who would worship his flirty fashion statements, which always whispered "class".

This bold designer journeyed on to Paris, where he quickly plunged into the world of couture before sailing off to New York two years later to design for Elizabeth Arden. On all of these peregrinations as a fashionista, de la Renta remembered the warm and vibrant range of colours in the Caribbean.

"From my island side comes my love for the exotic, for colour and light," he told *The New York Times*.

In 1965, he finally launched the Oscar de la Renta brand. "My customers are successful working women," he said. His dresses made women look smart, often including a contrast of severe angles and soft fabrics with intricate lace and bold colours – blues, reds, and black – and fitted bodices that flowed into dramatic skirts. De la Renta made women feel like Cinderella at the ball. Whenever he got a chance, de la Renta returned to his home in Punta Cana, on the eastern tip of the Dominican Republic. His home was palatial, on a fashion designer's terms.

"The many-columned, coral-stone house looks like Hollywood's dream of a colonial plantation," said writer Cathy Horyn, who travelled there to interview him. Cuban-born architect Ernesto Buch had designed de la Renta's Dominican home.

"The place says many things about him – maybe, above all, that he can't be contained by fashion. His life has always been bigger, more imaginative, than the clothes."

If there was one thing de la Renta did not possess, it was a big ego. "He's no snob," wrote Horyn.

On my first night in Punta Cana, as the houseboys were lighting the hurricane lamps for dinner, he was nowhere to be found. Eventually, I found him in the servants' quarters playing dominoes with several local men – contractors and gardeners who come in for the nightly game.

He could have been a ladies' man, drifting from one woman to the next in his glamorous life, but family was important to de la Renta. He married his first wife, Françoise de Langlade, former editor-in-chief of French *Vogue*, in 1967. She died of cancer in 1983, and six years later he married Annette Reed.

The de la Renta fashion empire unfurled through the decades as a balance between the delicate and the dramatic, as the designer pushed boundaries. De la Renta became a man of firsts. American first ladies wore his creations and the Boy Scouts wore his uniforms. JK Rowling, one of the world's best known authors, wore a soft green Oscar de la Renta strapless gown with pink flowers at the premiere of *Harry Potter and the Deathly Hallows: Part 2*. When the curtain rose for the 39th Grammy Awards at Madison Square Garden in New York, in 1997, there was Hillary Clinton dressed in a de la Renta long-sleeved lacy bodice flowing into an olive-green skirt as she accepted a Grammy Award for the Best Spoken Word category for her book *It Takes a Village*.

On the red carpet at the Academy Awards, countless stars wore his fashions. Penelope Cruz and Sandra Bullock were among the celebrities to don his feminine and opulent gowns. His clothes were woven into episodes of the drama series *Sex and the City*, with the character Carrie Bradshaw, journalist and style icon, dropping his name and comparing his designs to poetry. He was known for his evening wear, which somehow managed to give definition to voluminous skirts.

US President John F. Kennedy's wife Jackie wore Oscar de la Renta, as did every first lady after her at some point in the White House until Michelle Obama came along. Who can forget Ronald Reagan's wife, Nancy, in a long-sleeved, scarlet lace dress with a scalloped V-neck at the President's dinner in 1988? Clinton wore a gold de la Renta gown in 1997. She wore a brown leopardskin sleeveless dress with a long, shimmering, earthy-brown wrap for Nelson Mandela's 85th birthday party. First Lady Laura Bush wore an icy blue gown by de la Renta to the 2005 inaugural ball, Lady Bird Johnson, Pat Nixon, Betty Ford, Rosalynn Carter, and Barbara Bush had also embraced de la Renta designs on more than one occasion.

For most people it had been easy to get swept away in the beauty of his world, but it was not a particularly easy or predictable voyage from the Dominican Republic to become the fashion king who designed American first ladies' inaugural dresses. Born on July 22, 1932, de la Renta was the only son among seven children, which makes it all the easier to understand how his father would have reacted to his son's decision to be a designer.

"My father had different aspirations for me than I had for myself," he told the *Fashion Talks* audience. "If I ever told my father I would become a fashion designer, he would drop dead on the spot."

But he did become a designer, even revamping the image of the Boy Scouts in 1980, when he gave the organisation its biggest makeover in 60 years. De la Renta donated his services for a two-year project to remake all uniforms for Boy Scouts, Cub Scouts, Explorers, and both men and women adult Scouters. The military look vanished, giving way to a less starchy and more environmentally-friendly design. Boy Scouts wore short or long-sleeved shirts with red-ribboned epaulettes to designate the Boy Scouting programme. Shorts and trousers were olive green and they now sported large cargo pockets. The Boy Scouts still wear de la Renta's designs.

But if they could enthusiastically embrace Oscar de la Renta, why couldn't First Lady Michelle Obama? It seemed almost scandalous – at best a terrible break with tradition. But there it was: seven years into Barack Obama's administration, Michelle Obama had never appeared in a dress designed by Oscar de la Renta, let alone worn one of his gowns to an inaugural ball. But she finally came through when she wore a black sleeveless dress with a blue and silver floral pattern at an event where many of de la Renta's peers were present – a fashion education workshop she hosted at the White House on October 9, 2014. So De la Renta's record for dressing first ladies remained intact to the end of his life.

He had given up the title of chief executive of his company in 2004, but remained active at the design end, continuing to show his collections during New York Fashion Week.

When the news of his death was announced, de la Renta proved to have been much more than a couture icon. He was an avid patron of the arts, serving as a board member of the Metropolitan Opera and Carnegie Hall, among others, and he devoted considerable time to children's charities, including New Yorkers for Children. He also helped fund schools and day-care centres in La Romana and Punta Cana in his native country.

De la Renta died at home in Connecticut on October 14, 2014, surrounded by family, friends and "more than a few dogs", according to a statement by his stepdaughter Eliza Reed Bolen and her husband.

For his entire career, Oscar de la Renta created images of the Caribbean interpreted through fashion.

"I like light, colour, luminosity. I like things full of colour and vibrant," he once said. "My greatest strength is knowing who I am and where I came from – my island."

Through de la Renta, first ladies, movie stars, and fashionistas from the US to Europe reflected the beauty of the Caribbean. His designs brought new meaning to the West Indian saying, "making style".

Chapter 29

GEOFFREY HOLDER:
The Toast of the Town

He leaped across a Broadway stage like a gazelle; transformed himself into a voodoo villain in a James Bond movie; challenged a Coca-Cola-drinking generation on TV to sip lemon-lime 7-Up; and stepped away from the spotlight often to pursue his private passion – painting.

Geoffrey Holder made a name and a career for himself as the quintessential Trinidadian: a vivacious, dramatic figure sporting a Cheshire-cat grin, a booming voice with a hearty Trinidadian accent, and a rumbling, roaring laugh. His presence commanded attention in any room he entered. He towered over nearly everyone with his talent and a captivating personality that never lost its Caribbean charm.

When Holder died of pneumonia on October 5, 2014, the accolades rolled in.

Jennifer Dunning wrote in the *New York Times*: "Geoffrey Holder, the dancer, choreographer, actor, composer, designer, and painter who used his manifold talents to infuse the arts with the flavour of his native West Indies and to put a singular stamp on the American cultural scene, not least with his outsize personality, died on Sunday in Manhattan. He was 84."

Despite the range of his involvement in the arts, Holder was not a dabbler. He mastered every art form he chose: acting, dancing, painting, choreography, costume design. In the highest creative circles in the US, Holder earned praise.

"Few cultural figures of the last half of the 20th century were as multifaceted as Mr Holder, and few had a public presence as unmistakable as his, with his gleaming pate atop a six-foot-six frame, full-bodied laugh and bassoon of a voice laced with the lilting cadences of the Caribbean," wrote the *New York Times*.

People magazine had featured the larger-than-life Holder in its June 1975 edition. Wearing a white safari suit and "pounds of turquoise jewellery," sitting in his all-white West Side Manhattan apartment, Holder told the magazine, "I wear white when I want to look brown, and black when I want to pass."

At the time of that interview he had recently won two Tony awards – one for directing and one for costume design – of the seven presented to *The Wiz*, the hip black musical version of *The Wizard of Oz*. By then, every household in the US recognised Holder as 7-Up's spokesman: the "uncola" man dressed in white from head to toe – with the exception of the colourful scarf around his neck. Holder pitched the clear soft drink with no caffeine as a bold, natural choice – just like him. Sometimes he wore a crisp white suit, white shirt, white hat, and a powder-blue tie as he delivered his message: be an individual, make your own choices, be cool.

In many ways, he was defined by that 7-Up commercial for the better part of two decades, bridging the 1970s and 1980s. While that type of fame would have made a less confident man uneasy, Holder appeared to relish the role of the Caribbean man selling 7-Up. He certainly wasn't ashamed of it. When *People* magazine brought it up in an interview about his career, Holder proudly said, "I'm no snob. The commercial is an art form unto itself. After all, you are seducing people."

Noting he had "a voice as deep as Othello's and as smooth as Caribbean rum," *People* reported that Holder, 44 at the time of this interview, ranked painting at the top of his creative endeavours.

"Even when I am working in the theatre, there is always the smell of turpentine backstage. So I must be a painter first," he said.

He credited his family in Trinidad with his optimistic, broad-based, creative outlook on life. Holder's parents encouraged him and his older, equally talented brother, nicknamed Boscoe, to develop all their talents. Born into a middle-class family on August 1, 1930, in Port of Spain, Geoffrey Lamont Holder happened to be the youngest of the five children of Louise de Frense and Arthur Holder, who had immigrated from Barbados. Geoffrey attended Queen's Royal College, (QRC), a prestigious secondary school in the island.

If there was any secret in Geoffrey's life, it was that he struggled with a stammer throughout school and into early adulthood.

"At school, when I got up to read, the teacher would say, 'Next,' because the boys would laugh," he said. It would be years later, in the US, that Holder would lose his stammer. Without thinking, he stood up to defend his country at a well-attended function: he could not sit idly by while a speaker disrespected his culture by offering stereotypical images of a rum-and-calypso society.

Holder always held a deep respect and love for his culture and family, learning much from his older brother, Arthur Aldwyn, "Boscoe". He had taught Geoffrey painting and dancing, and recruited him to join a small folk-dance troupe he had formed, the Holder Dance Company.

Geoffrey Holder hit New York at a time when the scene was hopping.

"It was a period when all the girls looked like Janet Leigh and Elizabeth Taylor, with crinoline petticoats and starched hair," he told the *New York Times* in 1985. "The songs of that period were the themes from the *Moulin Rouge* and *Limelight*, and it was so marvellous to hear the music in the streets and see the stylish ladies tripping down Fifth Avenue. Gorgeous black women, Irish women – all of them lovely and all of them going somewhere."

While he established himself in the arts, he taught classes at the Katherine Dunham School, and he was a principal dancer for the Metropolitan Opera Ballet from 1956 to 1958. He continued to dance and direct the Holder Dance Company until 1960, when it disbanded. In the meantime, at a dance recital, he caught the attention of the producer Arnold Saint-Subber, who was putting together a show with a Caribbean theme.

Holder made his Broadway debut on December 30, 1954, as a featured dancer in *House of Flowers*, described by the *New York Times* as "a haunting, perfumed evocation of West Indian bordello life," with music by Harold Arlen. Directed by Peter Brook at the Alvin Theater, *House of Flowers* starred Diahann Carroll, Pearl Bailey, and Carmen de Lavallade – the future Mrs Holder.

In 1957, he landed a notable acting role, playing the servant Lucky in an all-black Broadway revival of Samuel Beckett's *Waiting for Godot*. That same year, he choreographed and danced in a revival of the George and Ira Gershwin musical *Rosalie* in Central Park, and received a Guggenheim Fellowship for painting. In 1959, he published a book on Caribbean folklore, *Black Gods, Green Islands*, written with Tom Harshman and illustrated by Holder.

When Holder plunged into the cinema, he played vivacious, exotic figures who, in the wrong hands, could have been nothing more than caricatures; if nothing else, Holder had fun with these roles and gave them a touch of elegance and sophistication, juxtaposed with raw earthiness. In *Doctor Doolittle* (1967), Holder portrayed a giant native who ruled a floating island as William Shakespeare (the 10th). In Woody Allen's *Everything You Always Wanted to Know About Sex but Were Afraid to Ask* (1972), he played a sorcerer. In *Annie* (1982), he was the exotic Indian servant Punjab. The noted exception to his flamboyant characters came in a 1992 romantic comedy, *Boomerang*, where Holder played a director of commercials working for Eddie Murphy's playboy advertising executive.

Above all, there's the character of Baron Samedi, James Bond's antagonist in the 1973 *Live and Let Die*. Samedi is the guardian of the cemetery and the spirit of death, sex and resurrection in Haitian Voodoo culture, and Holder injected the role with a spine-tingling dose of the macabre. This was the first of the Bond movies to star Roger Moore, and Samedi proved the perfect antagonist and character foil. In the movie, Samedi dances his way into infamy wearing a white top hat; a white tailcoat, open to expose his bare chest; and a loincloth under the sophisticated coat. With face half painted white, Samedi is quite a figure.

That year, 1973, also saw the publication of *Geoffrey Holder's Caribbean Cookbook*, with his recipes for orange rice, coconut chicken, and saltfish pie.

Holder could also often be found painting in his SoHo loft, where he captured the images of people inspired by his native Trinidad. He became a notable photographer and sculptor. His work was shown in Washington and at the Guggenheim Museum in New York. As *People* magazine noted,

> Holder's lush impressionist paintings hung in the Barbados Museum and Washington's Corcoran Gallery, as well as in the homes of such luminaries as showbiz legend Lena Horne and conservative political pundit William F. Buckley.

His love for drama, dancing, and painting all blended together in his costume design. Besides *The Wiz*, Holder's costume designs could be found in the 1982 production of *The Firebird* for the Dance Theater of Harlem, which transported the setting of a Russian fairytale into a tropical forest. He earned another Tony nomination for best costume design for the 1978 Broadway musical *Timbuktu!,* an all-black show based on the musical *Kismet* and which he also directed and choreographed.

Holder's designs for a 1999 revival of *Banda* by the Dance Theater of Harlem caught the attention of Anna Kisselgoff, who wrote in *The Times*, "Mr Holder is a terrific showman, and his mix of Afro-Caribbean rituals, modern dance and even ballet's pirouettes is potent and dazzling."

In 2005, he narrated the Tim Burton remake of *Charlie and the Chocolate Factory,* which starred Johnny Depp. Holder's deep, rumbling voice was still in demand, and he was still introducing children to the beauty of drama. He was the subject of documentaries as well, including *Carmen & Geoffrey* in 2009.

On his death, the *New York Times* wrote:

> Mr Holder said his artistic life was governed by a simple credo, shaped by his own experience as a West Indian child who had yet to see the world. 'I create for that innocent little boy in the balcony who has come to the theatre for the first time,' he

told Dance magazine in 2010. 'He wants to see magic, so I want to give him magic. He sees things that his father couldn't see.'

He had worked with Hollywood stars and icons like Josephine Baker. "We hit it off like nobody's business," said Holder. Hollywood stars never forgot him either.

When the news came of his passing, actor Samuel L. Jackson posted a picture of himself and Holder, then registered his feelings on Twitter: "I brush up against Fame all the time, but encountering GREATNESS is Rare! RIP Mr Holder!!"

Beyoncé uploaded a black-and-white portrait of Holder to her website with the caption, "Geoffrey Holder was a man with as much talent as he had charisma. May he rest in absolute peace. – B."

Oscar winner Marlee Matlin wrote, "RIP Geoffrey Holder – multi-talented Broadway star & true gentleman," and Edgar Wright remembered Holder as one of the best Bond villains, adding with a reference to the closing scene of *Live and Let Die*: "I would like to think that Geoffrey Holder is not dead but sitting on the back of a train laughing maniacally into camera. RIP Baron Samedi."

Always playful and powerful, Geoffrey Holder never lost sight of himself as a curious little boy discovering art. He presented an unforgettable picture of what it was to be Trinidadian. The boy who once stammered grew into a boy who loved to talk and explore the world around him. His advice to young people was simple: "Ask, 'What's that?' Ask 'Why?' 'Who?' Find the answers. Don't be satisfied until the answer really falls into your basket.

"We're all messengers. When you get information, keep it until you understand it, and then share it with your best friend."

His inquisitive nature served Holder well. He relished a challenge, and enjoyed challenging others. Geoffrey Holder's message was simply: Don't play life safe. Go to extremes. Who knows what you will discover when you go out on a limb?

On the red carpet at the 2017 Academy Awards ceremony in Hollywood, a reporter asked Lin Manuel Miranda, who wrote the musical *Hamilton,* about his all-time favoutite Oscar moment. Without hesitating, Miranda recalled being a spell bound child watching the 1990 Oscar Ceremony. "(It was) hearing Geoffrey Holder sing 'Under the Sea'," said Miranda.

On any given night, Holder could conjure up magic.

Chapter 30

PATRICK CHUNG:
The Wave of the Future

On a cold day in December, the New England Patriots prepared to do battle in New Jersey. It would not be a Christmas-Day attack like the one General George Washington and West Indian-born Captain Alexander Hamilton had planned for Colonel Rahl and the Hessian mercenaries fighting for the British in New Jersey on December 26, 1776. This battle would take place on December 27, 2015 between two American football teams: the New England Patriots and the New York Jets.

Jamaican-born Patrick Chung, a strong safety for the New England Patriots, could only look on in this more recent battle. A victim of friendly fire the week before when his own team-mate collided with him while he was making a tackle, Chung was sidelined with a hip injury. Normally, in this defensive position, Chung prowls the middle of the playing field on the strong side of the formation, playing closer to the line of scrimmage than the roaming free safety. As the strong safety he is the last line of defence to stop the opponent's running plays, and he guards the tight end on passing plays.

Growing up in Jamaica, where he once played cricket and soccer, Chung could not have imagined this foreign football field or the success he would achieve in the US, any more than Hamilton could have imagined his astounding success in battle or the political arena. Chung is a far cry from Hamilton, but in many ways, he is a reflection of those West Indians who made their mark on the US with poise, strength, and determination, shaped from a Caribbean brand of confidence and charisma.

Chung migrated to the US with his family when he was ten, and describes himself as a Jamaican-American. He still recalls missing Jamaica, and he especially remembers the challenge of settling in the US.

"When I got here, no one could understand me when I talked. I was a young kid speaking a different language, Jamaican Creole," said Chung, with a disarming ease that reflects his penchant for turning tough situations into a challenge.

It did not take him long to discover a way to immerse himself in American culture. One day, he came home from school and broke the news to his mother that he wanted to play American football.

"She said, 'Can't you be on the swim team?' She didn't want me to hit people," Chung laughs.

Chung finished secondary school and enrolled at the University of Oregon when he was sixteen, about two years ahead of American students. In Oregon, he became a Duck under American football coach Chip Kelley's tutelage. Off the football field, he spent a lot of time educating people about the ethnic diversity of Jamaica and the West Indies when they questioned him about his Chinese heritage and last name.

"Growing up in Jamaica teaches you about diversity, and it teaches you race doesn't matter. What's important is how you live life and how you treat people."

He sports tattoos that remind him of his roots.

"Kingston and August – the place I was born and the month of my birthday – are tattooed on my left bicep. I never forget my Jamaican roots."

Chung tells people that Jamaicans are down-to-earth, good people. He is a Bob Marley, hip hop and reggae fan, and he would eat jerk chicken every day if he could. He credits his Jamaican roots with shaping him into a hard-working, relentless NFL player, confident, but not cocky; outspoken and yet humble.

"I realise I come from a small place, but so many West Indians have shaped the US. I'm proud of that. And I know I can make a difference on the field. Jamaicans are fast and quick, and that helps us on the football field."

He adds, "I'm not just a Jamaican. I'm from the West Indies. That means pride, hard work, and being kind to people. My parents would slap me if they ever found out I wasn't kind to someone."

As New England battled on through late December and hopefully headed towards the Super Bowl of 2016, Chung could claim to be the most visible first-generation West Indian-born player ever to win a Super Bowl, the pinnacle of success in a popular American sport. He had played in the 2014/2015 New England team that beat the Seattle Seahawks in the Super Bowl of 2015. During that 2015/2016 season, the *Boston Herald* wrote that Patrick Chung "is in the midst of one of his best seasons as a professional".

His coach, Bill Belichick, a hard taskmaster known for his reticence and low-key personality, seemed unusually talkative when speaking of Chung in 2015.

"He has always been a good tackler that's played the run well, but he's also emerged as one of the Patriots' best players in coverage," said Belichick in an interview with *Boston Herald* reporter Chris Mason.

Mason said sports writer Jeff Howe's statistics showed opposing quarterbacks completed 16 out of 36 for only

214 yards when targeting Chung. In 2015, the defensive back surrendered only one touchdown up to December, and he had broken up eight passes. Belichick stressed that Chung had been good in his position since the Patriots drafted him in as the 34th player in the second round of the NFL draft in 2009, and he only departed to Philadelphia because Philadelphia offered a financial package the Patriots could not match.

"He's always been very competitive as a coverage player, whether it be on tight ends or slot receivers... He's obviously worked hard at that and continued to get better," said Belichick.

But when Chung left New England to play for the Philadelphia Eagles in 2013, it seemed his football career would crumble.

"He was awful. He was a laughing stock as an Eagle. One of those guys Eagles fans unanimously hated. Just the mention of his name drew disgusted looks, expletives, you name it," said sportswriter Frank Reuben.

> The Eagles thought they stole Chung from the Patriots when in 2013 they signed him to a three-year, $10 million contract with $4 million guaranteed after the 2012 season.

He was so bad in the 12 games he played, they quickly released him when the season ended. The cost? $715,000 in base salary, a $2,285,000 roster bonus, and $1 million in guaranteed salary in 2014. That's $4 million—for a guy who didn't make a play.

When the Patriots grabbed back Chung after his release from Philadelphia, sports reporters wrote there was no guarantee he would even earn a starting position with the Patriots. They had seen coming back from a dismal season as difficult if not impossible for many players in the past. But Chung quickly proved his worth, and his coach claimed he had no doubts Chung would rebound.

> Patrick has always been really good – smart, works hard...understands the team concept and is a versatile player, so he can do a lot of different things. Whatever you ask him to do, he embraces it and works at it and does the best he can,

said Belichick in an interview with sportswriter Reuben Frank.

> His skills, his attitude, his work ethic, dependability, toughness; he's always been a good tackler, always been a good coverage player, he runs well, he's a smart guy.

When he returned to New England, Chung signed a three-year deal with the Patriots worth US$8.2 million, including US$3.4 million guaranteed. He had a stellar season in 2015, covering some of the best receivers in the league, including the Indianapolis Colt's TY Hilton, the NFL's number one receiver. Belichick knew why he had made that decision – and all the other ones involving Chung.

> For a safety he's a good coverage player. He's got good quickness. He's got good playing strength, runs well, smart. He's been in those situations. He's comfortable in them. He does a good job.

When Chung became an integral part of the 2017 New England Patriots' Super Bowl winning team, he solidified his position as the most successful West indian in the NFL. Combining sheer determination and grit to reach the pinnacle of success, Chung tapped into the strength, charisma and confidence that certainly connect to his West Indian roots. And he found the perfect place to showcase those qualities. NFL football combines the spectacle of entertainment and the strategy of a battle. It demands the perseverance of a politician and the boldness of an explorer charting new territory. It is a place for individual athletes to shine and make their statement, like Chung's hard-hitting tackles that seem to come from nowhere, but it is also a team sport that demands a certain camaraderie.

Nearly all the West Indians who influenced US history had a keen social conscience – not just in politics, but in sports too, as the late, great baseball champion Roberto Clemente demonstrated. Chung is no exception. Early in his career, he and his wife Celia started the Chung Changing Lives Foundation to help children in poor areas to cope with school and life. Eventually Chung says he hopes to expand his charity work to Jamaica. The foundation supports musical programmes, one of Chung's passions because his mother, Sophia George, was once a singer in Jamaica, with a hit reggae song, "Girlie Girlie", released in 1985.

"Not everyone has the same opportunities in life," said Chung.

Like Shirley Chisholm, he feels the education he received in the West Indies shaped his life and career.

Looking back, it is easy to see he shares some of the traits and characteristics of famous West Indians of the past: the Jamaican pride and doggedness of Marcus Garvey, who picked himself up after he fell off a stage during his first speech and made a brilliant comeback; the fighting spirit and charisma of Stokely Carmichael; the leaping moves of Geoffrey Holder. On the football field, he commands attention as Alexander Hamilton and Shirley Chisholm did when they walked into a room.

Most of all, he shares a common characteristic with Jean Baptiste Point du Sable, William Leidesdorff and

Denmark Vesey: through sheer determination and a willingness to take risks, he has reached the pinnacle of success without most people even knowing what he looks like. Du Sable, Leidesdorff, and Vesey never had an official portrait; Vesey was never described physically; Chung earned his fame hidden under the helmet he wears on the football field. And yet Chung, covered with tattoos and wearing a helmet, shoulder pads and cleated shoes, represents the wave of the future: a West Indian in the US conquering new turf.

Afterword

It was bound to happen sooner or later. Confident with my cast of characters for *Making Waves*, I finally pressed the send button and settled down with a book I had wanted to read: *Devil in the Grove: Thurgood Marshall, The Groveland Boys*, and *The Dawn of a New America* by Gilbert King. There, in the first chapter, Zephaniah Alexander Looby hobbled his way into yet another story of how West Indians have shaped the US.

In 1946, Looby and Marshall, black lawyers for the National Association for the Advancement of Colored People (NAACP), who were "polite and gracious" in court, teamed up with their perfect character foil: the melodramatic white attorney Maurice Weaver. Together, the trio fiercely defended 25 black men in what had been deemed the Columbia, Tennessee Race Riot trial.

Looby, the "staunch Republican and an Episcopalian who loved poker and quoting Shakespeare to juries", had peppered his courtroom speeches with American idioms that he spoke in a slight West Indian accent.

Born in Antigua in 1899, Looby had grown up in Dominica where he spent his childhood sitting in court dreaming of becoming a lawyer.

Orphaned at 14, he fled a life of toiling in the fields cultivating cacao, nutmeg, sugar and bananas, signed on as a cabin boy for a whaling ship, headed for the US and jumped ship when he was 16 in New Bedford,

Massachusetts. There, he worked in a yarn mill, in a restaurant and in a bakery before he earned a law degree from Columbia University and a Doctorate in Law from New York University in 1926.

He started a law school for black students, fought prejudice through the legal system; argued for equal pay for black teachers, and worked to desegregate public spaces in Nashville during the 1940s and 1950s.

When the not-guilty verdicts poured in for the Columbia Race Riot trial on November 18, 1946, the stunned lawyers, who had expected to lose the trial, quietly packed their briefs and fled the courtroom. Looby lagged behind with a pronounced limp from a car accident. They drove out of Columbia as fast as they could.

Police stopped Looby's car just after Looby, Marshall and Weaver crossed the bridge over Duck River outside of Columbia. There, officers accused Marshall of drunk driving, ordered Marshall out of the car and demanded that Looby drive his car north. Police whisked away Marshall. The trio felt sure the police planned to lynch him. Marshall always loved telling the story. The car carrying Marshall bounced along a bumpy, unpaved road, and then it stopped. Out of nowhere a pair of headlights appeared casting a blinding spotlight on the grim scene. Looby stepped out of the car, limped towards Marshall and demanded the police set Marshall free. Zephaniah Alexander Looby saved Marshall's life.

Looby would become instrumental in the Civil Rights movement in Nashville where he would win cases on the ground level and fight cases in the Tennessee and US Supreme court. He served as a crucial link between Marcus Garvey and Stokely Carmichael in being an important West Indian voice in the Civil Rights movement.

He miraculously escaped death when someone blew up his home with 20 sticks of dynamite while Looby and his wife slept.

But that's a story for another day.

Acknowledgements

All it took to embark on this historical journey was the picture that Aaron Neville planted in my mind of New Orleans as a Caribbean island colliding with the US. Driven by the desire to remind history buffs in the Caribbean and the US of the important role the West Indies played in US history. I set my sights on that vast sea of information and gathered material to map out the vision of a glorious past.

I tested the waters with streamlined versions of two stories from *Making Waves*. One appeared as "John Paul Jones: Turning Point in Tobago" in Issue 99 and the other as "Tituba's Secrets" in Issue 121 of *Caribbean Beat*, the inflight magazine of Caribbean Airlines and Air Jamaica. Buoyed by the enthusiastic responses I received from Jeremy Taylor and Judy Raymond of *Caribbean Beat*, I stayed the course. I'm also grateful to *Caribbean Beat* for permission to use extracts from my interview with Patrick Chung (Issue 124).

The journey turned out to be smooth sailing, but I was quite surprised at every turn as I discovered a treasure trove of rare documents and books that led in unexpected directions. Chicago-born Luesette Howell, who settled in Trinidad after retiring from the International Labour Organization (ILO) of the United Nations (UN), led me in a new and unexpected direction when she told me about Jean Baptiste Point du Sable. This important West Indian did not make the US history books that I studied while growing up in the Midwestern state of Ohio. It has never really been the practice to recognise small islands as important contributors to US history.

My daughter, Ijanaya, provided constant encouragement and much-needed organisational skills. Every writer needs an editor, and Judy Raymond proved, as always, to be an exceptional editor.

Constable Roger Boodoo offered invaluable advice on staying the course and navigating a way through rough seas with confidence. Cpl. Neil Samaroo provided unwavering encouragement and uplifting advice in challenging times, reminding me of the importance of friendship and support on that long, lonely journey that leads to a book.

I am deeply indebted to former Editor-in-chief, Owen Baptiste, who taught me how to write stories about people when I worked for him at the *Trinidad Express* newspaper.

Before this voyage ended, my two CXC Caribbean History students, Kendell and Richard, received their marks. Kendell received a Grade 3 and Richard a 2. They had gone the traditional route – the one that portrays the US influence in the Caribbean. But at least now they know there is a sundry way to sea.

Notes

Abbreviations used:

l   location in an e-book
w   website
n   newspaper article
nw   newspaper article online
mw   magazine article online
i   interview

Introduction: Exploring the Myth
p. xiii

Kristin Downey, Columbus's Journey from Grenada, in
    Isabella: The Warrior Queen (New York: Doubleday,
    2014), 241.

Laurence Bergreen, "Obsessed with his God–given task," in
    Columbus: The Four Voyages (New York: Viking, 2011), 7.

"Weav(ed)[sic] a tale that mixed astronomy," Downey, 236.

"Made fun of what Columbus had to say," Downey, 236;
    Elias, Hiam Lindo. *The History of the Jews of Spain and
    Portugal* (1848; repr. New York: Brt Franklin, 1970).

The Story of Luis de Santángel, Downey, 242.

"A modest coral island in the Bahamas," Bergreen, 13.

p. xiv

Dates for possession of Caribbean Islands, http://www.
    historyworld.net.

John A. Knox, "The Knights of Malta in the Caribbean," *A
    Historical Account of S Thomas, WI: With Its Rise and
    Progress in Commerce, Missions and Churches, Climate
    and Its Adaptation to Invalids, Geological Structure,
    Natural History, and Botany: And Incidental Notices
    of St Croix and St Johns' Slave* (New York: Charles
    Scribner, 1852), 35.

Carrie Gibson, "The French bought back the islands," *Empire's Crossroads: A History of the Caribbean from Columbus to the Present Day* (New York: Atlantic Monthly Press. 2014), 53.

Donna Yawching, "The island of Tobago changed hands," *Caribbean Beat* 113 (November 1, 2012).

p. xv

James Brown Scott, "Danish West Indies Islands' history," *The American Journal of International Law* 10, no. 4 (1916): 853-59.

Chapter 1
Peter Stuyvesant: The Dutch West India Company's Disappearing Act

p. 1

John S.C. Abbot, Peter Stuyvesant's arrival, *Peter Stuyvesant: The Last Dutch Governor of New Amsterdam* (New York: Dodd & Mead, 1873), I, 203.

Residents of the small Dutch settlement..., Abbott, I 638.

Colin Woodard, "New Netherlands...where the Dutch had built a wall," *American Nations: A History of the Eleven Rival Regional Cultures of North America* (New York: Penguin Books, 2011), 65.

Population of the Dutch West Indies, Abbott, I, 243.

p. 2

"I shall govern you as a father does his children," Abbott, 1,273.

Stephen R. Bown, "When he looked around...windmills, gabled roofs and sprawling farms". *Merchant Kings* (New York: Thomas Dunne Books, 2009), 83.

He ordered vacant lots around the fort..., http://www.historyofholland.com.

p. 2-3

The main road, *Breede weg* (Broadway)...run by the Dutch West India Company, Woodard, 270.

p. 3

Stuyvesant's autocratic tendencies: History of Holland.com.

p. 3–5
The English in the Dutch West Indies, http://www.
   historyofholland.com.

p. 4
"If any one... appeal in that way," Abbott, 1,361.
"He sent two men," Abbott, I, 1,720.

p. 5
"would be like inviting the Trojan Horse," Abbott, I ,1,720.
"In Christina, the women were violently driven," Abbott, I, 880.
"I offered to leave," Abbott, I 1,881.
"A tough, sturdy, valiant," http://www.ancestry.com.
"The stakes were high...", Brown, 81.

p. 6
"Just leader and most satisfactory," http://www.biography.com.

p. 6, 7
"Stuyvesant's background," http://www.biography.com.

p. 6–9
"Leadership qualities," Bown, 80.

p. 7
Seventeenth-century surgical techniques, Bown, 81.
Return to the "Netherlands," Bown, 82.

p. 8
"His despotic character and his blunt manners," Bown, 82.
"The General," hhtp://www.ancestry.com.

p. 10
"Don't worry," Bown, 84–85.
"We are in hopes that," Bown, 59.
"was not apt to entertaine any thing of prejudice," Bown, 59.
"In his Majesties Name, I do demand the towne," Bown, 61.

p. 11
"your speedy answer is necessary," Bown, 61.
"I would rather be carried out dead," Bown, 61, 62.
"He tore up the terms of agreement," Bown, 62.
"misery, sorrow, conflagration," Bown, 62.

p. 12

"publicly accused him of cowardice," Bown, 62.

"shall keep and enjoy the liberty," Bown, 62.

"Modelled on its Dutch namesake..." Woodard 6, 66.

p. 12-13

"It is no wonder, historians point out," Woodard, 66.

p. 13

"It was a cosmopolitan place..." Bown, 101.

"Diversity, tolerance, upward mobility," Bown, 102.

p. 13-14

"Later, the hamlet of Groenwijck..." Woodard, 6, 66.

Chapter 2
Tituba: A West Indian Stirs the Cauldron in Salem
p. 15

Stacy Schiff, "Semi-itinerant Beggar," *The Witches: Salem, 1692* (New York: Little, Brown. 2015), 46.

Schiff, "caustic and insolent," 50.

Schiff, "deviant, cantankerous scolds...On all counts Tituba failed to fit the profile," 53.

Elaine G. Breslaw, "I rid upon a stick or poale," 127.

p. 16

Fourteen women and five men...(The number of people imprisoned and killed differs among sources. These numbers are taken from *The Witches*, Schiff, 3.)

Breslaw, Tituba's courtroom testimony, 126-27.

Breslaw, "like a man I think," 162.

Tituba's testimony in 1692: History of Massachusetts, w.

p. 17

Breslaw, A popular and unscrupulous historian, xxi.

p. 17-18

It all started on a late December day: Salem Library, Virginia w.

p. 18

Breslaw, By the time the New Year dawned, 18.

Breslaw, Description of events that spiralled out of control, 18.

Schiff, "tedious, mulish, sulky," 39.

According to Schiff, Parris was a West Indian merchant before becoming a preacher. Schiff, 36.

p. 18–20

The girls' behaviour in court is described in *The Witches*, 54–56.

p. 19

Schiff, "She was a brilliant raconteur," 54.

Schiff, "I am blind now. I cannot see" (Girls' behaviour in court.), 56.

Breslaw, "...the spirits of the dead, *opias* or *hubias*," 18.

p. 20

Breslaw, "Tituba the storyteller...", x.

Breslaw, "Tituba had lived in a Barbados society," 129.

p. 21

Breslaw, "Within a few years, a small group of Arawak," 6–7.

p. 22

Breslaw, Tituba's Amerindian background, 3–6, xxii.

Schiff, "Having lent the previous year its shape..." 356.

p. 23

Breslaw, "To dispose of his reluctant witch," 175.

"An unidentified person paid...", Breslaw, 175.

p. 23–24

Breslaw, "Tituba vanishes," 172.

Chapter 3

Jean Baptiste Point du Sable: The Haitian in the Onion Field

p. 25

Some reports say a Choctaw Indian: Bennett, 170.

Some say he came from what is now modern-day French Canada: Matson, 187.

Haitian slaves worked along the river: Bennett, 170.

He first settled in Peoria: Bennett, 171–172.

p. 25–27

Discovery of Chicago: Cortesi, 2

p. 26

Du Sable sketch found at the Du Sable Heritage Association
    website.

"And the weather was impossible": Bennett, 170.

p. 26-28

Description of Chicago at Du Sable's arrival: Bennett, 170-78.

Description of Du Sable's travels: Bennett, 170-178.

p. 27

"A great stench": Bennett, 170.

Du Sable's claim of being born in St Marc: PBS website.

He maintained excellent relations with Native Americans...
    Jean-Baptiste and Catherine had two children: Meehan,
    439-53.

p. 28-29

Du Sable's house and inventory in Chicago: Meehan, 439-53.

p. 28

Charles de Langlade, a pioneer in Wisconsin: Meehan, 171-78.

p. 28-29

The British and du Sable: Meehan, 439-53.

p. 28

"I had the negro Baptiste": Bennett, 175.

p. 29

Detention: Du Sable Heritage Association website.

p. 29-30

Return to Chicago in 1784 and his departure in 1800: Du Sable
    Heritage Association, w.

p. 29

Value of Du Sable's original property: Bennett, 175.

p. 29-30

Accounting records: Bennett, 171-78.

p. 30-32

Cortesi spins a sailor's yarn: Cortesi, 9; 12-18; 20-22.

Chapter 4
John Paul Jones: The Secret in Tobago
p. 33–34
John Paul Jones's background: Thomas, 11–14; 20–24.

p. 34–35
Trouble with Maxwell: Morison, 39; 43–45.

p. 35
Letter to Benjamin Franklin: De Coven, Vol II, 440–41.

p. 36
Appearance in the US: Morison, 45–49.
Command of the *Ranger:* Morison, 131.
Description of Paul Jones's battered East Indiaman: Seitz, 29.

p. 37
September 23, off Flamborough Head: Thomas, 178–192
"I have not yet begun to fight!": Thomas, 192.

p. 37–38
Description of Jones in Paris: De Kovan, Letters Vol II, 65–66,
     68.

p. 38
Post-war plans to build the American navy: Thomas, 300–303.
Service with Russian Empress: Thomas, 258.

p. 39
Coffin returned to the US: Morison, 482–83.
On January 26, 1913, John Paul Jones was laid to rest: Morison,
     482–83.

Chapter 5
John Hancock: Fame, Fortune and the West Indies
     Connection
p. 40–42
Description of the *Liberty:* Unger, *John Hancock: Merchant
     King,* 119–21.

p. 40
"The town is a blackguard town": Unger, *John Hancock:
     Merchant King,* 120.

p. 41

"heard the squeal of tackles hoisting goods": Unger, *John Hancock: Merchant King*, 120.

About 500 "sturdy boys and negroes": Unger, *John Hancock: Merchant King*, 120-24.

p. 41-43

John Hancock's background: Unger, *John Hancock: Merchant King*, 1.

p. 42

"vain, arrogant, egotistic....": Allan, x,

p. 43

"John Hancock did not set out to be a rebel": Unger, *John Hancock: Merchant King*, 1.

"The Hancocks were no different from other merchants;... analysing market conditions and minimising those risks": Unger, *John Hancock: Merchant King*, 2.

p. 44

"... lived as an aristocrat...in his splendid gilded coach": Unger, *John Hancock: Merchant King*, 5.

p. 45

"Boston's merchant plutocracy turned their city...More than 500 ships sailed out of the harbour each year": Unger, *American Tempest*, 26.

"Thomas Hancock's oil ventures": Unger, *Merchant King*, 32.

p. 45-46

"Rum by then had become New England's": Unger, *American Tempest*, 22.

p. 46

Sugar production in the British West Indies: Unger, *American Tempest*, 22.

"Rhode Island's 30 distilleries": Unger, *American Tempest*, 3.

Molasses Act: Unger, *American Tempest*, 23, and Molasses Act, Revolutionary War and Beyond, website.

"Hancock sent New England salted fish": Unger, *American Tempest*, 26.

Thomas Hancock turned to investment ...He traded rum for oil. Unger, *American Tempest*, 26.

The colonists had been sabotaging the British with their
    molasses trade even during the French and Indian War:
    Unger, Ame*rican Tempest,* 33.
Molasses smuggling: Revolutionary War and Beyond, w.

p. 46-49
Thomas Hancock's merchant bank: Molasses Act,
    Revolutionary War and Beyond, w.

p. 47-49
"The House of Hancock": Unger, *American Tempest,* 35, 53, 64.

p. 47
"Tea...was a negligible part of Thomas's stock": Allan. 44.

p. 48
Smuggling through St Eustatia as early as 1749...Salem
    merchants were importing...than the island's entire annual
    crop": Unger, *American Tempest,* 35.
"Two years later...". Unger, *Merchant King,* 33.

p. 48-49
"Hancock's assault on the British agent": Allan, 47.

p. 49
England's attorney general formally charged John Hancock
    and others with high treason: Farnsworth, 97.
"looking every inch an aristocrat from his dress" Unger,
    Merchant King, 176.
"prepare to fight": Unger, *American Tempest,* 176.
He quoted a passage from the Bible...Hancock wanted to keep
    his good name: Unger, *American Tempest,* 181.
"Hancock and other men of great wealth in Congress made
    huge loans": Unger, *American Tempest,* 177.

p. 50-51
Health in 1778: Unger, *American Tempest,* 220.

p. 50
"ornate yellow chariot ...": Unger, *Merchant King,* 264.
"Hancock's desk was the central command post...": Unger,
    Merchant King, 220.

p. 51
"Hancock had faults enough": Kindig, US, History.org.
Retirement and death: Unger, *Merchant King*, 262.

Chapter 6
St Eustatius: A Thorn in the Side of a Colonial Giant
p. 52
Andrew Doria: Tuchman, 5–15 and de Koen, *The Life and Letters of John Paul Jones,* Vol II, 20.

p. 53
"...Seldom has an island port": Jameson, w.

p. 54
"The island is different": Burke, 301.

p. 54-55
Role in America's independence: Jameson lecture, w.

p. 54
"A Dutch rear-admiral": Jameson, lecture, w.

p. 55
"Many passages in the diplomatic history": Jameson, lecture, w.

John Adams often mentioned St Eustatius: Jameson, lecture, w.

"An informant of Lord Suffolk": Jameson, lecture, w.

"As early as March 1776, Abraham van Bibber...taking care of cargoes sent or underwritten by the state": Jameson lecture, w.

p. 56
"By the end of the year 1774": Yorke correspondence.

"If you continue, we will cut off your supply": Yorke to Suffolk correspondence.

"...as the Dutch have discover'd": Yorke correspondence.

Chapter 7

George Washington: How Barbados Saved the General
p. 58-59
Details of Washington's crossing: Fisher, 206–210, Chernow, 269.

p. 59

Alexander Hamilton's role: Chernow, *Washington: A Life*, 276.
Washington's leadership: Chernow, 276.
Special relationship with Lawrence: Ellis, 9–10.

p. 59–63

Journey to Barbados: Chernow, 16, 24–25.
Details of Barbados trip, Washington's house and stay in
    Barbados: Washington's Diaries and the Barbados
    National Trust.

p. 62

"In retrospect, George's brush with a mild case of smallpox":
    Chernow, *Washington: A Life,* 25.

p. 63

Because he had contracted smallpox in Barbados, Washington
    was spared…would have died, leaving the American rebels
    to find a new leader: Ellis, 86, 87.

p. 63–64

"Historians have long known…a policy of inoculation was the
    most important strategic decision of his military career":
    Ellis, 86–87.

Chapter 8
Alexander Hamilton: The West Indian
Who Defined the US
p. 66

Morning of July 11, 1804: Randall, 1–6.
Physical description of Hamilton: Cerami,
24, Shea, 45, MacLane, I 530.

p. 68–70

Burr/Hamilton duel and its aftermath from "The Wish of My
    Heart" in *Alexander Hamilton: A Life* and in the chapter
    "Fatal Errand" in *Alexander Hamilton*, Chernow, 695–710.
Hamilton/Burr feud: Isenberg, 86–89.

p. 67

Hamilton insisted…he never intended to kill Burr: Chernow,
    702.

p. 69
"Mrs Mitchell is the person": Chernow, 697.

p. 70
Fluent in French: MacLane, I 395.
James Hamilton: Randall, 20.
Early life: Randall, 6-9.
Description of Nevis: Randall, 11.

p. 71
"yearning for an aristocratic heritage": Randall, 18.

p. 70-71
History of Nevis: Dyde, pp17, 92.
Support in the Virgin Islands: Cerami, 23-25, Chernow, 35-39.

p. 71
His dreams of becoming a physician vanished: Randall, 25.

p. 72
"Few West Indians educated in North America":
    O'Shaughnessy, 25.

p. 72-73
Princeton rejection; Washington's acceptance: Chernow,
    47-48.

p. 73-74
Defence of former loyalists: Jasanoft, 319.
For Burr, Republican Vice President of the United States
    under the Democratic-Republican President of Thomas
    Jefferson: Note: During the early years of the US, the
    candidate who received the most votes became the
    president and the runner-up became vice president, so
    a president and a vice president could be from different
    parties.

p. 73
Work on Constitution: Cerami, 2.
"Hamilton's tendency to be noticed": Cerami, 27.
General Alexander Hamilton as field commander: Fleming, 1-2.

p. 74
Hamilton's achievements: Chernow, 200-201; Randall, 421.
"Hamilton was...the proponent of banks, factories and stock
    exchanges": Chernow, 3-4.

Budget and tax system, central bank, customs service and the
 coast guard. Arguments for a dynamic executive branch
 and an independent judiciary: Chernow, 6.
"Nearly everyone described him as a genius": Chernow, 4-5.
"Today we are indisputably the heirs": Chernow, 6.

p. 74-75
Personal scandal: Randall, p5.

p. 75
"Even some Hamilton admirers": Chernow, 3.
"the most interesting in the early history": Chernow, 3.
"the most brilliant American statesman": Chernow, 4.
"our greatest constructive statesman." Chernow, 4.
"Hamilton is the foremost political figure": Chernow, 4.
Relationship with father: Randall, 23.
US credit rating under Hamilton: Fleming, 19.

p. 76
"If they break this union, they will break my heart": Chernow,
 708.
"He was incapable of turning the other cheek": Chernow, 683.

Chapter 9
South Carolina: Nothing Sweet from Barbados Comes
p. 78-79
Sir John Colleton's trip to England: Wood, 13-15.
Early South Carolina history: Alleyne, 6-7.

p. 79
"a very rich and fertile soyle": Alleyne, 13-14.
Sugar trade between Carolina and Barbados: Wood, 32-33.
"Apart from politics": Alleyne, 21.
"...During the early decades of its establishment": Wood,
 32-33.
"James Colleton appears to have frequently come to South
 Carolina": South Carolina Historical Society.

p. 80
"The Gold Bug": Wood, 170.
Gullah language: Alleyne, 64.

p. 81
"The Deep South was founded": Woodard, 9.
"For most of American history": Woodard, 9.
"Beginning from its Charleston beachhead": Woodard, 9.
A "near-carbon copy": Woodard, 82.
"By the eve of the American revolution": Woodard, 84.
History of Barbados: Alleyne, 2–5.
As sugar plantations grew, they squeezed small farmers out:
    Alleyne, 5.

p. 82
"good men, formerly proprietors": Alleyne, 5.
"along the coastal plain of the North American continent...
    known for the past three centuries as 'South Carolina'":
    Alleyne, 5.

p. 83
"From that single square mile": Woodard, 270.

Chapter 10
**Toussaint L'Ouverture: From Slave to
Iconoclast**
p. 85–86
Description of the events leading to
the revolution in "Opening the Gate"
from *Toussaint Louverture: A Biography,*
Madison Smartt Bell, 19–23, 113.

p. 86
An "exterminating war": Dubois, 116.
American cities with Haitian refugees: Dubois, 8; Clavin, 33;
    Kukla, 148.

p. 87–88
Description of the slave hierarchy, birth and death rate:
    Dubois, 19, 37, 40, 42.

p. 88
Toussaint Bréda as *médecin général*: Smartt Bell, 9.

p. 88–89
"The insurrection of 1791": Dubois, 101.

p. 89
Slave rituals and torture: Dubois, 30.
Description of Makandal: Dubois, 51.
Ogé return home: Dubois, 85–88.

p. 90
"the rest of his glorious life": Dubois, 88.

p. 90–91
"A growing army": James, 155.

p. 91
Letter to L'Ouverture dated June 7, 1802 from General Brunt:
    Beard, I 4607.

p. 92
"Dessalines... gets the credit as the liberator": Bell, 4.
"As the leader of the only successful slave revolution": Clavin, 9.

p. 92–93
L'Ouverture's letter in prison: Beard I 4688, 4699, 4728, 4820.

p. 93
As a freedom fighter: Clavin, 1.
English portrait of Toussaint: Gibson, 292.

p. 94
"You think you have rooted up the tree of liberty": Clavin, 2.
"The significance of L'Ouverture": Clavin, 23.
"The Haitian Revolution had a profound effect": Clavin, 29.

Chapter 11
Saint-Domingue Changes America's Landscape
p. 95
Jefferson's French visitor: Fleming, 1–4.

p. 96
John Adams' position on Haiti and Edward Stevens' visit to
    Cap-François: Fleming, 4–5.

p. 97
Jefferson's fear of Haitian piracy: Fleming, 5.
Napoleon's view of the US: Fleming, 7–9.

p. 98
Madison's meeting with Pichon: Kukla, 219–29.
US position on Florida and the French: Fleming, 15–16.

p. 99
L'Ouverture sensed something was up: Fleming, 27.
Leclerc threatened Henri Christophe: Fleming, 27.
Leclerc and L'Ouverture at Gonaïves: Fleming, 31–32.

p. 100
Yellow fever ...Napoleon's intentions to reinstate slavery in
 Guadeloupe and Santo Domingo: Fleming, 45.
Leclerc lacked men and money and his health further
 deteriorated: Fleming, 47.
The US did not want a French occupation of Louisiana:
 Fleming, 47–48.
Jefferson and Madison dispatch Robert Livingston to France:
 Fleming, 26.

p. 101–102
The US was playing its own games, sending diplomats to
 Saint-Domingue to congratulate L'Ouverture: Fleming,
 26–27.

p. 101
Livingston chipping away at France's confidence...which
 needed huge investments to build back devastated
 economies: Fleming, 51.
Louisiana Purchase: National Archives, Louisiana Purchase.

p. 102
"Without Secretary of State James Madison's hard-headed
 realism": Fleming 183–84.

Chapter 12
Denmark Vesey: The Man Who Bet on Freedom
p. 103–104
Description of Denmark Vesey's meetings: Egerton, 151–54.

p. 103
Vesey had quit taking carpentry jobs: Egerton, 172.

p. 104
"I don't understand such talk": Egerton, 155. (Incident on the
 wharf described in the e-book *He Shall Go Out Free: The
 Lives of Denmark Vesey.*)
Peter divulges the plot: Egerton, 173.

Governor requests federal troops: Egerton, 163.

"Good God," Vesey admits knowing the wigmaker: Egerton, 186.

Vesey wins the lottery and purchases his own freedom: A and E Biography, w.

"Denmark Vesey in 1822 organised": Robertson, 4.

p. 105

Vesey's plot: Robertson, 4.

His religious activity: A & E. Biography, w.

p. 106

Early life outlined in *He shall go out free: The Lives of Denmark Vesey by Douglas Egerton and Denmark Vesey The Buried Story of America's Largest Slave Rebellion and the Man Who Led It* by David Robertson.

In 1815, whites in Charleston moved to block black Methodists: PBS, A & E Biography, w.

"Over 4,000 black members left": PBS, w. A & E Biography, w.

p. 107

"...in the habit of reading": Clavin, 33.

"We can conquer the whites": Clavin, 33.

Vesey's company of black supporters: Clavin, 33–34.

"The Court were [sic] not only satisfied": Egerton, 189, and the South Carolina Department of Archives, w. Court Proceedings Vesey case.

p. 107

"He folded his arms": Robertson, 6.

Vesey cross-examined each witness: South Carolina Archives Court, w: proceedings and testimony regarding the Vesey rebellion.

p. 108

Vesey's background revealed in court: Robertson, 6–7.

Monroe refused to recognise Haiti: Robertson, 5.

...in 1822, the revolution in Haiti mentioned nearly 20 times: Clavin, 16.

p. 109

Portrait of Vesey: Robertson, 3 and 114.

"That a conspiracy": Higgins, *Atlantic Monthly*, w.

p. 110
"For nearly 200 years": Kaplan, *Washington Post*, w.

Chapter 13
Jean Laffite: The Legend of a Pirate
p. 111–12
Description of Jean Laffite: Davis, 51–52, 56, 57.

p. 113
Background of the brothers Laffite: Davis, 2, 4.
Pierre in Savannah, Georgia...Pierre's plans: Davis, 6–7.
"From the moment of his birth": Davis, 25.

p. 114
"He felt at home": Davis, 26.
Records show more than one Captain Laffite: Davis, 26.
"wild and scarcely inhabited place": Davis 26–28.

p. 115
"All that was needed": Davis, 32.

p. 115–16
Claiborne and the Laffites: Davis, 11, 43, 31,123–25, 132.

p. 116
Rumour of Laffite in Napoleon's army: Davis, 129.

p. 117
Jean suddenly found himself an American patriot: Davis, 131.
He did not volunteer to defend New Orleans: Davis, 165.
The US government would offer pardons: Davis, 165–68.

p. 118
Jean Laffite had only about two per cent of Jackson's forces: Davis, 180.

p. 119
Jean Laffite played by Clark Gable. Lux Radio Theatre, *The Buccaneer*, November 13, 1948 (audible.com).

p. 118
Pierre Laffite's death: Davis, 221–25.
Jean Laffite's death: Davis, 463.

Chapter 14
Oliver Perry: "We have met the enemy..."
p. 120
Description of Ethan Allen and his Green Mountain Boy taken
from *Ethan Allen: His Life and Times* by William Sterne
Randall, 361–365.
Plans to take over Canada: Altoff, 1–3.
"For two long weeks the British pounded": Altoff, 3.

p. 120–21
Perry's personality and the British Battle: Altoff, 9.
Perry's problems and correspondence for new commission:
Altoff, 9–11.

p. 122
"You are the very person I want": Skaggs, 45.
Perry's crew: Altoff, 12–13, 21.
"Sail ho!": Altoff, 30.

p. 123
"I don't care, to windward or to leeward": Hickey, 132.

p. 123–25
Description of the Battle of Lake Erie: "The Battle of Lake
Erie," Chapter 5, *A Signal. Victory: The Lake Erie
Campaign 1812–1813* by David Curtis Skaggs and Gerard T
Altoff. Altoff, 35, 42, 48, 54, 69 and Hickey, 132.

p. 125
Rededication of the Oliver Hazard Perry Gateway: Jacob,
Trinidad Guardian.
"Oliver Perry is among the most celebrated American naval
heroes...and several cities": Welters, speech.

p. 125–26
In 1819 President James Monroe dispatched Perry to
Venezuela...Perry's journey and illness: Skaggs, 208–209.

p. 125
Ceremony at Lapeyrouse: Skaggs 209, 210.

p. 127
"He was still presiding over": Homer, Tr*inidad Express*
"Perry's burial in Lapeyrouse": Homer, *Trinidad Express.*
Perry's remains brought back to US: Skaggs, 210 - 211.

p. 128

Description of monument in Lapeyrouse Cemetery: Homer, *Trinidad Express.*

Eventually vandals stripped the monuments: Homer, *Trinidad Express.*

Chapter 15
William Alexander Leidesdorff: All that Glitters is not Gold

p. 130

Leidesdorff's background in Danish West Indies: The Black Past on Blackpast.org.

Leidesdorff's engagement: "Forgotten San Francisco" Hu, *San Francisco Travel*, w, and *Pioneers of Negro Origin in California* by Sue Bailey Thurman. San Francisco : Acme Pub Co.

p. 131

Leidesdorff in San Francisco: Hu, *San Francisco Travel*, w.

January, 30, 1846 ordinance from California Star from Chief Magistrate Washington A Barlettt: Gibbon, 178–179.

p. 132

"intelligent, fairly well educated": Hu, *San Francisco Travel*, w.

p. 133

California Gold Rush: from "Aspiration, Acculturation and Impact: Immigration to the United States"...Harvard University Library Open Library Collection, w.

p. 133–34

Leidesdorff obituary: *Maritime Heritage Project.*

p. 135

He is said to be the first Afro-American millionaire: blackpast.org.

Chapter 16
The Invisible West Indians of the Panama Canal
p. 135-36
Dr Edward Cullen's expedition: McCullough, 22-23.
The Panama Canal...one of the least known areas of the world: McCullough, 22.

p. 136-37
Geology of Panama Canal: Senior, 11.

p. 137
The journey around South America took...the narrowest point it would take only 5,200 miles: Senior, 24.
Nicaragua, consideration of a canal: McCullough, 27.

p. 137-38
Descriptions of conditions in Panama: McCullough, 34, 26.

p. 138
"The difficulty in throwing up just 47.6 miles of rail": Senior, 30.
"The opening of work on the isthmus": Senior, 40.
Cholera: Senior, 45.
Colón was being called "the new Jamaica": Senior, 64.

p. 139
Strikes in Panama: PBS, *The American Experience*.
"The engineers could not have chosen an unhealthier spot": Senior, 29.

p. 139-40
World-famous Ferdinand de Lesseps "charming, pervasive and indomitable": McCullough, 45.

p. 140
De Lesseps accused of mismanagement: McCullough, 241.
In 1906 alone 80 per cent of the total workforce was hospitalised: PBS, *The American Experience*.
"Skilled white workers": McCullough, 471-72.

p. 140-41
Workers' conditions: PBS, *The American Experience*.

p. 141–42
"The West Indian's every movement": McCullough, 474.
p. 142
"The police had to be on hand": McCullough, 475.
Description of West Indian jobs: McCullough, 476–47.
"The West Indian": McCullough, 579.
"From March to the end of 1905, 34 Americans had died":
McCullough, 501.

p. 142–43
Diseases and death statistics: McCullough, 501–503.

p. 143
"In the United States the public had little if any conception":
McCullough, 575.
"In the United States the public had little if any conception":
McCullough, 575.
"The West Indian worker...": McCullough, 579.

Chapter 17
Hazel Scott: A Class Act
p. 145
Introduced on the big screen as
herself: Chilton, 73.
"How's the piano, Hazel?" "I guess it
will hold up.": *Takin' a Chance*, movie.

p. 146
"I've got rhythm": *Rhapsody in Blue*, movie.
"No woman would see her sweetheart": Chilton, Smithsonian,
w.
"I've been brash all my life": Chilton, pxiv.

p. 146–47
Scott's background, grandmother and mother: Chilton, 2–4,
29.

p. 147
Scott heads for New York: Chilton, 9–10
Audition at Julliard: Chilton, 22.
Child prodigy: Ledbetter, *New York Times* w.
Childhood: Chilton, 11–12

"Hire Hazel Scott.": Chilton, xiii.

p. 148
"Who's that?": Chilton, xiii.

First public appearance: Chilton, xiii.

"The wrong place for the right people": Chilton, 49.

"...where others murder the classics": Chilton, Smithsonian, w.

"She loved the limelight": Chilton, 69.

p. 148–49
Marriage to Adam Clayton Powell: Chilton, Smithsonian, w;
    Biography.com ACP; Ledbetter, The *New York Times*, nw.

p. 149
"They were stars": Chilton, Smithsonian, w.

p. 150
Death: Ledbetter, *New York Times*, nw.

"Although jazz was her forte": *New York Times*, nw.

"It was witty, daring": *New York Times*, nw.

"She can be a musical chameleon": *New York Times*, nw.

Chapter 18
Marcus Garvey: The Black Star Line
p. 153
"intolerant and punitive" father: Grant, 10.

Garvey's father: Grant, 11.

Travels: Grant, 2, 31, 77.

p. 154
"There was startling chutzpah": Grant, 78.

First appearance in Harlem: Grant, 79.

Description of Garvey: Grant, 16.

"...mounted the platform shaking like a leaf...": Grant, 79.

"upbeat,": Grant, 80.

p. 155
"A style of speech": Grant, 91.

West Indian community in Harlem: Grant, 76–77.

Description of Harlem parade: Grant, 91, 245.

"...to compose the constitution of the brave new UNIA": Grant,
    119.

p. 156
"We have been very spiritual": *Negro World* , 4 July, 1919, w.
Black Star Line: Grant, 187.

p. 156-57
UNIA's ships: *Marcus Garvey*, PBS.
p. 157
Description of Cockburn: Grant, 200, 241.
Garvey shooting: Grant, 212–13.

p.159
Speech at the First International Conference of the Negro
    Peoples of the World: Grant, 246–47.
Arrested for mail fraud: PBS.

p. 160
Stroke, decline and death: Grant, 1–3.

p. 161
"Endowed with a dynamic personality": Grant, 2.
CLR James... would have a change of heart: Grant, 3.

Chapter 19
Fidel Castro: An American Obsession
p. 162-63
Lands in Cuba: Szulc, 19–23; 26–33.
Ramonet, p266 (Castro Spoken
Biography).

p. 164-65
Background and childhood: Szulc, 101, 19.

p. 164
Vito Genovese arrival in Cuba: English, I 675.
Lansky and the mob in Cuba: English, I 675, 781.
Graduates as doctor of law: Szulc, 193.

p. 165
"Don't shoot. You can't kill ideas": Szulc, 282–91.

p. 165-66
Castro in prison: Szulc, 301, 311–12.

p. 166
"...he had the inner certainty of triumph": Szulc, 20.

p. 167
Business in Havana after World War II: English, I 90, 96, 101, 107, 259.
Estimate of Cuban migrants to the US: Ramonet, 335, 339.

p. 168
CIA plan to assassinate Castro: Kennedy library, w.

p. 168-69
"Since the end of World War II, the focus of American anxieties": Kennedy, Edward, 174-75.

p. 169
Kennedy's radio/TV address to the nation, October 22, 1962: Chang, 160-61.
"Neither side wanted war...by the other side": Kennedy, Robert I 534.

p. 170
"Dear Comrade" (Castro's letter): Chang, 387.
"Each hour the situation": Kennedy, I 719.
CIA's position on the crisis: Chang, 150
"We are going to have to face the fact": Kennedy, I 727.

p. 171
"Mr President, we have a preliminary report": Kennedy, Robert, I 609.
"No ships will be stopped": Kennedy, Robert I 610
"The whole world was becoming more and more alarmed": Kennedy, Robert I 632.
"extraordinarily rapid pace": Kennedy, Robert I 666.
"The actions of the US with regard to Cuba": Kennedy, Robert I 687.

p. 172
"You wish to ensure the security": Chang, 207.
"The crisis abated": Chang, 243.
Castro's refusal to allow inspections of Cuba: Chang, 243.
Soviet Union's final departure from Cuba: COHA (Cuban—Russia Now and Then)

p. 173
Castro's assessment of Cuba: Ramonet, 584.

p. 174

"Today, the United States of America is changing its
relationship": White House.gov, w. Obama speech:
Statement by the President on Cuba policy changes.

"The handing over of the flag by three old men": Sopel, BBC
online.

"After all, these fifty years have shown": White House.gov.
Obama speech, w.

"At the time the CIA had reported...fight to the death":
Foreword, *The Cuban Missile Crisis, 1962,* McNamara, xi.

Chapter 20
**Stokely Carmichael: Stoking the Fires of the Civil Rights
Movement**

p. 176

FBI description of Carmichael speech and speech itself: FBI
files, Stokely Carmichael.

p. 177

"When I first heard about the Negroes sitting in at lunch
counters": Kaufman, *New York Times,* nw.

p. 178

Memorandum on the activities of Carmichael: FBI files.

Carmichael's first arrest: Kaufman, *New York Times,* nw.

"This area [the West Indies] is a stepping stone": FBI files,
Stokely Carmichael,

p. 179

"...the Southern Negro...": Carmichael, *Stokely Speaks.*

"How in the world can the FBI allow a person": FBI files,
Stokely Carmichael.

"...whose avowed purpose is to abolish the House Committee
on Un-American Activities": FBI files, Stokely Carmichael.

p. 180

"I meant it literally – not figuratively": FBI files, Stokely
Carmichael.

"Stokely Carmichael's belief that black political power":
Joseph, 87.

p. 180-81

"Our country does not run on reason": FBI files, Stokely
  Carmichael.

p. 181

"In a remarkably short time": Joseph, 29.

Carmichael and the Freedom Rides: Joseph, 20-34.

"quintessential penal farm, the closest thing to slavery that
  survived the Civil War. Its story covers the panorama of
  race and punishment in the darkest corner of the South.":
  Oshinsky, 36.

p. 182

"One of the memorable scenes from Parchman": Oshinksy, 36.

Carmichael's work on voter registration in the south can be
  found in Joseph, 20-74.

"Barely a month after his selection, Mr Carmichael raised the
  call for black power": Kaufman, *New York Times*, nw.

He organised the all-black Lowndes: Joseph, 88.

Alabama registration in Lowndes County: Kaufman, *New York
  Times,* nw.

p. 183

"We are engaged in a psychological struggle in this country":
  Carmichael speech, American Radio Works, University of
  California at Berkeley.

"I maintain that every civil rights bill in this country":
  Carmichael, *Stokely Speaks*, 47.

p. 184

Carmichael interview with mother: YouTube.

"Though his active participation": Kaufman, *The New York
  Times,* nw.

Chapter 21
Sidney Poitier: The Big Picture
p. 186–87
Poitier's description of first audition:
Poitier, *Life Beyond Measure,* 106–107.

p. 187
Life on Cat Island: Poitier, *The Measure of a Man,* 20–21, 27.
"I didn't think about the colour of my skin": Poitier, *The Measure of a Man,* 37.

p. 188
"...more of an observer than most": Poitier, *The Measure of a Man*, 105.
"The Harlem that I knew": Poitier, *The Measure of a Man,* 93
"About 125,000 citizens" "Poitier was both inside and outside the West Indian milieu": Goudsouzian, 34.
No Way Out: Goudsouzian, 111, and Poitier, *The Measure of a Man,* 132.

p. 189
"[I] came very much back down to earth": Poitier, *The Measure of a Man,* 80.
"He drummed his fingers": Goudsouzian, 216.

p. 190
"We're in the adrenalin section. It's knee-knocking hour here, and I won't delay any more...Because it is a long journey to this moment": YouTube: Sidney Poitier Wins Oscar, 1964.

p. 192
"...fundamental questions of life, survival and death": Poitier, *Life Beyond Measure,* 6.
"One of my few advantages..." Poitier, *Life Beyond Measure,* 60.

p. 192–93
Journey to New York City at 16: Poitier, *Life Beyond Measure,* 95–98.

p. 193
"So I arrived in America with nowhere to turn": Poitier, *Life Beyond Measure,* 105.

"For over a decade, from the late 1950s to the late 1960s,
Poitier was Hollywood's lone icon": Goudsouzian, 1.
"The civil rights movement had shaped": Goudsouzian, 2.
"...the only actor I've ever worked with who has the range
of Marlon Brando – from pathos to great power":
Goudsouzian, 2.
Never seen a mirror: Poitier, *Life Beyond Measure,* 35.

Chapter 22
Shirley Chisholm: A Barbadian in the House
p. 194
Chisholm's description of the House of Representatives:
Visionary Project, YouTube.

p. 195
"Speaking for them at this moment": Chisholm, l 219.
"I do what my conscience": Visionary Project, Shirley
Chisholm.

p. 196
"warm, kind, hardworking": Visionary Project.
"It is important to notice": Chisholm, l 288.
"So early in 1928 a diminutive young black woman": Chisholm,
l 290.
Description of grandmother: Chisholm, l 316, 328.

p. 197
"When all seven classes were at work": Chisholm, l 369.
"Years later I would know": Chisholm, l 359.
Chisholm's father and Garveyism: Chisholm, l 484.
"There I heard my first black nationalist oratory": Chisholm, l
516.

p. 198
"shrewdest, toughest, most hard-working": Chisholm, l 858.
A "stocky, quiet, handsome Jamaican, Conrad Chisholm":
Chisholm, l 1147.
University education: Chisholm, l 803.
"take over the entire Seventeenth": Chisholm, l 1188.
"made a lot of noise": Chisholm, l 1199.

p. 199
Steinem's opinion of Chisholm's candidacy for
    president: Steinem, *Ms.* magazine, w.

p. 200
"George Wallace liked me": Visionary Project.
"This is not the way we do this": Visionary Project.

Chapter 23
Roberto Clemente: Faith, Hope and Charity
p. 202
"Roberto Clemente felt he had two strikes": Cepeda, Orlando,
    PBS, *American Experience.*
"He told me that, that it was very lonely": Orlando, PBS,
    American Experience.

p. 202-203
Clemente's early childhood: UPI, 1-6 and Schwartz, *A Sports
    Century* feature for television.

p. 203
"While in high school, Clemente signed": Schwartz, *A Sports
    Century.*
"He wasn't an instant hit": Schwartz, *A Sports Century.*
"He had a wicked right arm": Schwartz, *A Sports Century.*

p. 203-204
Early baseball career: Schwartz, *A Sports Century.*

p. 204
Courtship with wife Vera: *The Blade,* nw.
"He wanted to marry quickly": *The Blade,* nw.
Health issues: UPI 5.
"People saw him as a hypochondriac": UPI 5.

p. 205
Lifetime batting average: Pittsburgh Pirates' website.
Clemente and the 1972 World Series: Pittsburgh Pirates'
    website.

p. 206
"My greatest satisfaction": PBS, *American Experience.*
"You were black or you were white in Pittsburgh": PBS,
    American Experience.

Clemente's charity work: PBS, *American Experience.*

p. 207

"...bobbed and bucked and wheezed": PBS, *American Experience.*

"The baseball world did not need time and distance": Schwartz, *Sports Century.*

"At the plate he would stretch and coil": Schwartz, *Sports Century.*

"You're going to a town": Schwartz, *Sports Century.*

p. 208

"If you don't play in a big city": Schwartz, *Sports Century.*

"He had the audacity to speak": Schwartz, *Sports Century.*

"Clemente is the first athlete to transcend both race": Schwartz, *Sports Century.*

Chapter 24
Euzhan Palcy: Making Waves in Hollywood
p. 210

Background: Paddington, *Caribbean Beat,* mw.

p. 211

"I found people, people from the streets": Keaton, *Feminist Wire,* mw.

p. 212

Palcy received death threats: Keaton, *Feminist Wire,* mw.

p. 214

"When you are safe and well-off": Ebert, rogerebert.com.

A Dry White Season review: Ebert, rogerebert.com.

p. 216

"Dry White Season, which opens today at Loews New York": Maslen, *New York Times.*

Chapter 25
Bob Marley: "Rastaman Vibration"
p. 217

"free-living, free-loving sanctuary": Goldman, *Exodus,* 54.

"Give me a juice, nah!": Goldman, *The Guardian,* nw.

p. 218

"... like Jimmy Cliff in *The Harder They Come*." Goldman, *The Guardian,* nw.

"Even though this was the moment": Goldman, *The Guardian,* nw.

"volatile bars and brothels of the Kingston waterfront": Goldman, *The Guardian,* nw.

p. 219

"long-estranged husband": White, 114.

Early days in Trenchtown: Sheridan, 11.

When that gig didn't work out: Sheridan, 31.

The songs "Natural Mystic": Discography.

p. 220

"There's a natural mystic": *Exodus* album lyrics.

"They've got so much things to say": *Exodus* album lyrics.

"movement of Jah people..." *Exodus* album lyrics.

"Don't worry 'bout a thing..." *Exodus* album lyrics.

p. 221

Description of Zimbabwe independence: Griffith, YouTube.

Wailers' early days at Studio One: Marley, Rita, 15–17, 19, 25.

Lee "Scratch" Perry, who climbed from being a cleaner: Marley, Rita, 121.

"In Jamaica, Rasta was the last thing": Marley, Rita, 38.

p. 221–22

"There was this strange sensation... and we felt we were going to die": Griffith, YouTube.

p. 222

Rita said Marley feared cutting off his toe: Gilmore, *Rolling Stone,* mw.

p. 223

"On stage, with his Medusa locks spiralling": Steffens, 25.

Bob Marley sold more than 20 million records: Biography.com, Bob Marley.

"No Woman No Cry" ranked 37": *Rolling Stone,* mw.

p. 223–24

Ishmael Beah speaks: Beah, 161–64.

p. 224

"one of their own": Steffens, 264.

In Nepal, there are people: Steffens, 264.

Mario Vargas Llosa speaks: Vargas Llosa, 228-24.

"...on the sad streets of Trench Town": Vargas Llosa, "Trench
     Town Rock," 56.

"...is probably the best known secular figure": Toynbee, 7.

"Rebel music, Babylon, freedom, rights, justice": Toynbee, 219.

p. 225

"His music represents a resource of hope": Toynbee, 220.

"Bob Marley is probably the most enduringly influential
     popular songwriter": Stephens, 148.

Chapter 26

Kool Herc: Trenchtown Rocks Hip Hop

p. 226

Popular music of 1973: Music Outfitters.

Cindy had her eye on some clothes: Batey, *The Guardian*, nw.

Cindy roped her parents into her plan: Chang, 67.

With her parents' help, she booked the first-floor recreation
     room: Chang, 67.

p. 227

Their father, a record collector: Chang, 66.

On August 13... Kool Herc pumped up a party: Batey, *The
     Guardian*, nw.

"Along with his immigrant friend Coke La Rock.": Chang, 78.

p. 228

"No one had heard of DJ Kool Herc": Batey, *The Guardian*.

"When I started deejaying back in the early '70s": Batey, *The
     Guardian*, nw.

"to spin the percussion breakdown from two copies": Batey,
     The Guardian, nw.

When Herc hit the scene: Till, interview with Kool Herc on
     YouTube.

p. 229

Kool Herc found a way to blast music louder: Chang, 67, 79.

"To me, hip-hop says, 'Come as you are Herc": Introduction to
    Can't Stop, Won't Stop.
Concept of the merry-go-round: YouTube, Kool Herc explains
    his merry-go-round technique.
The merry-go-round became the blueprint for hip hop: Batey,
    The Guardian, nw.
"Them said nothing good ever come outta Trenchtown. Well,
    hip hop came out of Trenchtown.": Chang, 22.

p. 230

"The part of his set he came to call 'the merry-go-round'":
    Batey, *The Guardian*, nw.
"With the merry-go-round, Herc played two copies" Chang,
    79.

p. 231

Felt a knife stab him three times in the side: Chang, 84.
"The way you walk, the way you talk": Herc, introduction to
    Can't Stop, Won't Stop.
"DJ Kool Herc spent his earliest childhood years": Chang,
    22–23.
"When Kool Herc first came on the scene...Bambaataa
    changed the game with his programming genius": Chang,
    111.

Chapter 27
Janelle Commissiong: Stealing the Show
p. 233
"Miss Universe was in its heyday in 1977": Sassoon,
    I 3296.

p. 234
"It was more than just gorgeous girls": Sassoon, I 3299.
"There was always much interest in the girl": Sassoon, I 3300.

p. 235
Slim Fast hit the market and Annie Hall: All PopCulture Trivia
    1977, w.

p. 237
"We jumped up and down on the bed": Jacob, i.
"When it came to the final judging": Sassoon, I 3296.

p. 238

"I remember the simple things...": Jacob, i.

"Responsibility dictates behaviour...That was the only
    reason I was really there": Jacob, i.

"Don't think you're the most beautiful...": Jacob, i

p. 240

" I wanted to continue what Brian..." *Trinidad Express*

"She increased the brand's visibility" *Trinidad Express.*

"Nothing at this stage bothers me..." Jacob, i.

"I think becoming Miss Universe... Jacob, i.

I wanted to continue what Brian... *Trinidad Express*, w.

She increased the brand's visibility... *Trinidad Express*, w.

Chapter 28
**Oscar de la Renta: The Man Who Dressed
First Ladies**
p. 241

After Francesca Lodge commissioned the
Dominican: Oscar de la Renta web site.

"I was picking pins off the floor": Mower,
Vogue, mw.

...had time to dance with the glamorous
American actress Ava Gardner: Mower,
Vogue.

p. 242

"From my island side comes my love for the exotic": Nikas,
    New York Times, nw.

"My customers are successful working women": Nikas, *New
    York Times*, nw.

"From my island side comes my love for the exotic": Nikas,
    New York Times, nw.

Whenever he got a chance de la Renta returned: Horyn, *New
    York Times*, nw.

"The many-columned, coral-stone house": Horyn, New York
    Times, nw.

"The place says many things about him..." Horyn, New York
    Times, nw.

"And he's no snob": Horyn, New York Times, nw.

p. 243-44

American first ladies wore his creations: Nikas, *The Guardian*, nw.

p. 243

On the red carpet at the Academy Awards: Mower, *Vogue,* and Nikas, *New York Times,* nw.

p. 244

First ladies who wore Oscar de la Renta: Jackie Kennedy-Michelle Obama. CNN news.

"My father had different aspirations for me": Ahmed, CNN news.

p. 244-45

In 1980, Oscar de la Renta gave the Boy Scouts its biggest makeover in 60 years: Peterson, *Scouting Magazine.*

p. 245

First Lady Michelle Obama: Ahmed, CNN news.

p. 246

"I like light, color, luminosity": Oscar de la Renta website.

Chapter 29
Geoffrey Holder: The Toast of the Town
p. 247

"Geoffrey Holder, the dancer, choreographer": Dunning, *New York Times*, nw.

p. 248

"Few cultural figures of the last half of the 20th century": Dunning, *New York Times*, nw.

"I wear white": Silverman, *People* Magazine, mw.

"I'm no snob": Silverman, *People* Magazine, mw.

p. 249

"Even when I am working in the theatre": *People* Magazine, mw.

"At school, when I got up to read": YouTube, Holder interview.

p. 250

"It was a period when all the girls": YouTube, Holder interview.

"House of Flowers": Dunning, *New York Times,* nw.

p. 251

"Never one to be lost in the spotlight": Silverman, *People Magazine*, mw.

p. 252

"Holder's lush impressionist paintings": Silverman, *People Magazine*, mw.

"Mr Holder is a terrific showman": Dunning, *New York Times*, nw.

"Mr Holder said his artistic life was governed": Dunning, *New York Times*, nw.

p. 253

"We hit it off like nobody's business": YouTube, Holder interview.

"Ask, 'What's that? ...We're all messengers...' : YouTube, Holder interview.

Chapter 30
Patrick Chung: The Wave of the Future
p. 255-56

All background information and quotes: Jacob, *Caribbean Beat*, mw.

p. 257

"is in the midst of one of his best": Mason, *Boston Herald*, nw.

"He has always been a good tackler": Mason, *Boston Herald*, nw.

"He's always been very competitive": Mason, *Boston Herald*, nw.

p. 258

"He was awful": Frank, CSN Philly.com.

"The Eagles thought they stole Chung": Frank, CSN Philly.com.

p. 259

"Patrick has always been really good": Frank, CSN Philly.com.

"His skills, his attitude, his work ethic": Frank, CSN Philly.com..

"For a safety he's a good coverage": Frank, CSN Philly.com.

"Not everyone has the same opportunities": Jacob, *Caribbean Beat*, mw.

Afterword
p. 262

"polite and gracious" in court... (King, 10).
 The "staunch Republican..." Houston, 37.
He worked in a yarn mill..., O'Brien, 224.

p. 263

Description of Looby saving Marshall's life King, 17.

Select Bibliography

Books

Abbott, John S.C. *Peter Stuyvesant: The Last Dutch Governor of New Amsterdam*. New York: Dodd & Mead, 1873.

Allan, Herbert. *Patriot in Purple*. 2nd ed. New York: The Beechhurst Press, 1953.

Alleyne, Warren and Henry Fraser. *The Barbados–Carolina Connection*. Basingstoke: Macmillan Caribbean, 1988.

Altoff, Gerard T. *Oliver Hazard Perry and the Battle of Lake Erie*. Put-in-Bay: The Perry Group, 1999.

Ambrose, Douglas and Robert W.T. Martin, eds. *The Many Faces of Alexander Hamilton: The Life Legacy of America's Most Elusive Founding Father*. 1st ed. New York: New York University Press, 2006. E-book.

Beard, JR. *Toussaint L'Ouverture: A Biography and Autobiography*. Heraklion Press, 2013.

Bell, Madison Smartt. *Toussaint Louverture: A Biography*. New York: Vintage Books, 2013.

Bergreen, Laurence. *Columbus: The Four Voyages*. New York: Viking, 2011.

Bown, Stephen R. *Merchant Kings*. New York: Thomas Dunne Books, 2009.

Breslaw, Elaine G. *Tituba, Reluctant Witch of Salem: Devilish Indians and Puritan Fantasies*. New York: New York University Press, 1996.

Burke, Edmund. *The Speeches of the Right Honourable Edmund Burke*. 1st ed. Vol. 2. London: Oxford University Press, 1781.

Carmichael, Stokely. *Stokely Speaks: Black Power Back to Pan-Africanism*. New York: Lawrence Hill Books, 1965.

Cerami, Charles. *Young Patriots: The Remarkable Story of Two Men, their Impossible Plan and the Revolution that*

Created the Constitution. Naperville: Sourcebooks, Inc., 2005.

Chang, Jeff. *Can't Stop, Won't Stop: A History of the Hip-Hop Generation*. New York: St Martin's Press, 2005.

Chang, Laurence, and Kornbluh, Peter, eds. *The Cuban Missile Crisis, 1962: A National Security Archive Documents Reader*. New York: The New Press, 1992.

Chernow, Ron. *Alexander Hamilton*. New York: Penguin Books, 2004.

——. *Washington: A Life*. New York: Penguin Press, 2010.

Chilton, Karen. *Hazel Scott: The Pioneering Journey of a Jazz Pianist from Café Society to Hollywood to HUAC*. Ann Arbor: University of Michigan Press, 2008.

Chisholm, Shirley. *Unbought and Unbossed*. 40th ed. Take Root Media, 2010. E-book.

Clavin, Matthew J. *Toussaint Louverture (sic) and the American Civil War: The Promise and Peril of a Second Haitian Revolution*. Philadelphia: University of Pennsylvania Press, 2010.

Colpys, John. *Captain John Colpys: Letters to Vice Admiral James Young*. Basseterre: Department of the Navy, 2014.

Cortesi, Lawrence. *Jean du Sable: Father of Chicago*. Philadelphia: Chilton Book Company, 1972.

Davis, William C. *The Pirates Laffite: The Treacherous World of the Corsairs of the Gulf*. Orlando: Harcourt, Inc., 2005.

De Koven, Reginald (Mrs). *The Life and Letters of John Paul Jones*. Vols I, II. New York: C Scribner's Sons, 1913.

Downey, Kirstin. *Isabella: The Warrior Queen*. New York: Doubleday, 2014.

Dubois, Laurent. *Avengers of the New World: The Story of the Haitian Revolution*. Cambridge, Mass: Belknap Press of Harvard University Press, 2004.

Dyde, Brian. *Out of the Crowded Vagueness: A History of the Islands of St Kitts, Nevis and Anguilla*. Oxford: Macmillan Caribbean, 2005.

Egerton, Douglas R. *He Shall Go Out Free: The Lives of Denmark Vesey*. New York: Rowman & Littlefield, 2004.

Ellis, Joseph J. *His Excellency: George Washington*. New York: Vintage Books, 2004.

English, T.J. *Havana Nocturne: How the Mob Owned Cuba—and then Lost it to the Revolution*. New York: William Morrow, 2008.

Farley, Christopher John. *Before the Legend: The Rise of Bob Marley*. New York: Amistad, 2006.

Farnsworth, Paul, ed. *Island Lives: Historical Archaeologies of the Caribbean*. University of Alabama Press: Tuscaloosa, 2001.

Federal Bureau of Investigations. *Stokely Carmichael—The FBI Files*. Kentucky: Filiquarian Publishing. N.d.

Fischer, David Hackett. *Washington's Crossing*. Oxford: Oxford University Press, 2004.

Fleming, Thomas. *The Louisiana Purchase*. Hoboken: John Wiley and Sons, 2003.

Garvey, Marcus. *Selected Writings and Speeches of Marcus Garvey*. New York: Dover Publications. E-book.

Garvey, Marcus, and Blaisdell, Bob. *Selected Writings and Speeches of Marcus Garvey*. Mineola: Dover Publications, 2004.

Gibson, Carrie. *Empire's Crossroads: A History of the Caribbean from Columbus to the Present Day*. New York: Atlantic Monthly Press, 2014.

Goldman, Vivien. *The Book of Exodus: The Making and Meaning of Bob Marley and the Wailers' Album of the Century*. New York: Three Rivers Press, 2006.

Goudsouzian, Aram. *Sidney Poitier: Man, Actor, Icon*. Chapel Hill: University of North Carolina, 2004.

Grant, Colin. *Negro with a Hat: The Rise and Fall of Marcus Garvey*. Oxford: Oxford University Press, 2008.

Hamilton McLane, Allan. *The Intimate Life of Alexander Hamilton*. London: Duckworth & Co., 1910. E-book.

Hickey, Donald R. *The War of 1812: A Forgotten Conflict*. Urbana: University of Illinois Press, 1989.

Houston, Benjamin. *The Nashville Way: Racial Etiquette and the Struggle for Social Justice in a Southern City*. Athens: U of Georgia, 2012. Print.

Hubbard, Vincent K. *Swords, Ships & Sugar: History of Nevis to 1900*. Corvallis, Oregon. Premiere Editions International, Inc., 1998.

Irving, Washington. *Knickerbocker's History of New York, Complete*. Chicago: WB Conkey Company Publishers, 1809.

Isenberg, Nancy. *Fallen Founder: The Life of Aaron Burr.* New York: Viking, 2007.

James, C.L.R. *The Black Jacobins: Toussaint L'Ouverture and the San Domingo Revolution*. 2nd ed. New York: Vintage Books, 1963.

Jasanoff, Maya. *Liberty's Exiles: American Loyalists in the Revolutionary World*. New York: Alfred A Knopf, 2011.

Joseph, Peniel E. *Stokely: A Life*. New York: Basic Civitas Books, 2014.

Kennedy, Edward M. *True Compass*. New York: Twelve, Hachette Book Group, 2009.

Kennedy, Robert F., and Arthur Meier Schlesinger. *Thirteen Days: A Memoir of the Cuban Missile Crisis*. New York: WW Norton, 1969. E-book.

King, Gilbert. *Devil in the Grove: Thurgood Marshall, the Groveland Boys, and the Dawn of a New America.* New York: Harper, 2012. Print.

Knox, John. *A Historical Account of S Thomas, WI: With Its Rise and Progress in Commerce, Missions and Churches, Climate and Its Adaptation to Invalids, Geological Structure, Natural History, and Botany: And Incidental Notices of St Croix and St Johns, Slave.* New York: Charles Scribner, 1852.

Kukla, Jon. *A Wilderness So Immense*. New York: Anchor Books, 2003.

Marley, Bob, and Hawks, Noel. *Complete lyrics of Bob Marley: Songs of Freedom*. London: Omnibus, 2001.

Marley, Rita. *No Woman, No Cry: My Life with Bob Marley*. New York: Hyperion, 2004.

Matson, Nehemiah. *Jean Baptiste and Father Bonner*. 2nd ed. New York: Princeton, 1874.

McCullough, David. *The Path Between the Seas: The Creation of the Panama Canal, 1870-1914*. New York: Simon and Schuster, 1977.

Miller, Ira, and United Press International. *Roberto Clemente*.
New York: Grosset & Dunlap, 1973.

Morison, Samuel Eliot. *John Paul Jones: A Sailor's Biography.*
Annapolis: Naval Institute Press, 1959.

O'Brien, Gail Williams. *The Color of the Law: Race, Violence,
and Justice in the Post-World War II South.* Chapel Hill: U
of North Carolina, 1999. Print.

O'Shaughnessy, Andrew Jackson. *An Empire Divided:
The American Revolution and the British Caribbean.*
Philadelphia: University of Pennsylvania Press, 2000.

Oshinsky, David M. *"Worse Than Slavery": Parchman Farm and
the Ordeal of Jim Crow Justice.* New York: Simon and
Schuster, 1996.

Pares, Richard. *War and Trade in the West Indies, 1739–1763.*
London: Routledge, 1936.

Poitier, Sidney. *Life Beyond Measure: Letters to My Great-
Granddaughter.* New York: HarperOne, 2008.

———. *The Measure of a Man: A Spiritual Autobiography.*
California: Harper San Francisco, 2000.

Ramonet, Ignacio. *Fidel Castro: My Life: A Spoken Biography.*
New York: Scribner, 2008.

Randall, Willard Sterne. *Alexander Hamilton: A Life.* New York:
Harper Perennial, 2004.

Robertson, David. *Denmark Vesey: The Buried Story of
America's Largest Slave Rebellion and the Man Who Led
It.* New York: Vintage Books, 1999.

Sassoon, Vidal. *Vidal: The Autobiography.* London: Macmillan,
2011.

Schiff, Stacy. *The Witches: Salem, 1692.* New York: Little,
Brown, 2015.

Sedgwick, John. *War of Two: Alexander Hamilton, Aaron Burr,
and the Duel that Stunned the Nation.* New York: Berkley,
2015.

Seitz, Don Carlos. *John Paul Jones, His Exploits in English
Seas During 1778–1780, Contemporary Accounts Collected
From English Newspapers, With a Complete Bibliography.*
New York: EP Dutton and Co., 1917.

Senior, Olive. *Dying to Better Themselves: West Indians and the Building of the Panama Canal.* Jamaica: University of the West Indies Press, 2014.

Shea, George. *The Life and Epoch of Alexander Hamilton: A Historical Study.* Boston: Houghton, Osgood and Company, 1879.

Sheridan, Maureen. *Bob Marley, Soul Rebel: The Stories behind every Song, 1962–1981.* New York: Thunder's Mouth Press, 1999.

Skaggs, David Curtis. *Oliver Hazard Perry: Honor, Courage, and Patriotism in the Early US Navy.* Maryland: Naval Institute Press, 2006.

Skaggs, David Curtis, and Altoff, Gerard T. *A Signal Victory: The Lake Erie Campaign 1812–1813.* Maryland: Naval Institute Press, 1997.

Soulé, Frank, Gihon, John H and Nisbet, James. *The Annals of San Francisco: Containing a Summary of the History of the First Discovery Settlement, Progress, and Present Condition of California, and a Complete History of All the Important Events Connected With Its Great City.* New York: D Appleton & Company, 1855. http://www.archive.org/stream/annalsofsanfranc00soul#page/n7/mode/2up.

Steffens, Roger. *Bob Marley, Rasta Warrior: Chanting Down Babylon.* Kingston: Ian Randle Publishers, 1998.

Szulc, Tad. *Fidel.* New York: William Morrow and Co, Inc., 1986.

Thomas, Evan. *John Paul Jones: Sailor, Hero, Father of the American Navy.* New York: Simon and Schuster, 2004.

Toynbee, Jason. "How Do You Solve a Problem Like Bob Marley?" in *Bob Marley.* Cambridge: Polity Press, 2007.

Tuchman, Barbara W. *The First Salute: A View of the American Revolution.* New York: Ballantine Books, 1988.

Unger, Harlow Giles. *American Tempest: How the Boston Tea Party Sparked a Revolution.* Massachusetts: Da Capo Press, 2011.

———. *John Hancock: Merchant King and American Patriot.* 2nd ed. Edison: Castle, 2005.

———. *The Last Founding Father.* Philadelphia: Da Capo Press, 2009.

Vargas Llosa, Mario. "My Son the Rastafarian," in *Making Waves*. New York: Faber and Faber, 1996.

Venable, Sarah. *From Bush Hill House to George Washington House: The Story of a Restoration*. Bridgetown: Bush Hill Tourism Trust, Inc., 2007.

Washington, George. *The George Washington Papers at the Library of Congress: The Diaries of George Washington*. Vol 1. Charlottesville: University Press of Virginia, 1976.

White, Timothy. *Catch a Fire: The Life of Bob Marley*. 9th ed. New York: Henry Holt, 2006.

Wood, Peter H. *Black Majority: Negroes in Colonial South Carolina from 1670 through the Stono Rebellion*. New York: Knopf, 1974.

Woodard, Colin. *American Nations: A History of the Eleven Rival Regional Cultures of North America*. New York: Penguin Books, 2011.

Film, Music

Marley, Bob. *Exodus*. Island Records, 1977.

Minnelli, Vincente, dir. *I Dood It*. Metro-Goldwyn-Mayer, 1943.

Rapper, Irving, dir. *Rhapsody in Blue*. Warner Brothers, 1945.

Journals, Newspapers, and Magazines

Anderson, Christopher P. "Geoffrey Holder, the Un-Cola Man, Is an Uncommon Wiz on Broadway and at Home." *People* 3, no 23 (June 16, 1975). Accessed December 12, 2014. http://www.people.com/people/archive/article/0,,20065353,00.html.

Appelbaum, Yoni. "The Fight for Equality in Charleston, from Denmark Vesey to Clementa Pinckney." *The Atlantic*. Washington, DC. Accessed June 18, 2015. http://www.theatlantic.com/politics/archive/2015/06/denmark-vesey-clementa-pinckney/396251.

Batey, Angus. "DJ Kool Herc DJs His First Block Party (His Sister's Birthday) at 1520 Sedgwick Avenue, Bronx, New York." *The Guardian*. August 13, 1973. Accessed October 31, 2014. http://www.theguardian.com/music/2011/jun/13/dj-kool-herc-block-party.

Bennett Jr., Lerone. "The Negro Who Founded Chicago."
   Ebony. December 1963, 170–78.

Brown Scott, James. "The Purchase of the Danish West Indies
   by the United States of America." *The American Journal
   of International Law* 10, no. 4 (1916): 853–59.

Cohen, Stefanie. "Alexander Hamilton to Get a Hip-Hop
   Musical." *Wall Street Journal*. Mar 6, 2014. Accessed
   November 20, 2014. http://www.blogs.wsj.com/
   speakeasy/2014/03/06/alexander-hamilton-to-get-a-hip-
   hop-musical.

"The Colleton Family in South Carolina." *The South Carolina
   Historical and Genealogical Magazine*. Oct 1900: 325–341.
   Web May 5, 2015. http://www.jstor.org/stable/27574930.

Drebinger, John. "Pirates Win 10-9, Capturing Series on Homer
   in 9th Mazeroski Hit Beats Yanks, Lifts Pittsburgh to First
   World Title in 35 Years." *New York Times*. October 14,
   1960. Accessed March 12, 2014. http://www.nytimes.com/
   packages/html/sports/year_in_sports/10.08.html.

Dunning, Jennifer and William McDonald. "Geoffrey Holder,
   Dancer, Actor, Painter and More, Dies at 84." *New York
   Times*. October 6, 2014. Accessed January 20, 2015.
   http://www.nytimes.com/2014/10/07/arts/geoffrey-
   holder-dancer-choreographer-and-man-of-flair-dies-
   at-84.html?_r=1.

Friedman, Vanessa. "Oscar de la Renta's Legacy." *New York
   Times*. October 22, 2014. Accessed December 26, 2014.
   http://www.nytimes.com/2014/10/23/fashion/oscar-de-la-
   renta-legacy.html.

Gilmore, Mikal. "Bob Marley: How He Changed the
   World." *Rolling Stone*. March 10, 2005, 68–78.

Headley, Joel Tyler. "Darien Exploring Expedition, Under
   Command of Lieut Isaac Grier Strain." *Harper's New
   Monthly Magazine* 10 (1855). Accessed October 12, 2014.
   http://www.wikisource.org/wiki/Darien_Exploring_
   Expedition_(1854).

Higginson, Thomas Wentworth. "Denmark Vesey." *The Atlantic
   Monthly* 7, no. 44 (June 1861): 728–44. http://www.
   theatlantic.com/past/issues/1861jun/higgin.htm.

Homer, Louis B. "Trinidad cemetery pays tribute to US naval
    hero." *Trinidad Express*. October 31, 2011. Accessed
    November 9, 2012. http://www.trinidadexpress.com/news/
    Trinidad_cemetery_pays__tribute_to_US_naval_hero-
    132900923.html.

Hu, Cindy. "William Alexander Leidesdorff: Forgotten San
    Francisco Pioneer." *San Francisco Travel*. Aug 22, 2014.
    Web July 25, 2015. http://www.sanfrancisco.travel/article/
    william-alexander-leidesdorff-forgotten-san-francisco-
    pioneer.

Jacob, Debbie. "From Island to End Zone." *Caribbean Beat* 124
    (Nov/Dec 2013).

———. "Singing the Spirit of New Orleans: Aaron Neville
    headlines Sando Jazz Fest." *Trinidad Guardian*. September
    28, 2007.

———. "This is Sixty." *Trinidad Express* Women's Magazine. July
    21, 2013. Accessed April 12, 2015.

Jameson, J. Franklin. "St Eustatius in the American
    Revolution." *The American Historical Review* 8, no. 4
    (1903): 683–708. http://doi.org/10.2307/1834346.

Kaplan, Sarah. "For Charleston's Emanuel AME Church,
    Shooting is Another Painful Chapter in Rich History."
    Washington Post. June 18, 2015. Accessed July 22, 2015.
    http://www.washingtonpost.com/news/morning-mix/
    wp/2015/06/18/for-charlestons-emanuel-a-m-e-church-
    one-of-the-oldest-in-america-shooting-is-another-painful-
    chapter-in-long-history.

Kaufman, Michael T. "Stokely Carmichael, Rights Leader
    Who Coined 'Black Power,' Dies at 57." *New York Times*.
    November 15, 1998. Accessed January 3, 2015. http://
    www.nytimes.com/1998/11/16/us/stokely-carmichael-
    rights-leader-who-coined-black-power-dies-at-57.htm.

Keaton, Trica Danielle. "The Defiant One: Euzhan Palcy." *The
    Feminist Wire*. May 9, 2011. Accessed January 5, 2015.
    http://www.thefeministwire.com/2011/05/the-defiant-
    one-euzhan-palcy.

Lehmann, Karl. "John Hancock: Patriot in Purple. By Herbert
    S. Allan." *William and Mary Quarterly*. January 1, 1949,

136–40. Accessed December 5, 2014. http://www.jstor.
org/stable/1921870?seq=1#page_scan_tab_contents.

Mason, Chris. "Bill Belichick Not Surprised by Patrick Chung's
Success in Coverage." *Boston Herald*. December 1, 2015.
hhtp://www.bostonherald.com/sports/patriots/the_
blitz/2015/12/bill_belichick_not_surprised_by_patrick_
chungs_success_in_coverage.

Meehan, Thomas A. "Jean Baptiste Point du Sable, the First
Chicagoan." *Journal of the Illinois State Historical Society*
56, no. 3 (1908–1984), (1963): 439–53.

Nikas, Joanna, Safronova, Valeriya, and Oliver, Simone S.
"Oscar de la Renta's Life Through the Years." *New York
Times*. October 21, 2014. Accessed April 9, 2015. http://
www.nytimes.com/interactive/2014/10/21/fashion/21-
OSCAR-DE-LA-RENTA-TIMELINE.html#/#time352_10440.

Paddington, Bruce. "Euzhan Palcy: Making Waves." *Caribbean
Beat* 1 (March 1, 1992). Accessed December 27, 2014.
http://www.caribbean-beat.com/issue-1/euzhan-palcy-
making-waves#axzz3MOjqEjTi.

Parker, Adam. "Denmark Vesey Monument Unveiled in
Hampton Park Among Hundreds." *Post and Courier*.
Charleston, South Carolina. February 15, 2014. Accessed
March 1, 2014. http://www.postandcourier.com/
article/20140215/PC16/140219534/denmark-vesey-
monument-unveiled-in-hampton-park-before-hundreds.

Paquette, Robert L. "Jacobins of the Low Country: The Vesey
Plot on Trial." *William and Mary Quarterly*. 2002:185–92.
http://www.latinamericanstudies.org/slavery/WMQ-2002.

Trinidad Express newspaper. "Janelle Penny Commissiong-
Chow: Simply Phenomenal". www.trinidadexpress.com/
womanmagazine (September 21, 2012).

Vargas Llosa, Mario. "Trench Town Rock." *American Scholar*
(2002):53–56.

Yawching, Donna. "Tobago's Hidden History." *Caribbean Beat*
113 (November 1, 2012).

Online sources

Academy of Motion Picture Arts and Sciences. "Sidney Poitier
Wins Best Actor: 1964 Oscars". *YouTube*. http://www.
youtube.com/watch?v=qCzTyxXPy1o.

Bailey Thurman, Sue. "William Alexander Leidesdorff." Virtual Museum of the City of San Francisco. N.d. Accessed July 2, 2015. http://www.sfmuseum.net/bio/leidesdorff.html.

Black Past Organization. "Janelle Penny Commissiong" N.d. Accessed May 12, 2015. http://www.blackpast.org/gah/commissiong-janelle-penny-1953#sthash.OhNZ6XiE.dpuf.

Carmichael, Stokely. "Stokely Carmichael Interviews Mother in Sweden." 1967. http://www.youtube.com/watch?v=cXKZdw49b3l.

Ebert, Roger. "A Dry White Season." September 22, 1989. Accessed April 15, 2014. http://www.rogerebert.com/reviews/a-dry-white-season-1989.

Frank, Reuben. "Bill Belichick Explains How Patrick Chung Reinvented Himself." *CSNPhilly*. http://www.csnphilly.com/football-philadelphia-eagles/bill-belichick-explains-how-patrick-chung-reinvented-himself.

Furlong, Jeffrey. "Sports Century—Roberto Clemente." *YouTube*. December 10, 2012. Accessed September 4, 2014. http://www.youtube.com/watch?v=APaxP5eOLqg.

Goodwin, Liz. "Denmark Vesey and a Battle Over History in Charleston." Accessed June 21, 2015. http://www.yahoo.com/politics/denmark-vesey-and-a-battle-over-history-in-122041235761.html.

Harvard University. *California Gold Rush (1848–1858): Aspiration, Acculturation, and Impact Immigration to the United States, 1789–1930*. Harvard University Library Open Collections Program. N.d. Accessed January 3, 2015. http://www.ocp.hul.harvard.edu/immigration/goldrush.html.

John F. Kennedy Presidential Library and Museum. "The Bay of Pigs." N.d. Accessed December 24, 2014. http://www.jfklibrary.org/JFK/JFK-in-History/The-Bay-of-Pigs.aspx.

Kurutz, Steve. "Kool DJ Herc: All Music." N.d. Accessed November 1, 2014. http://www.allmusic.com/artist/kool-dj-herc-mn0001254243/biography.

Louisiana Purchase Treaty. America's Historical Documents. National Archives. April 30, 1803. Accessed February 2, 2014. http://www.archives.gov/historical-docs/document.html?doc=5&title.raw=Louisiana%20Purchase%20Treaty.

Maritime Heritage. "Sea Captains: San Francisco 1800s." Ship Passengers–Sea Captains. The Maritime Heritage Project, San Francisco 1846–1899. N.d. Accessed March 2, 2014. http://www.maritimeheritage.org/captains/leidesdorffWilliamA.html.

"Miss Universe Pageant, 1977 – Full Show." *YouTube*. Accessed June 6, 2014. http://www.youtube.com/watch?v=2Du1NQsTOsM.

"New York Illustrated: The Irrepressible Shirley Chisholm." NBC News Special. 1969. http://www.youtube.com/watch?v=ERGWEG4Lcpl.

Obama, Barack. "Statement by the President on Cuba Policy Changes." The White House. December 17, 2014. Accessed December 26, 2014. http://www.whitehouse.gov/the-press-office/2014/12/17/statement-president-cuba-policy-changes.

Rose, Charlie. "Hamilton." *60 Minutes Overtime. 60 Minutes*, November 8, 2015. http://www.cbsnews.com/news/hamilton-broadway-musical-60-minutes-charlie-rose.

Schwartz, Larry. "Clemente Quietly Grew in Stature." Sports Century Biography ESPN Classic. N.d. Accessed January 3, 2015. http://www.espn.go.com/classic/biography/s/Clemente_Roberto.html#.

Serjeant, Jill. "Broadway's Buzzy 'Hamilton' Music to the Ears of Founding Father's Fans." Reuters. June 30, 2015. Accessed July 10, 2015. http://www.reuters.com/article/2015/07/31/us-theatre-hamilton-musical-idUSKCN0Q51BH20150731.

St Eustatius Historical Foundation. "St Eustatius History and Archaeology." 2010. Accessed May 2, 2015. http://www.steustatiushistory.org/StatiaHistoryandArchaeology2.htm.

Sopel, Jon. "US Flag Raised Over Reopened Cuba Embassy in Havana." *BBC News*. August 15, 2015. Accessed August 15, 2015. http://www.bbc.com/news/world-latin-america-33919484.

Steinem, Gloria. "From the Archives: 'The Ticket That Might Have Been.'" *Chisholm '72: Unbought & Unbossed. PBS*. February 7, 2005. Accessed December 15, 2014. http://www.pbs.org/pov/chisholm/special_ticket.php.

"The Workers." *American Experience*. PBS. N.d.
    Accessed April 14, 2014. http://www.pbs.org/wgbh/
    americanexperience/features/general-article/panama-
    workers.
Willis, Cheryl. "Late Brooklyn Congresswoman to Receive
    Presidential Medal of Freedom." Warner Cable
    News. November 23, 2015. http://www.ny1.com/
    nyc/all-boroughs/news/2015/11/23/late-brooklyn-
    congresswoman-to-receive-presidential-medal-of-
    freedom.html.

Other
Welters, Beatrice. "Speech at the Rededication of the Oliver
    Hazard Perry Gateway." Port of Spain: US Embassy. April
    4, 2012.

Index

www.ingramcontent.com/pod-product-compliance
Lightning Source LLC
Chambersburg PA
CBHW032147080426
42735CB00008B/621